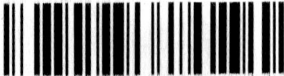

U0720846

文
景

———————

Horizon

社 科 新 知　文 艺 新 潮

徐梵澄 全集

孙波 主编

小学菁华

徐梵澄 著

贺佳 译　孙波 校

上海人民出版社

主 编 的 话

　　徐梵澄（1909 年 10 月 26 日—2000 年 3 月 6 日），原名徐琥，字季海，湖南长沙人。幼塾就学于近代湘中巨子王闿运（湘绮）之再传弟子，其师杨度、杨钧辈，尝讲汉魏六朝古文。后进新式小学，开国领袖毛泽东为其地理老师。再后入教会所办之雅礼中学，接受全面现代教育，并得到了良好的英语训练。1926 年春，遵父命考入湘雅医学院。1927 年春，自作主张转入武汉中山大学历史系，开始发表文章，谋求自立。1928 年春，又考入上海复旦大学西洋文学系。同年 5 月，因聆听鲁迅讲演并作记录，遂与鲁迅通信，从此结下了深厚的师生情谊。1929 年 8 月至 1932 年 7 月，梵澄赴德留学修艺术史专业，分别就读于柏林大学和海德堡大学，其间为鲁迅搜求欧西版画，并自制作品寄与恩师，其作品为中国现代版画最早之创作，被业界誉为"第一人"者。回国以后，寄寓上海，为《申报·自由谈》撰写杂文和短篇小说，并受鲁迅之嘱，有规模地翻译尼采著作，包括《尼采自传》（良友公司 1935 年），《朝霞》（商务印书馆 1935 年），《苏鲁支语录》（含《人间的、太人间的》节译，生活书店 1936 年），《快乐的智识》（商务印书馆 1939 年）和《葛（歌）德自著之〈浮士德〉》（商务印书馆 1939 年）。又译出《佛教述略》

（英译汉，上海佛教协会 1939 年）。

抗战爆发后，梵澄随国立艺专前往湘西，复又辗转昆明。1940 年底，艺专回迁至重庆，梵澄遂入中央图书馆，独自编纂《图书月刊》，并授课于中央大学。值 1945 年抗战胜利，梵澄加入中印文化交流计划，于年底飞赴印度加尔各答之桑地尼克丹的泰戈尔国际大学，任教于该校之中国学院，尝讲欧阳竟无唯识思想，并编辑《天竺字原》（佚失）。1950 年，梵澄赴名城贝纳尼斯（今名瓦拉纳西）重修梵文，其间译出印度文学经典《薄伽梵歌》和《行云使者》（迦里大萨）。1951 年春，梵澄又入南印度琫地舍里（今名本地治理）之室利·阿罗频多（Sri Aurobindo）学院，并受院母密那氏（Mira）之托任华文部主任。1950 年代，是梵澄于印度韦檀多学古今经典的译介期，古典有《奥义书》（梵译汉）五十种，今典有阿罗频多的《神圣人生论》，《薄伽梵歌论》，《瑜伽论》（学院版，六册，1957 年、1958 年、1959 年、1960 年），《社会进化论》（学院版 1960 年）和《伊莎书》，《由谁书》（学院版 1957 年），皆英译汉；以及院母的《母亲的话》（学院版，四册，1956 年、1958 年、1978 年），为法译汉。1960 年代，是梵澄于中国传统学术菁华的宣扬期，其以英文著译《小学菁华》（学院版 1976 年），《孔学古微》（学院版 1966 年），《周子通书》（学院版 1978 年）和《唯识菁华》与《肇论》。1970 年代，是梵澄将中、西、印三大古典文化思想之玄理整合的会通期，其标志乃为疏释室利·阿罗频多《赫拉克利特》之《玄理参同》（学院版 1973 年）。

1978 年底，梵澄回国。1979 年春，入中国社会科学院世界宗教研究所任研究员，直至 2000 年春殁世。此一末期，先生隐然有着确立中国精神哲学之努力的倾向，他的工作成果也不断被推向社会：1984 年，《五十奥义书》(中国社会科学出版社) 和《神圣人生论》(商务印书馆) 出版；1987 年，《肇论》(中国社会科学出版社) 和《安慧〈三十唯识〉疏释》(梵译汉，中国佛教文化研究所) 出版；1988 年，《异学杂著》(浙江文艺出版社) 和《老子臆解》(中华书局) 出版；1990 年，《唯识菁华》(新世界出版社) 出版；1991 年，《周天集》(英译汉，生活·读书·新知三联书店) 出版；1994 年，《陆王学述——一系精神哲学》(上海远东出版社) 出版。先生故去以后，《薄伽梵歌论》于 2003 年面世 (商务印书馆)；又由编者所辑《徐梵澄文集》十六卷于 2006 年推出 (上海三联书店)。

纵观先生一生，注重非在某一学，如印学、西学或中学，尽管其治思于各家研讨极为深湛，要其着力所在仍为精神哲学，正如他自己所言："最是我所锲而不舍的，如数十年来所治之精神哲学。"这一端头是依鲁迅 ("立人""改造国民性") 启始，这一线索是从希腊古哲赫拉克利特 (永恒之"变是") 和德国近哲尼采 (精神之回还)，到印度古"见士" (由"无明"见"明") 和近代"圣哲"阿罗频多 (自性高栖，有为人生，终与"至上者"合契)，再回吾华儒家，并以中国文化为本位 (变化气质，转化人生与社会)，收摄、重冶三家并塑模自家学说之雏形。于此可问：先生的尝试成功与否？或许"成功"不见！又有可说者，这是一"渊默而雷声"之事，影响或在久远的将来，它是浑融在中华民族未来希望之曙色中的，并渐行渐起，直趋"午昼" (阿罗频多语)。再问：到了"午昼"又如何呢？一个更高远的、更阔大的目标在上，即"超心思"之域，也可以称之为"精神道"。50 年前，国内"文革"尚未消歇，只身寄寓南印度一海隅的梵澄就发出了其深情的期待，他说："将来似可望'精神道'之大发扬，二者（哲学与宗教）双超"(《玄理参同》学院版）。复问："'精神道'之大发扬"为何种境界？乃光明倾注天理流行矣！

先生著、译述，除佚失和未采者，文集之收录约合 650 余万字。据他本人的想法，全部文字可分为三个部分，他说："编拙稿成集，细思只合分成三汇。属'精神哲学'者一，则《薄伽梵歌·序》等皆收。属'艺术'者一，则论书画者收之，当待大量补充。属'文学'者一，则自诌之俚句，及所译文言诗，并诗说者属之，犹待大量补充。"(《梵澄先生》，上海书店出版社 2009 年）其中三汇之"艺术"者和"文学"者，极为粲然，可入乎美学畛域，编者无似，读者自鉴。此就"精神哲学"者略说，这一宗学问在我国古代属内学、玄学，也即形而上学，有伦有序而不违逻辑，立义黏柔而超乎知识，故"从此一学翻成西文，舍哲学一名词而外，亦寻不出恰当的称呼。"(《陆王学述》）

那么，当解"精神"二字，与寻常概念不同，他以人"型"(the Ideas)来打比方的：

> ……而人，在生命之外，还有思想，即思维心，还有情感，即情感心或情命体。基本还有凡此所附丽的身体。但在最内中深处，还有一核心，通常称之曰心灵或性灵。是这些，哲学上乃统称之曰"精神"。但这还是就人生而说，它虽似是抽象，然是一真实体，在形而

上学中，应当说精神是超乎宇宙为至上为不可思议又在宇宙内为最基本而可证会的一存在。研究这主题之学，方称精神哲学。这一核心，是万善万德具备的，譬如千丈大树，其发端初生，只是一极微细的种子，核心中之一基因（gene），果壳中之仁。孔子千言万语解说人道中之"仁"，原亦取义于此。（《陆王学述》）

这"精神"，在徐先生的语境中，也被称为"知觉性""力""气"，即一超乎现象的基本力，在黑格尔或叫作"自然"；亦被称为"心灵""性灵"，即那"极微细的种子"，在柏拉图或叫作"灵魂"。前说好比大树之整个，后说有似其发芽破土的"种子"，二者是一事。又可表之：在本原性东西（宇宙之树）之内的一种自由（心灵或仁）。

先生所治之精神哲学，又分次第，初赫拉克利特和尼采，中诸《奥义书》和《薄伽梵歌》，后阿罗频多和儒家。初则赫氏与尼采之思想，不为"大全"，其精神只行进在半途，盖因赫氏不言"本体"，只说一永恒的"变是"，尼采否定"上帝"，只认一不歇的"心思"力。中则诸典，因受"空论"和"幻论"的消极影响，其真精神泯漠不彰垂二千余年。后则阿罗频多，欲挽沉滞，力振国运，重铸韦檀多哲学，并以《薄伽梵歌》为经，以诸《奥义书》为纬，教示其人民：以工作实践化除私我，以瑜伽精神奉献上帝。而阿氏之学，又与我国未明儒家心学一路符契，梵澄说："鄙人之所以提倡陆、王者，以其与室利·阿罗频多之学多有契合处。有瑜伽之益，无瑜伽之弊。正以印度瑜伽在今日已败坏之极，故室利·阿罗频多思有以新苏之，故创'大全瑜伽'之说。观其主旨在于觉悟、变化气质，与陆、王不谋而合。姑谓为两道，此两道有文化背景之不同，皆与任何宗教异撰。亦与唯物论无所抵牾，可以并行不悖。"（《梵澄先生》）

又说先生之勤力，中年以后主要当在印度古典和阿罗频多诸书。其中翻译《薄伽梵歌》有句，"盖挥汗磨血几死而后得之者也"（佛协版"序"）；又有翻译《神圣人生论》曾云："'母亲'的精神力量是巨大的，我能够把室利·阿罗频多那样精深的《人生论》翻出来，没有精神力量支撑是不行的。"（《梵澄先生》）其自著之书，《老子臆解》也是颇费了不少心神，曾与友人说道："这是'狮子搏兔'的工作，是用过全身气力的，几十年来断断续续，不知费了多少功夫。"（《徐梵澄传》）对于这些文字的研读，仿佛有见一条基线，引向那本深而末茂的幽隧、高山而仰止的化境……于此可想，入躁者定会兴味无尽，昭晰者必能疑窦释然，因为那是一注"神圣之泉"（阿罗频多），"没有汲桶放下去不能汲满着黄金和珠宝上来"（尼采）！而先生的自著文字，皆是简洁、雅健、灵犀、深锐，其中传映着他优游涵泳、从容论道的儒者气象，使人读来每每如沐春风而怡然自适，如饮醇醪又不觉自醉。

然而，说到自己的工作，他尝言："我的文字不多，主要思想都在序、跋里了。""我的英语文字多于文言文字，文言文字多于白话文字。"惜乎在本次文集的编辑过程中仍未能如意尽收，可知其一生有多少劳作皆付之东流了，这又是人生无可奈何之事。好在"基线"昭然，于是可问：先生为什么要去印度并且一滞就是 33 年呢？回答：是为了实现鲁迅的理想，即

挹取彼邦之大经大法。百余年前，鲁迅就已明示："凡负令誉于史初，开
文化之曙色，而今日转为影国者，无不如斯。使举国人所习闻，最适莫如
天竺。天竺古有韦陀四种，瑰丽幽瓊，称世界大文。其摩诃波罗多暨罗摩
衍那二赋，亦至美妙。"（《摩罗诗力说》）故先生去国，译出经典是首要任务，
因为"若使大时代降临，人莫我知，无憾也，而我不可以不知人，则广挹
世界文教之菁英，集其大成，以陶淑当世而启迪后人，因有望于我中华之
士矣"（《薄伽梵歌论》案语）。

　　诸《奥义书》乃韦檀多学之经典，韦檀多乃韦陀之终教，为刹帝利族
所擅，其陈说巫术祭祀少，探讨宇宙人生多，被称为韦陀之"知识篇"，与
婆罗门族所执之"礼仪篇"相对。大致公元前 750 年后，战事稍息，农耕
始稳，刹帝利支配力扩大，王庭成为教学的中心，王者成为主宰者，一
转婆罗门"祭祀万能"之外求，诉诸内中"心灵"之醒觉，迈出了寻求普
遍性的步伐，憧憬最高者、最广者、最完善者，也即"真理"者——"大
梵""上帝""逻各斯""道""太极"等等。德哲雅斯贝尔斯将其称为人类
的"轴心期时代"。诸《奥义书》首推《伊莎书》与《由谁书》，是为其体
系之两柱石。《伊莎书》主旨在：**揭示宇宙本然之大经大法，乃彰显大梵圆
成之境。此是为入道者说法**。《由谁书》所表在：**由用达体，描述求道之过
程，只止于"阿难陀"之境。此是为普通人说法**。前者可看作精神哲学，
后者应当作精神现象学。尤其《伊莎书》，其密接韦陀之根本，反映古韦
陀圣人之心理体系，即精神实用者也。徐先生指出：阿氏"疏释"之简约
一卷，"而韦檀多学之菁华皆摄。有此一卷，即是书古今余家注疏皆可

不问。"（前记）

阿罗频多为印度近世韦檀多学之集大成者，其学说又可以称之为"大全瑜伽论"。1972 年，阿氏百年诞辰，院母为其出版全集，煌煌然三十巨册。徐先生采译最重要者，乃其中四部，分属世界观者《神圣人生论》、人生观者《薄伽梵歌论》、修为观者《瑜伽论》和历史观者《社会进化论》。四者实"而一而四、而四而一"之论。设若以《薄伽梵歌论》为寻常本（俗谛义），后二者则皆为其系论；如果以《神圣人生论》为超上本（真谛义），余三者则又皆为其系论。《瑜伽论》补白"从成熟的低地（身体）出发"（康德），《社会进化论》注目集团、民族、国家的命运。四者或可一言以蔽之，曰：神圣人生本体论！于此足觇先生印学工作的重要性。我们说，他在这方面的贡献至少表现在二个方面：第一，于《薄伽梵歌》和《五十奥义书》之雅言风格的翻译与经典范式的注释——是基础性的；第二，于阿罗频多博大与精深之思想的介绍与显扬——是方向性的。阅读徐先生的文字，需要跳出寻常知觉性加以体会，或许我们能得出这样的结论：一方面，他造就了一种属于自己的思维风格和语言风格；另一方面，他指出了一个新的哲学工作的方向。

时光迅迈，陵谷替迁，《徐梵澄文集》出版已然 17 年了，先生示寂也 23 年了。这期间国家发生了多大的变化，何可计量？回想起上世纪 90 年代初，先生曾在街头看到一拨拨的农民工穿着西服，于是高兴得像小孩似的回来逢人便讲；又在 90 年代末，他尝与友人聊天，感慨地说道："南水北调如果成功了，南方没有水灾，北方也不干旱，那中国就是天堂了。"

《徐梵澄传》）如今，这梦想已经一步一步地变成现实。若果他在天有知呢，会对我们再说点儿什么？也许，他会勉励我们要把这一和平的局面再坚守"一世"（30年），或"两世""三世"……"子曰：'善人为邦百年，亦可以胜残去杀矣。'""子曰：'如有王者，必世而后仁。'"（《论语·子路篇》）他会希望我们将中国人和平发展的理想推及全世界。因为我们无论多么强大，其根柢都是以"文教"立国的理念，它保证了吾华族"宜尔子孙绳绳兮"之不竭的国运。今兹文集分期再版，正为长久，因为先生的目光始终是发到前方的。而前方正是我们的期许，也是现代文明世界所有人的期许，即"人类同一"的世界。虽然，这"期许"从未在人类社会实现过。然而，正如先生所言：

> 直至今日，这理想仍然只是理想，然而无论这一理想有多广大，却并非不可企及，仍属物理世界，终将实现于有限未来的某一刻，为一普遍真理的最终胜利。（《孔学古微》）

孙 波　写定于癸卯雨水日　2023年2月19日

目录

CONTENTS

编者说明

《小学菁华》，为梵澄于 1963 年编辑的一部汉英字典，后在法国学者的催促下，于 1976 年晚出于南印度；2006 年以《徐梵澄文集》卷二在中文世界出版；今经汉译，以中英对照单行本出版。

此书序后，是汉语史的一个简略概说，书末为现代（文字改革之前）的语音符号系统，亦给出一些书写方法的规范示例，读者可依此作字帖加以临摹。字典正文部分，在其所属的偏旁、部首之下，给出每一字的原形和拼音，字形三体并列：印刷楷体、小篆、楷书；在对应之英文名词及其汉译下，又给出同一字之篆体的不同写法；其下是英文注解及其汉译。（参见下页"体例示意"）书末索引经编者重新编制，以便利读者查阅。

梵澄指出：汉语自古以来虽无一套成文字的语法规则，但是它的语法结构却很完善，有佛经翻译为其明证。另外，汉字在书写和印刷上有节约空间之优点；更重要的是，它有高度的化合性，即这种单音节的文字之不同组合，会生成新的概念与意义，从而较顺利地增益我们汉文字之语言宝库，以适应时代发展的需要。每一个受过教育的中国人都有这样的体会：我们今天阅读二千五百年前之孔夫子的箴言，并没有什么障碍。

英文版印刷体字形

现代规范楷体字形

序号

氷 （冰）

10

bīng/Ping₂

现代汉语拼音 / 拉丁化转写

中文字义 ——— 冰，冰锥

英文释义 ——— Ice, icicles

小篆字形　楷书字形　注音符号

其他书体的中英文注解

其他古代书体 ———
a

"a" 是另一古体，上面部分与前文给出的字形相同，表冰之裂纹。下部的起源不明。

"a" is another antique form, the upper portion retaining the same form as given above, which represents the cracks of ice. The origin of the lower portion is unknown.

*《段注》："以冰代仌，用别制凝字"。邵英《群经正字》："冰冻作仌，坚凝本字作冰。俗以冰代仌，凝代冰字，而仌字遂废不用。"

译者注

体 例 示 意

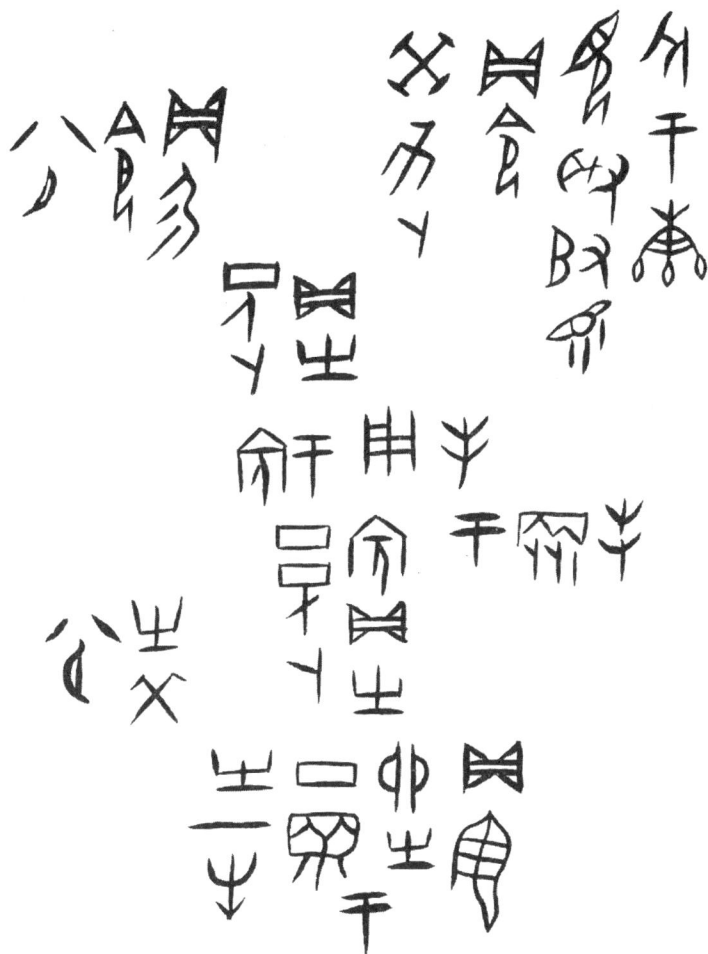

拓片 2　集自甲骨卜辞的汉字

Plate II　Words gathered from inscriptions on tortoise shells

埶	宎	及
1	2	3
啟	牧	攲
4	5	6
羔	既	即
7	8	9
射	饗	是
10	11	12
宿	印	嵒
13	14	15
則	頡	野
16	17	18
漁	臽	春
19	20	21

拓片 3　拓片 2 中汉字的现代正体书写

Plate III　The words in Plate II written in modern "proper" script

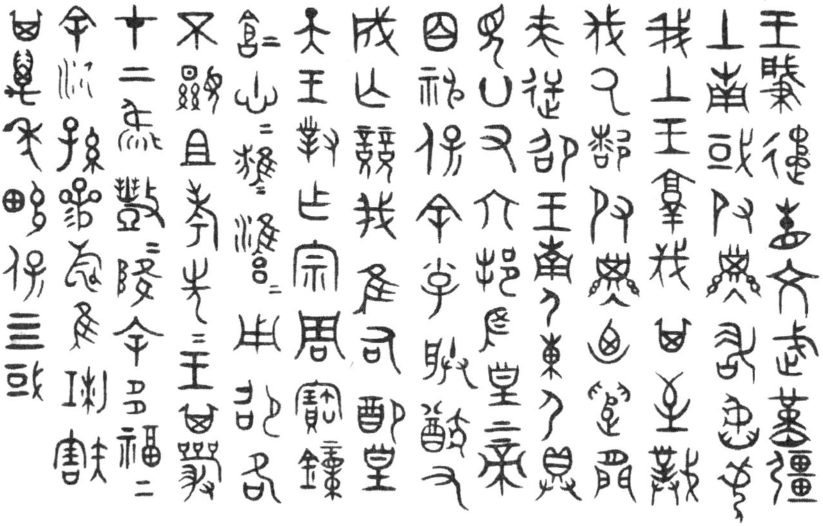

拓片 4　西周王朝（公元前 1122—前 770 年）[1] 的大篆

Plate IV　Major Script of the Western Chow Dynasty (1122–770 B.C.)

拓片 5　西周青铜器上的大篆铭文

Plate V　Major Script of the Chow Dynasty engraved on a bronze plate
.

1.　今通常以公元前 1046 至前 771 年为西周时期。——编者注

序言

在过去 60 年甚至更长一段时期里，中国知识分子付出了巨大的心力，以期使汉字简化，并消除各种方言使民族语言标准化，逐渐减少乃至最终消除文盲，至今成就已粲然可观。然中国人口众多，汉语复杂深奥，过去几十年之种种成就皆只可谓漫漫旅程之一初步。

首先，作为此书之序言，不妨先谈谈语言学习本身。近年来，由于对汉语知识需求的增大，外国人对汉语学习的困难抱怨亦多。据我所知，中国学生过去学习外语也有类似的抱怨。克实而论，学习何种语言都不是简单的。即便是英语，这门使用广泛且在当今世界极为重要的语言，要熟练掌握也非易事，于中国人尤其如此。语言是鲜活的，随时代不断地发展和变化。除了极少数天才的诗人、散文家、戏剧家和语言学家之外，一般人单是完全掌握并使用好自己的母语都十分困难。设若论及希腊语、拉丁语、梵文等古老的语言，学习就更加烦琐了。各种名词的词形变化、动词变位以及冗长的复合词（如梵文），一开始就让学习者如临深渊。

印欧语系语种繁多，彼此关系密切，在过去虽无一种印德语实际存在过，但这些语言从基础结构来看，皆具有共同的语音系统、语法以及句法，犹如开辟铺就好的路径，可供学习者摸索前行。以英语和法语为例，这两种语言极为相似，约有 6000 词几乎相同，唯有拼写和含义上略有差异，正是因为这些词多属同一拉丁词源。特别是如今英语和法语皆使用广泛，英国人学习法语自然容易，法国人学英语亦然。现在约有 1.3 亿人使用法语作为官方语言，此一事实不禁让人想起法语辉煌的过去——自 17 世纪开始，法语一直是外交和高雅文化的主流语言。然今之趋势已然是，英语不断扩张并愈加占优。根据最新统计，除了普通话之外，全世界以英语为第一语言的人数已经远远超过了其他语言。

汉语虽然是世界上使用人数最多的语言，却仍局限于本国范围之内。与诸印欧语不同，汉语不是拼音系统的文字，没有成文的语法。实际上，汉语的方方面面都是不同的。但不可否认，拥有近 5000 年历史的汉字具有高度的文明，至今仍生气勃勃。于此不妨一问：如果学习汉语真是困难重重，那么它何以能经久流传并被广泛使用呢？

学习汉语困难，原因纷繁复杂，但归根结底与现代教育体制有关。通常汉语作为第二语言，学习时没能遵循正确的方法。从心理学看，困难还不在语言本身，而在学习者的心态。人皆受到成见和习惯之束缚，形象地说，人极少能如器具那般地空净自己，从而注入新的溶液。儿童学习新知识较成人容易，正是因其无知和自由。当大脑太过拥挤，阴云密布，外部的光亮如何能照射进去，内中的光亮又如何能透射出来呢？

其次，今之社会随着时代的变化，生活愈加繁忙。有略通外语者亦无闲暇和耐心深入异域文化，浸润熏陶。而语言一旦脱离文化背景，极易忘却。橄榄树乃雅典娜女神所赐之神树，落地生根，30 年后方才结果，却能百年果实不断，至枯而方休。今人追求知识，虽谈不上野心勃勃，却不免急功近利；总希望缩短求知的过程，使之如寻常购物一般，更为轻松和舒适。此现象不难解释，亦可以理解，因为现代文明的基本准则之一便是，人人追求更简单、更快乐的事物。那么我们学习外语之目的何在呢？当然是为了认识其他民族，了解彼邦的习俗、思想和文化，以及他们在物质和精神领域所取得之成就，以期能共同向着更高之生活目标迈进，最终为人类创造出一个更美好的世界。通过语言，我们得以学习和吸收异邦民族之菁华，同时帮助落后的地区加快发展。正如室利·阿罗频多在《未来诗集》中所言："去了解其他国家，不会贬低我们自己的国家，反而帮助它变得更加强大。"[1] 而要实现这一切，语言是关键。然而，还有一个重要因素不能忽视——时间。科学家为了某一研究往往耗费毕生精力，而一些实验的完成，如植物学，需要几代人的努力。学习外语亦是如此，必须从一开始就做好长年学习的准备，切不可急于收获。学习汉语，尤其如此。

学习外语的另一困难与教学方法有关。现代的教学方法大抵是成功的，但结果并非尽善尽美。通常是集中若干年龄相仿的学生于一室之内，由老师讲授知识，有时亦采用教材。针对一些综合性和专业性的课程，辅助以录音磁带和影像资料。学生须独立完成大量功课，或撰写论文，或阅读补充材料。在一阶段学习结束后，会组织考试。考试合格者颁发一证书或文凭，课程就此结束。这是现代的民主式教学，其优点是向大众普及教育，使学习有所规范，此法实可称道。不幸的是，其教学方法也是一张普罗克汝斯忒斯之床[2]。设若老师学识渊博，循循善诱，且教法得当，则多数学生可以达到标准，但另一部分学生却无法企及；而最优秀者原本可以超出平均水平许多，却不能进一步发展。有经验的老师都知道，这好比是朝某一方向无的放矢，只能希望多数箭中的，但也明白肯定会有脱靶者。或许有人会说，这是教育机构的性质所决定的，别无良策。事实上，教育标准和考试方法皆有待完善。然而每年求学者数量众多，仅考虑到这一事实就很难寻出更好的办法。

这不禁使人想起中国古代之教育。旧的教育系统固然不适合现代社会，但就民族语言的教学而言，仍不失为一种好方法。在古希腊罗马社会想必亦如此。每逢文化繁荣，学者和文人便纷纷涌现——历朝历代皆有类似的繁荣期，或长或短——然其绝不可批量制造，如工厂之产品一般。集体主义在某种意义上一直存在，但每个人的个性也应受到尊重。教学的特点是，一位或几位老师轮流或同时给一名学生独立授课。这好比是开垦

---

1.   p. 328, Ashram edition, 1953.

2.   Procrustes，希腊神话中的强盗，海神波塞冬之子，以铁床之长短齐睡者之身，长者截短，短者拉长。含义近似汉语中的"削足适履"。——译者注

一片荒地，于学生为未知，于老师却是熟悉的；学生扶着老师的手，尽可能向远处探寻，而不受学年之限制。求学的过程中，也不必存有竞争和奖励。一位名士门下可能有成百上千的弟子和门生，他会针对各人的情况单独授课，或者有所选择地分小组指导，而对于初学者，则指派年长的学生担任私人教师。考试由国家统一组织。隐退的大臣和政府官员、知名的学士、考取功名以及落榜的读书人，都可以成为塾师，给贵族和富家子弟授课。与古罗马时代的希腊家庭教师不同，塾师享有较高的社会地位。他可以在村庄创办私学，招收少量学生，并受到民众的尊崇，类似于印度婆罗门教的导师。政府在各城镇和省份设有学府，最高一级的学府隶属于中央政府。较大的城镇或风景秀美的地区也普遍设有高等书院，在那里每位学生有单独的师傅指导，但同时也接受其他老师的授课。学生可以参加综合课程，并开展独立的研究，不定期撰写论文以检验其学习进展。各书院的学习年份没有限制，学术荣誉取决于师出何门以及个人成就。如此，青年人受到训练、教育和熏陶，要之，他们接受的是独立教育，并以个人发展为目标。这种教育体制在中国一直沿用，直到50年前才被废止。

此法在现代社会却很难通行，因为只有极少数人能够负担私教的费用。而人天性喜欢群居，自觉或不自觉偏好数量众多之事物。即使是百万富翁，也宁愿资助以大众教育为目标的机构，并送子女前往就读，而不愿意花更少的钱让子女接受私家教育。许多知名学者也不愿出任私人教师，宁可给一群而非几个学生授课。但问题的关键在于：要完全精通一门语言，必须接受单独教育，由一良师采用恰当的方法，弥之以岁月，成之于无形，而不必以寻常标准为绳。此实为一贵族式的教育，亦是更为自由的教育。

除了任意附加的标准，各类考试制度也应取消。全国性考试和学术性考试的作用是完全不同的，此处不予讨论。西方许多教育机构已经部分废除考试制度，代之以其他必要之测试[3]。于此，论及一归旨性问题：学习中文的目的是为了切合当下之实际需要，如在商务领域；还是为了更高上之目标，当然最终亦有其实用价值。如前文所言，还必须考虑时间因素。克实而论，学习新知识是越年轻越好。一般而言，培养一名普通的梵语专家大致需要 14 年，于中文而言，因日常生活中仍在使用，时间可能稍短，也不少于 10 年。开始学习的时间以稍晚为宜，可在完成高等教育之后。无论个人或民族都应先学母语，后习外语，外语终是第二位的。待之应如同宾客，不能喧宾夺主。学习外语之前，应先掌握母语，因为所学的新知识经由母语传授，才容易被本族人接受。年龄稍大的人理解力更强，正可以弥补记忆力之不足。

某些人确有学习语言之特殊才能，然则是极少数，不能期望人人有此天资，故不能作普遍情况考虑。也有不少优秀的汉学家，按照自创之特殊方法而掌握了汉语。但普通人最好还是遵循常法，一步一个脚印地学习每

---

3. 本书初版时，中国大陆的大学已经废除常规的考试制度多年，但他们的学术水平和质量似乎并未因此降低。所以就结果而言，废除考试制度是积极而有益的。

个汉字的读音、含义和书写规范。汉语是单音节字，每个音节有少则四种、多则五种的声调，学习时必加以区分。每个汉字都有特定的书写规范，也是最便于书写的方式。严格地说，正确的书写规范与书法有关。书法是一门精妙的中国艺术，必须经年潜心练习（通常是临摹一种或多种石刻拓片）——外国学习者倒不必在此用功，只需掌握每个汉字的正确写法，坚持练习方能熟练书写。初学时如不加以训练，则永远无法知道这些点、钩、折、横是如何组合在一起的。而字母 a，b，c，d 则无此困难，只须连笔书写即可。学习汉语若不能区分五种声调，不了解基本的韵律知识，则无从欣赏诗歌和韵文；若没有适当的书写训练，则无法辨认形近字；学习越深入，困难越多，最终不堪重负，彻底失去学习的兴趣。笔者以为，多数学习者的抱怨都源于此——初学时没能掌握此两项基本技能。对于声调变化，成年人一小时之内便可掌握，当然，每个字的读音之后仍须单独学习；对于汉字的书写，以每天练习一小时计，则最多需要一年。那么，学习中文真的很难吗？当然，中文的音韵学，尤其是古代之韵律，词源学以及古文字学皆可独立成为一门学科，穷尽毕生研究，然而初学者不宜在此用力。

于此，自然生出一问题：若中文全无字母系统，每个汉字必须单独学习，那么需要学习多少个汉字呢？这当然因人而异。近年，有一项针对小学的调查，根据统计数据，以每天平均学习 4 到 5 个字计算（每周28字），4 年后可掌握 4864 个字，其中包括 3861 个常用字，574 个不常用字，以及 429 个生僻字。这对于任何实用之目的已是不可胜用。⁴ 一间印刷厂，配备 7000 个汉字已可谓完备，只须偶尔增铸新字即可。有一部现代词典名叫《辞海》，收录了约 13 000 个汉字，其中许多为非常用字，还有许多已然废用。

其次，谈谈语法和句法。任何语言自创立之初必有其语法，汉语亦有一些基本的语法要素，但实际使用中并无成文的规定。汉语的名词没有阴阳性和单复数变化，动词亦无变位，而是借用辅助词来表达一个名词或动词的确切含义。梵语以语法繁复著称，但佛经自梵文译成汉语却毫无障碍。然而，欲将汉语"复原"或回译成梵文却十分困难，因其在汉译的过程中，原文一些精确的表达常被省略了。

学习语法应配合文学欣赏，而不必另作一课程。上世纪末（约 1875—1908 年间），一位名叫马建忠的中国学者被公派到法国留学。归国后，他参照法语的模式，写了一部中文语法书《马氏文通》。此书名气虽不大，却胜在能以欧洲之语法系统释义中国之古典名著和历史。此书对于学者是有所裨益的，但不适合教学之用。简括言之，汉语或有不足和缺陷，至若语法体系则无可诘难。较之拉丁文和希腊文，英语语法可谓松散，甚至较德语和法语亦然，但在实际使用中并不觉得含糊或不便。

本文将对汉字的形成作概要说明，并列出一些示例。旨在阐明其基本原则，且仅限于适度的范围，因为对汉字的过度阐释有时反而让人愈加困

---

4. 中国大陆有一种汉语"速成班"，让农民在很短时间内学习 1500 个汉字。但这种情况不在本书讨论范畴，因为学习者都是已经会说汉语的本国人。

感，何况许多汉字现在已经不使用了。17 世纪末，有一位大学者顾亭林开始深入研究古代汉语。此项工作经过几代学人之努力，持续了近 300 年，直至近几十年才声势渐弱，其结果引出了一个极具争议性的观点，即研究古代文学应先识汉字，然而字典所录之汉字不必尽数习之，这只于语言专家为必要。本书收录了现在最常用的汉字，注以古体写法、读音、字义及所属类别。正文之前是汉字简史，后面是现代音标。书中亦附有规范的书写示例。所有字体皆可作字帖临摹，久之方可掌握书法。

至此，不应忽略，学习汉语尽管有上述诸多困难，但作为一种单音节语言，汉语自有其优势。汉语诉之于口，简洁而优雅，较之当下的任何流行语言毫不逊色。汉语中绝不会出现三个以上的辅音单独发声而不与元音相拼的情况；也绝无同一元音重复五六次之多——尤其是"a"音。汉语中甚至没有德语的"r"音。但其最大的优势一直被忽略了：在大多数语言中一个单词由几个音节组成，只表达一词之意；而汉语中几个音节相拼可表示数个词，传达出一整句话的意思。显然，汉语省时，并且省力。我们注意到，今人写作有一倾向，偏好用三个音节以下的词，此文风常被斥为不雅。尽管如此，社会关系的日益复杂却加剧了这一倾向，促使人们愈加惜字如金。字母本身并不传达任何意思，一些前缀和后缀也只能表示话语的形式。学习汉语应从最简单、最基本的汉字入手，而不是字母。字与字可组合成复合词或短语，含义即各部分相加之和。这对推广基础教育十分有利，特别是对于未受过教育之民众，更容易理解新的复合词。既已识得各个简单部件，复合词之义便一望而知，可省下不少学习新词的功夫。这一简单的语言之"化学反应"，下文将举例说明：

　　火、水、河、手、口、人、牛、马等，皆为常用汉字，对于不会读写、未受过教育的成人，也是自然知道的。如若"火"和"水"合为复合词"火－水"，则不难理解是指易燃之液体，如"石油"或"汽油"。反之，若言"水－火"，稍加思索便知是"相互敌对的"意思，因为水火自不相容。"河"和"马"合为复合词"河马"（hippopotamus），与希腊词源之"马"（hipopo）和"河"（tamus）正好对应。若以英语"hippopotamus"一词提问英国孩子，而他未曾学过，便会不知所云；而对于中国孩子，"河马"是一目了然的，根本不必费力去拼写和记忆一长串的字母"h-i-p-p-o-p-o-t-a-m-u-s"及其重读音节。"人"与"口"合为"人口"（population）；"水"加"牛"即"水牛"（buffalo）；"水"并"手"即"水手"（sailor）；"人"和"马"皆作复数，即"人马"，指"部队"（troops）等。以此类推，汉字由简单的词语组合，造出成倍的复合词，却无有混淆。这种造词法与梵语之复合词类似，却无后者之极度冗长。由此可知，学习汉语是相对简单和轻松的。中华民族世代的智慧凝结成汉语之一贯原则，言极简而意深切。这正是汉语固有之特殊价值——高度的灵活性和兼容性；也是汉语流传至今的原因。无论是新思想、新术语，抑或新法典，汉语皆兼容并收，从而适应科学之发展，是以为证。

　　汉语省力，自然也省时。但汉字书写另有一优点关乎空间。寻常是一汉字占据约 1 厘米见方的空间。较之英语，一个单词往往由一串字母组成，从 1 到 20 个不等。假设每个单词平均包含 5 个字母，此估算当然偏低，则单词与字母之比为 1∶5。如若印刷一汉字所占的空间同于一英语字母——事实亦常如此，则印刷英文所用的空间将远远超过汉语。此优势常常被忽略，因为英语字母是横向排列的。倘若换一种方式对比英语单词和与之对应的汉语，例如：

（英语）	（汉语）	（英语）	（汉语）
hippo potta mus	河 马	po pu la ti on	人 口
more	多	less	少
great	大	small	小

则英语和汉语所占空间之差异便一目了然。

中文和英文的这种差别在印刷中更为明显。寻常是一页英文资料翻译并印刷成法语，大抵也只有一页，反之亦然。而同一资料翻译成汉语，无论是白话文还是今之口语，取相同字号印刷，如 10.5，则汉语译文往往不足一页，大致可省下 1/8 到 1/6 页。如若以文言文或古文翻译，则字数还会减半。然而汉语与英语所占空间之比例绝不为 1∶5，因为一个英语单词往往对应 2—3 个汉字。尽管如此，汉语仍可节省出不少空间。印刷大部头书籍时，汉语在纸张使用、销售以及人工方面的优势就非常明显了。

汉语还有一个重要特点常被忽视，即为保存人类知识之巨大贡献。汉字作为一门语言，其书写鲜有变化。同一词在不同方言中的发音和读音或有差别，但书写和含义却是一致的。在中国，阅读两千年前之古书与阅读今之书籍无甚差异。然而，在欧洲欲就某一问题求得如此久远之史实，必借助希腊文和拉丁文。这两门语言因受圣经文化影响，多年来已极少使用。如若想了解中世纪之知识，除了学习现代英语和近代高地德语之外，必求之于古英语、中世纪英语、高地德语和低地德语[5]。古法语时期之"奥克语"（Language d'oc）和"奥伊语"（Language d'oïl）[6] 情形也差不多。以西方学术界眼光视之，此为高等教育和高雅文化必不可少者。克实而论，不同国家和民族之间的语言障碍已颇受重视，然而极少人关注到母语自身之历史障碍，每一代人为此额外耗费了（且不谓浪费）不少的精力和时间。将来又会如何呢？生活于 30 或 40 世纪之人类能否理解今之 20 世纪呢？以

---

5. 德语的形成大致经历了六个阶段：日尔曼语（Germanisch：公元前 2000—650 年）；古高地德语（Althochdeutsch：650—1050 年）；中高地德语（Mittelhochdeutsch：1050—1350 年）；早期近代德语（Frühneuhochdeutsch：1350—1650 年）；近代高地德语（Neuhochdeutsch：1650—1900 年）；现代德语（Gegenwartsprache：1900 年至今）。——译者注

6. 公元 9—13 世纪是古法语时期，也称"中世纪法语"，语言学家根据"是"字在不同地区的发音，把方言大体分为两类：卢瓦河以南地区的南方方言"奥克语"（Language d'oc，普罗旺斯语中 oc 表示"是"）和卢瓦河以北地区的北方方言"奥伊语"（Language d'oïl，oïl 即现代法语中的 oui，表示"是"）。奥克语后来演变为普罗旺斯语，奥伊语则最终演变为现代法语。——译者注

过去之发展看，一种基于构架和形式的语言会更有生命力。它犹如一永恒之舟承载着各种知识——物质的或精神的——不断前行，驶向远而愈远的前方，可以是人类最好的守护者。由此，人类可望赢得我们永不停步的朋友——时间。

在此有一词源学上的门径。本书的初衷并非作为汉语词典或教材使用。读者若能怀着愉快的心思阅读、临摹并思索书中的各种字体，可逐渐掌握汉字，而无须死记硬背。所谓哭丧着脸学习一门语言，只能算成功了一半，因为学习任何语言原本不是痛苦的事，怀着快乐而自由的心思足矣。通习此书，可以减少许多背诵汉字的功夫，亦可了解汉字的本源。本书的初始目的在于帮助初学者学习汉语。如若有读者对汉字的象形和象征特性感兴趣，亦可资参考，但这是次要的，亦非本书之目的。书中的汉字均给出词源学注释，故而也是最为可信的，读者可用作阅读理解古籍的基础工具，特别是哲学古籍。因为随着岁月的流逝，一些文字的释义逐渐变得含混不清了。此乃本书之高上目标，亦是其真正价值之所在。但这也只合为通向更高层次学习之一初步，此外别无捷径了。

最后，谨以此书作为微薄之礼献给我们的神圣母亲，是她的远见以及无上力量乃促成此书。愿所有读者皆荣享她的神圣恩慈。

徐梵澄 于瑲地舍里 1963 年 7 月

INTRODUCTION

During the past sixty years or more, great efforts have been made by the intelligentsia in China towards the simplification of the language, and, with the abolition of many dialects, towards the standardization of the national tongue with the idea of a gradual reduction and final disappearance of illiteracy. Much indeed has been done, but in view of the immensity of the population and the complexity and profundity of the language itself, even the considerable achievement of the past decade can only be regarded as a first step on the long journey ahead.

First, as a prelude to this *Analysis*, a word must be said about learning the language. As a result of the great demand for knowledge of Chinese in recent years, there have been many complaints about the difficulties non Chinese have in learning it. But as far as I know, Chinese students in the past have made similar complaints about the difficulty of learning foreign languages. In fact, no language can be easy. Even English, a language so widely used that it has assumed an international importance nowadays, can by no means be described as easy, especially for us Chinese. Since every living language must be growing and changing all the time, it is difficult for anyone except an occasional great poet, prosaist, dramatist or philologist to justly say that he has a complete mastery and command of his own mother tongue. With the ancient languages such as Greek or Latin or Sanskrit, the case is even more burdensome. Even at the very first, the numerous inflections of nouns, conjugations of verbs, and, in Sanskrit, the lengthy compounds carry the student into deep waters.

Within the Indo-European family the diverse tongues have still somehow an affinity to each other, though there was in the past actually no one Indo-German language in existence. In their fundamental structure, they all have a phonetic system, a grammar and a syntax, all comparable to well-hewn, well-paved paths for travellers to follow. English and French are examples of this; they are so similar to each other that between them there are approximately 6,000 words more or less alike, with only slight differences of spelling or meaning, as they are mostly of a common Latin origin. Naturally an Englishman can learn French easily, and vice versa, especially as both are popular and commonly used nowadays. About one hundred and thirty million people in the world use French as an official language, a fact reminiscent of its glorious past when, beginning in the seventeenth century, it was used chiefly in the diplomatic as well as in high cultural fields. But the tendency of the present day is more and more towards the expansion and predominance of English. Apart from Mandarin Chinese, English is now spoken as a first language by more people than any other language in the world, according to the most recent statistics.

Yet Chinese, though now used by the largest population of the world, is still confined within the boundaries of its realm. As opposed to any language of the Indo-European family, Chinese has neither an alphabet nor any written grammar. In fact everything about it is different. Yet no one can deny that it is a language of high culture with a history of nearly 5,000 years, and it is a living one still. Let us then sensibly ask: could it have lasted so long and been so widely used if it were actually so difficult to learn?

The difficulties arise for many reasons. The problem is a very complicated one, and in the end it is even connected with our modern educational system in general. Usually as a second language it is not learned in the right way. Psychologically speaking, the difficulty is not so much with the language itself as with our own mental attitude. We are all in a sense bound by our prejudices and habits, and figuratively speaking, one may say that there is scarcely anyone who can empty himself like a vessel of its contents for the new liquid to be poured in. A child learns things more readily than an adult because he is empty or free. If that upper chamber is crowded or clouded, how can light shine upon it from outside or any ray shine forth from within?

Moreover, society in modern times has changed and life has become much busier. We have neither the leisure nor the patience to dive deep and immerse ourselves in the cultural atmosphere of another land, even when we have partially learned its language; and what is learned apart from its cultural context can easily be lost. The blissful olive tree, a gift from Athene, begins to bear fruit only thirty years after planting, yet it yields fruit for a hundred years before it withers away. In seeking knowledge in general, we are nowadays often too anxious, if not too ambitious, for its fruits; and we want to hasten the process of acquiring it, to make it easier and more comfortable like the commodities of our daily life. This phenomenon is explicable and excusable because, as one of the underlying principles of our civilisation, it is our common urge to make things easier and happier. But why do we want to learn a foreign language? It is because we want to understand the other people, their living habits, their mentality, their culture, all their achievements both in the material and spiritual fields in order to march together to the higher goals of life and eventually to create a happier world for all. By this means we can learn and assimilate what is best in another race, and when the other people are backward we may hasten their progress. As Sri Aurobindo once remarked in *The Future Poetry*, "To know other countries is not to belittle but enlarge our own country and help it to a greater power of its own being".[1] For all this, language is of course the key. But there is one important factor which we should never ignore — Time. Scientists must often devote an entire lifetime to certain researches, and some experiments, such as in botany, must be carried on through generations. The same is the case with learning any foreign language. From the very beginning we must be prepared to spend many years in study, possibly without thinking of reaping the fruits. With the Chinese language that is especially true.

Another difficulty is connected with the method of teaching. Most modern methods are successful to a large extent, but the result is never total or complete. Nowadays a number of students of approximately the same age gather in a classroom where the knowledge is imparted by the instructor, using a textbook if available. Tape recordings and films are used as an auxiliary to lectures on general and on special subjects. The student is asked to work a great deal by himself writing essays, doing extra reading etc. Then after a certain period of time an examination is given. When that is passed, the student receives a certificate or diploma and the course is ended. This is the modern democratic way, and considering its merits in extending education to the masses and in bringing about some sort of standardization of learning, it is even admirable. Unfortunately it is also a bed of Procrustes. Assuming that the professor is quite competent, his influence inspiring, and his method of teaching ideal, a good number of students may come up to the standard, still others may fall below the level, and the best ones may shoot far above the level and then not proceed farther. Experienced professors can see that it is still a matter of firing shots at

.

1.   p. 328, Ashram edition, 1953.

random in a certain direction, expecting that many may hit the mark, knowing that some may fail. But they would say that there is no better way, due to the nature of the educational institutions. In fact not only the standardization but also the ways of examination are not free from imperfections. But it seems that scarcely any better way can be found, considering the simple fact that so many students have to be taught every year.

Coming to this point one cannot keep from thinking of the ancient Chinese way. The system of education in China in ancient times is indeed unsuitable to our modern age, but with regard to the teaching of its national language, the method was an excellent one. This must have been true also in the ancient Graeco-Roman world. Scholars or men of letters were too numerous to be counted in those times when culture flourished—as there must be periods of such flowering, whether short or long, in every dynasty—but they were never, mass-produced like goods from a factory. Collectivism in a certain sense always existed, but the individuality of each person was respected. The special characteristic is that everyone was taught individually and separately by a teacher or several teachers successively or at the same time. It was like exploring a foreign land unknown to the pupil but well-known to the master, and, taken by the hand, he might proceed as far as he could for an unlimited period of years. In the course of learning there was no need for competitions or prizes. With a great master, disciples and followers might amount to hundreds or thousands, yet each one was taught by him separately and individually, or else he placed them in very small groups according to his choice, and for the newcomers he would appoint some of his old disciples as private teachers. Examinations were undertaken by the state. Retired ministers and high officials of the government, eminent learned men, and scholars who had passed or not passed the various examinations of the state could be private tutors of one or more children in a noble or wealthy family, and, unlike the Greek tutor in the Roman world, the social standing of a teacher was an honourable one. In a village a scholar could establish a sort of grammar school of his own with a small group of pupils and, not unlike the Brahmin Guru in India, he was highly revered by the common people. In every town there was an educational directorate established by the government, and also one in each province, and finally the highest one was in the central government. Colleges for higher learning were common in large towns, or in localities with beautiful landscapes, and in those the student had the director as his private master, though he might be taught by different teachers. He could attend general lectures and he had to do independent research work, and every now and then he had to write theses to test his progress. The number of years of his stay in this or that college was unlimited, and his academic honor lay in having been the disciple of this or that famous master, and in his personal achievements. The youths were, in this way, trained and educated and cultured, but all in all, they were taught separately for their individual development. That system lasted in China until about fifty years ago.

In modern times this is well-nigh impossible, and very few people can afford individual tuition. The herd instinct is always there in our human nature, and knowingly or unknowingly we like things in great quantities and large numbers. Even a millionaire might be inclined to contribute funds to an institution for the education of many and send his children there instead of having them trained by private tutors at a small expenditure. Many eminent professors refrain from taking a job as a private tutor, preferring to teach a multitude at a time instead of a few. Here then we have come to the kernel of the problem: if the learning of this language is to be entirely successful, each student must be taught individually and separately by a good teacher using correct methods for a number of years, without regard to the general standard, which will shape itself. This is a rather aristocratic but more liberal way.

Together with the superimposed standard, which is quite arbitrary, the unnecessary examination system can be done away with. The use of examinations to a state is entirely different from that of the academic field, but we need not dwell upon that subject here, since many of the educational institutions in the West have partially abolished the examination system and have resorted to other means of testing when necessary[2]. But at this juncture we come across the problem of the initial orientation: whether to learn the Chinese language for an immediate practical purpose, say, for its use in the commercial field, or to learn it for a larger and higher purpose, though in the end that must be practical as well. The time to be spent must be taken into consideration, as said before. Indeed, it is easier to learn a new thing when one is young. Generally it takes fourteen years to develop an ordinary Sanskrit scholar, and for Chinese, since it is daily used, the term may be shorter, but no less than ten years. Yet it is advisable to begin this career fairly late, that is to say, after one has completed his higher education. Naturally, for any people or nation, learning a foreign language must come after learning the native one and it must occupy a secondary place. It is to be treated as a guest, and according to a Chinese proverb, even a noisy (i.e. presumptious) guest cannot take the place of the host or hostess. Before learning a second language it is better to have mastered one's own, because it is through that, after all, that any new knowledge thus acquired can be readily imparted to one's own people. However, better understanding at a riper age compensates for shortcomings in memory ability.

There are certain people with a special talent for learning languages, but such people are rare, and we cannot expect everyone to have such an

2. At the time of publication of this book we have learnt that the ordinary examination system has been abolished in the universities of mainland China for several years, and this does not seem to have lowered the level or lessened the quality of academic achievements there. The results of this practice have presumably been quite positive and salutary.

innate aptitude, so in general they cannot be brought into consideration. Many a good Sinologist has mastered this language quite well following his own special method. But with the average man it is still the usual practical way of learning that must be followed; the path must be trodden step by step, and the sound, the meaning and the correct way of writing each word must be learned. And in learning the pronunciation of each syllable, as Chinese is a monosyllabic language, five or at least four different tones must be distinguished. Each word has to be written in a definite way which is also the most convenient way. Strictly speaking, the correct writing is connected with calligraphy, which is by itself an elevated art in China, one which demands practice (usually by copying the rubbings from stone inscriptions of a definite style or different styles) for many years; but a foreigner need not go to such lengths. Only learning the proper way of writing each word is required and gradually after constant practice one can write a word easily. Without this training from the very beginning, one is permanently at a loss as to how to put a number of dots, hooks, dashes and strokes together. Simply to write a, b, c, d, with the letters joined gives no such trouble. Without knowing the distinction of the five tones, together with a common knowledge of rhyme, no poem or rhythmic prose can be read and appreciated and, without the proper training in writing at first, similar words cannot be easily distinguished; difficulties will increase as one advances until finally they become so heavy a load that one drops the study altogether. Most of the complaints, I suppose, must have come from this source — one has not mastered these two essential things at the very beginning. Yet the variation of tones can be learned by adults within an hour, with of course the tone of each word learned later, and the writing course would require a maximum of one year with one hour of practice every day. Is that then actually so difficult? Chinese phonology, especially ancient euphonics, etymology and paleography are different subjects that can occupy one's whole life in research, but they are not for beginners.

The natural question arises: if there is no alphabet at all in Chinese and every word must be learned separately, then how many words should we learn? It is very flexible. A general estimate has been made for primary schools in recent years. The number of words usually mastered after four years of learning, beginning with 4 or 5 words a day (28 words a week) amounts to 4,864, including 3,861 most commonly used, 574 less common, and a reserve of 429 uncommon words. This would be more than sufficient for all practical purposes.[3] A printing press equipped with 7,000 words is said to be complete, with a few occasional supplements from the foundry. A modern dictionary called "The Ocean of Phraseology" contains about 13,000 words, but many are rare and infrequently used and many others are obsolete.

.

3. In the mainland a "crash course" of 1,500 words is taught to the agrarian population in a very short time, but this is of less consideration here as these people already speak the language.

The next question is that of grammar or syntax. By its very construction every language must have some grammar of its own and, in Chinese, we find the same elements of grammar in existence, but there is no written set of rules in use. We do not have distinctions of gender, inflections of nouns, or changes of verbs, yet by using auxiliary words we can convey the idea of every noun or verbal form precisely. In fact, there was almost no trouble in translating Buddhist texts into Chinese from Sanskrit, a language well known for its complex grammar. However, to "restore" or rather to re-translate them into Sanskrit presents some difficulty because the meticulous exactitudes of the originals were often ignored in Chinese translations.

In learning the language grammar is taught along with literature, and there need not be a separate course for it. At the end of the last century (somewhere between 1875 and 1908) a Chinese scholar named Ma Chien Chun 马建忠 was sent by the Chinese government to France for studies. On returning to China he wrote a Chinese grammar called "Ma's Grammar" 《马氏文通》 patterned after a French one. His book, not too well known, had some merit in helping to elucidate the texts of ancient classics and histories in the light of European grammar and it proved useful to scholars to a certain extent, but nobody used it for teaching purposes. On the whole we may say that there may be other defects or deficiencies in the Chinese language, but with regard to grammatical construction there are none. English is much loose in its grammar than Latin or Greek, or even than German and French, but it is neither defective nor inefficient for our modern usage.

A general idea is given in this treatise, with a number of examples, of the formation of Chinese words. Since the purpose here is only to elucidate the fundamentals, and that also only to a limited extent because sometimes by further analysis of a word one is led to greater perplexities, many words are not employed. At the end of the seventeenth century a great scholar named Ku Ting Ling 顾亭林 began a profound study of ancient Chinese. This study was continued by many generations of scholars for nearly three hundred years and it began to diminish in fervour only a few decades ago. But finally a great controversy arose when it was argued that in order to study the ancient literature one must of course first recognize the words, but one should not be required to learn every word in the dictionary. That would only be necessary for specialists. Here we take only those words most commonly used today; the original form of every word is given with its pronunciation and meaning under the category to which it belongs. Preceding this is a very brief survey of the history of the Chinese language, and the modern system of phonetic signs is at the end. Some examples of the correct method of writing are also given. Also all the written words may be used as models for copying, in order to master calligraphy.

Now at this point we must not fail to note that this monosyllabic language has certain advantageous characteristic of itself, in spite of all the difficulties in learning which have been mentioned. In speaking it can be just as easy and pleasant as any of our popular languages today. Three or more consonants to be pronounced together without a vowel, or five or six repetitions of the same vowel —especially 'a' —in a word are never found. Even the sound of a German 'r' is not present. But the greatest advantage which remains usually unnoticed is that in most languages we must utter several syllables to say a word, and then only the idea of one word is expressed; whereas when we utter several syllables in Chinese, several words are said and the idea of an entire sentence is stated. Obviously there is a certain economy of effort and of time as well. We note that in modern writing there is a tendency to use words of no more than three syllables, and that is considered to be a lack of elegance in style. Be that as it may, the tendency toward economy of words is accelerated by the increasing complexity of our social relationships. Letters by themselves do not convey any sense, and certain prefixes and suffixes can only indicate forms of speech. In Chinese simple and elementary words are learned instead of alphabets, and when they form compounds or terms, the meaning can be recognized through their components, this being a great convenience in elementary education, especially that of the illiterate masses. Therefore it is easier for them to comprehend new complex terms. If one understands a term spontaneously through the simple components one already knows, then one is spared much effort in learning new words. This simple linguistic chemistry can be illustrated by a few examples:

Fire, Water, River, Hand, Mouth, Man, Ox, Horse... all these are common words. These words are naturally known to the illiterate adult who can neither read nor write them. If we combine the two sounds of 'fire' and 'water', forming a compound of 'fire-water', he can easily understand that this means that liquid which is combustible, i.e. 'petroleum' or 'petrol'. Conversely, if we say 'water-fire' then by a slight turn of mind he can think of the idea of 'being antagonistic', because these two things are mutually exclusive. 'River' and 'horse' combined into one compound means 'hippopotamus', just as its Greek origin of 'horse' and 'river'. If you say this word to an English child and if he has not learned it he may be puzzled, wondering what gibberish you are uttering. But to a Chinese child a 'river-horse' is almost self-evident. He is spared the effort of spelling and memorizing the long word 'h-i-p-p-o-p-o-t-a-m-u-s' together with its correct accent. 'Man' and 'mouth' together means 'population'. 'Water-ox' is the 'buffalo'. 'Water-hand' is the 'sailor'. 'Man' and 'Horse', both understood in the plural, means the 'troops', and so on. In this way very simple words are multiplied into a great number of compounds without confusion. The process is very much like the formation of compounds in Sanskrit but without its extension to any great length. In this respect the Chinese language is comparatively simple and easy to learn. Its underlying principle, forged through the ages by the wisdom of the race, is always the same, i.e. to express the most by means of the least without ambiguity. And herein lies an important and inherent value of this language, a high flexibility and adaptibility, which is revealed by its entrance into the modern world. The rich inflow and steady absorption of new ideas, new terminologies, and new codifications to meet the requirements of the advancing sciences attest to this.

Less effort means less time. With regard to the written language there is yet another advantage so far as space is concerned. In hand-writing a Chinese word is normally written in a square form of about one centimeter. We may take English as a comparison. An English word may be composed of a number of letters varying from one to twenty. Let us suppose an average of five letters per word, which is of course a very low estimate. The ratio between the number of words and the number of letters is then 1 to 5. If a printed Chinese word occupies only as much space as an English letter, as is often the case, then printed English requires far more space than printed Chinese. We forget this because the letters are arranged in a horizontal line. If we put them together in another way and compare their equivalents in Chinese, for example:

(English)	(Chinese)	(English)	(Chinese)
hippo potta mus	河 马	po pu la ti on	人 口
more	多	less	少
great	大	small	小

then the difference between the space occupied by an English word and that by a Chinese word becomes remarkable.

This is more evident in printing. Usually a page in English printed and translated into French is still approximately one page, and vice versa. Rendering the same into Chinese, in Pei Hwa or the spoken language of today and printing it with types of the same size, say of $10^{1}/_{2}$ points, it covers usually less than a page. It may be less by 1/8 to 1/6. Putting it into Wen Yen, or classical style, the reduction of the words may come to half of the former. Yet it can never come to that ratio of 1 to 5, because an English word is usually expressed in Chinese by two or three words. Nevertheless, much space can be saved. When a thick volume is to be printed, the economy of paper, chasing and all labour costs involved can be clearly seen.

There is still another important characteristic which is often overlooked that contributes greatly to the conservation of human knowledge. In a language like Chinese the written forms scarcely change. The sound or pronunciation of a word may vary according to different dialects, but its written form and its meaning remain always the same. In China people read books written two thousand years ago just as we read books of today. Whereas in Europe if we want to acquire some historical knowledge on a subject of such antiquity we must resort to Greek and Latin, and both these owe much of their fragile existence throughout the ages to the Bible. For obtaining knowledge of the Middle Ages one must also go through Old or Middle English, or

High or Low German, all to be learned apart from Modern English and New High German. With Langue d'oc and Langue d'oïl, the case is no better. Intelligentsia in the West regard this as a natural part of higher education and culture. Indeed, the language barrier between nations or races has attracted a large measure of attention, but few people have reflected upon the problem of the extra energy and time which whole generations have spent, if not wasted, on this historical barrier within the realm of their mother tongue. And what will be the condition in the future? Shall we people of the twentieth century be understood by man in the thirtieth or fortieth century? Judged by developments in the past, a language based on form or shape lasts longer. A solid mass of knowledge, physical or spiritual, conveyed by an everlasting vehicle, rolling and progressing ever farther and farther, can be the greatest guardian of humanity. And by that means we shall have won back our ever fleeing friend—Time.

Here then is an etymological approach. This book is not meant to be a dictionary or a textbook. If these scripts are read and copied or meditated upon in a joyful mood, gradually they can be mastered without the need of cramming. To say that any language is learned without tears declares only its partial success, because no language should be learned with tears. Only a happy and free state of mind is needed. Thoroughly studying this book should greatly lighten the effort of memorizing the vocabulary, and by this one can understand the language in its essence. The immediate purpose of this book as a help to beginners ends here. It may also be interesting to those who have natural inclinations toward pictorial or symbolical forms, but that can neither be of primary importance nor is it the intention of this book. But since the authentic etymological and hence the most reliable explanations arc given, this affords a substantial means for the correct understanding of ancient texts, especially those of philosophy, upon which vague and misty annotations have gradually accumulated throughout the ages. The far-reaching consequences of such a work go up to this point where presumably its true value lies. This serves as the first step on a royal way to higher studies, though there is as yet no royal way.

Finally it must be said that this book is essentially meant as a small offering to our Divine Mother under Whose providential guidance with Her supramental force alone it has come into being. May all readers enjoy Her Blessings.

F. C. Hsu   Pondicherry   July 1963

汉语简史

一

中国古文字上可追溯到结绳记事时代，结绳记事法的影响至今可见，某些语言的字母是纵向书写的，如梵文。古希腊字母亦可能源于这一习俗。人类早期文明中，结绳记事之法必非常普遍，至今南美洲一些原住部落仍然沿用。随着时代发展，此法逐渐废用，其间的发展已无从知晓。大抵从亚述人建造独立城邦，埃及人修建金字塔开始（约公元前 3000 年），中国人创立书写文字，为人类文明带来新的曙光——从此进入一新的历史时期。扩大观之，古代的标记、符号、图案、象形文字等，皆可算作书写文字的基础和来源。根据传说，八卦是由圣君或名士庖牺首创，后世亦称宓牺（伏羲，因古汉语中没有轻唇塞音——译者）。卦与卦重叠排列，又创出 64 种卦象。在上古社会，此类图案极可能具有某些社会功能，故有其社会学上的价值。此只存为一假说，然亦不能排除八卦与早期文字可能存在某种联系。八卦之首为"乾"，指"天"，书写时微倾即为"气"字[1]，指"空气"或"气息"。这两个字的读音也几乎相同，只是音调略有差异。八卦之"坎"[2]横向书写即为古体之"水"字，指"注水入器"，这在"益"字中亦有所体现。此类古代字体后来逐渐发展成神秘的玄学系统，用于占卜神谕，进而失去了日常语言和交际的功能。此仅为理论上一假设，然较为可信。[3]

据称，汉语文字之始创者为圣贤苍颉。于其生平，只知道时在中国第一任君王黄帝（前2698—前2598）统治时期，他在朝中担任史官，并创造出所有汉字。然而，即使是超凡的圣贤或天才，亦很难凭一己之力创立一整套的书写规范，并印刷出来（时人还很难想象出印刷术），公开发行使用。至若口头语之字母表，历史上曾有一二人为本族创出之先例，然此为另一事。可能的情况是，当时已有许多古代社会创出的文字在使用，直到苍颉这位饱学之士出现，才使汉字规范化。此后，汉字有了固定的写法，进而减少了书写之混乱。苍颉收集和编撰的书写规范则被奉为权威。传说故事止于此，也就不必再深究了。

此后的历史学家普遍认为，中国约于公元前2698年进入有史时期。随

.

1. 见本书第114页（II.4）。

2. 见本书第117页（II.9）。

3. 卫礼贤（Richard Wilhelm），德国著名汉学家，他发现"Yes"表示为一条未折断的线，而"No"表示为一条折断的线，并认为古汉字与三角图形（trigram）有关，此结论的依据何在，笔者不得而知。—Vide *I Ging*, Diederichs Taschenausgabe, S. 11, 18. *Book of Changes*, trl. by C. F. Baynes, Ldn., ed., 1951, pp. xxix, xxx, xxxviii, xxxix.

着时代的发展，朝代更替，许多历史遗迹后人已无从寻觅。现存最古老的文字遗迹中，必论及甲骨文。1899 年，中国中部之河南省出土了大量龟壳残片（见前文"拓片 1"），经研究其上所刻文字为卜辞。这一发现为语言学和古代史研究开辟出新的领域。现代学者以此为题的著述颇多，最著名的是加拿大裔传教士兼学者明义士（Menzies）之文集《殷墟卜辞》（*Oracle Records from the Waste of Yin*）。至今，已发现的甲骨文约有 5000 字，然而近半数仍待识别。经学者确定且普遍认同的文字不足 1000。近年，中国科学院有一著名学者，根据现有资料重新制出一张殷代（前 1766—前 1122）[4] 的历法年表。此项工作难度极大，耗费精力亦巨，可存希望为古代史研究提供新的线索。目前，该研究尚未完成。除甲骨文外，还必须提到周代（前 1122 [5]—前 256）著名的青铜器及青铜鼎上之铭文（见拓片 4，5）。

在周代，儿童 8 岁而入文法学校或"小学"，由保氏教授六类符号和文字（即六书）。此"小学"后世成为一门大学科，即今之"文字学"。据称，这些符号和文字是自苍颉流传下来的传统写法。公元前 827 至前 781 年，朝廷中有一官员或史官开创出新的字体，后世称为"籀书"（可能是发明者姓籀，亦可能取籀的字面含义"可读"）。籀书形态优美、结构复杂，在小学中亦有教授。此新创之书写体被整理编纂成一部词典，共 15 章，又称"大篆"，与秦朝（前 246—前 207）[6] 之小篆对举，分别表示"早期"和"晚近"的字体。[7] 至秦朝为止，大致已存三种字体：

（一）古文，又称古体，据说上起苍颉，沿用至秦朝，儒家之经典——秦亡后约 100 年才发现——多采用此字体；

（二）籀书，又称大篆，见于周代青铜器上；

（三）小篆，兴于秦，由大篆发展演变而来。

三种字体或多或少有些差异，以近三千年文字发展观之，文字大抵是趋于简化的。

秦王朝虽短，中华文化却遭遇巨变，因暴君专制之下，大量书籍被焚毁，学者受迫害，手段之残酷，不亚于中世纪欧洲之宗教审判。政府还强制颁行了另一种方形字体，即隶书。较之前代字体，隶书更为简洁，便于书写。隶书最初是为了政府部门节省时间，以便满足国家的紧迫需要，集中大量人力提供公共服务，并管理众多的强制劳力等。至此，前文归为第一类的古体字逐渐被废用。

学习中国悠久的历史，必须重视"五经"。周代文化之繁荣，超过了前两代，尤其是在礼教方面。中文称后者为礼，英文中无完全对等的词，常译为"风俗"（mores）或"礼仪"（rites）。礼类似于绅士的行为规范，但内涵更为丰富，旨在培养人之高上行为，并在形与质上兼具善良、美丽和丰盈。当今世界各大博物馆展出的周代几何图案、装饰纹样、青铜器铭文以及乐器，皆体现出极高的审美意识和情趣。无疑，大篆体（上文第二类）不

4. 今通常以公元前 1600 至前 1046 年为殷代。——编者注

5. 今多认为周代始于公元前 1046 年。——编者注

6. 今通常以公元前 221 至前 206 年为秦代。——编者注

7. 这两种字体刻于印章之上，沿用至今。

适合日常使用；而小篆（上文第三类）虽更为简化且线条优美，但书写时仍十分烦琐，较之其他字体并不省时。秦朝宰相李斯是一位饱学之士，也是一位精通小篆的书法家，为后世留下诸多石刻碑文，但也正是他建议焚毁古籍，施行了诸多专制手段。他还编纂过一部字典，名叫《苍颉篇》，但仅仅给出了 3000 个字的标准写法。此外，还有两位学者，也是朝廷的高级官员，做过类似的工作：其一编纂之字典包含六章，另一位编纂之字典包含七章，二者皆广泛参考了籀书。汉代（前 206—220）初期，一些不知名的私塾校长将上述三部字典合而为一，仍叫《苍颉篇》，共 55 章，每章 60字。后世亦称此集合本为"三苍"。

关于古代词典的编纂，此处不作深究，但新字典从此层出不穷。至公元前 1 世纪，在原有集合本上又增加两卷，共收录 7380 字。该字典合编为一册，仍称《三苍》。此外，亦有少数字典收录了《三苍》以外的新字。

于此，对各种字体稍作回顾可知，汉代初年已存如下八种字体：

（一）大篆，前文已述，本书多有收录，作为古代字体之示例。

（二）小篆，本书几乎所有汉字皆在第二个位置给出小篆体。

（三）刻符或刻于符木上的字体，通常为竹质，在军队中使用。

（四）虫书，旗帜上使用的特殊字体。

（五）摹印或印章字体。

（六）署书或标题字体，常用于信封或大标题。

（七）殳书，仅篆刻或浇铸于兵器上。

（八）隶书，前文已述。

根据目的不同，每个汉字可选择以上八种字体之一书写。字为同一，形却相异。八种字体中，第二种至今仍广泛使用，第一种和第五种亦有使用和研习，其余四种（第八种隶书除外——译者）则很少见。

值得注意的是，第六和第七种字体的名称并非重复或印刷错误。两种字体的名称在中文里读音相同（shu），写法却各异，声调亦不同，故而不会发生混淆。但对于不熟悉汉字的人而言，此类同音字"shū—shú—shǔ—shù……"竟像是绝望的叹息。此姑且不论，汉字之拼音化也面临重重困难，因为许多汉字的读音和声调相同，意思却各异。这些字只有在特定语境和书面体中，理解起来方不致混淆。汉语的一大特点是用不同声调标注同一个音，通常是字，以扩大词汇量，因之语音的数量终究是有限的。汉字为方块字，在四角上用弧线标注声调是很容易的（通常为逆时针方向）。如若字的四角皆无标记，则按普通的音调发声。无疑，此法对于汉字的拼音化既不适合，也不实用。

既然汉字的发音必须配合声调学习，则须创立相应的注音方法。过去，常是于汉字下方标出 1，2，3，4，5，此法只适用于字典，而不致引起混淆，本书亦予采用。另一较新的方法是用横线、曲线、左斜线、右斜线标注于元音之上，分别表示不同的声调。此法更为简便，且不易与英语中的长、短音，法语中的爆破音（*l'accent aigu*）和低音（*l'accent grave*）标记相混淆。总体而言，汉字的拼音化并非完全无功，其有助于学生学习普通话，同时为掌握欧洲语言奠定了基础。然而拼音化的汉语，即使汉语专家辨认起来也很吃力；再者，即便熟练掌握汉语的拼音系统，对于汉语本身仍可能一无所知。这也印证了序言所言，学习汉语必须遵循特殊的训练方法。值得注意的是，汉语的拼音化虽收效甚微，然其简化工作却成就卓然。寻常汉字以简化形式写出，笔画更少，自然更省时。汉字之书写几乎呈现出一全新面貌。然而历史证明，过度的简化或缩写也会导致不确定和混乱（尤其是数量词，在法律文件中容易被替换），故往往又回复采用繁体字。这或许将是汉语未来的发展趋势。

在一定程度上，汉语更多地诉诸视觉器官，而非听觉器官。较之听觉发达者，视觉敏锐和天生偏爱图形的人更易掌握汉语。学习梵文则恰恰相反。

汉代初年有一规定，凡年满 17 岁者，欲在政府担任书记或秘书等公职，必须先通过一项考试，内容为识别籀书中 9000 字的八种字体。成绩优异者将委以要职，但倘若日后在书写公文或诏书时犯错，朝廷将予以惩罚和罢免。此规定后来逐渐放宽，考试也于公元前 128 年被废止。由于隶书（上文第八种字体）被广泛采用，对于古体字的认知自然普遍减少，深入学习其他古体字亦无必要。然而这门知识与个人教育和民族文化皆紧密相关，必须予以保存；有两位皇帝——宣帝（前 79 [8]—前 49）和平帝（1—5）进行了鼓舞人心的复兴，以振词源学研究之衰。全国各地的有识之士、士大夫和知名学者都被召集到殿前讲学，优异者予以赏赐。由此，许多失传的知识得以恢复，《三苍》乃成。

随着时代的推移，学术不断进步，知识日新月异。此时中国文字学史上出现了第一位大家——许慎（约 58—147），为民族文化做出了巨大贡献。

他编纂出一部综合性语源学词典《说文解字》——意指"分析和解释各种符号及文字"。该词典自问世以来一直被尊为权威，至今亦然，后世的研究必以此为基础。许慎是一位享有盛誉的学者，时人为之语曰"五经无双许叔重"，其生平极简，可见于范晔《后汉书》。《说文解字》收录 9353 字，重字 1143 个，分 14 卷列于 540 首之下。根据该书序言记载，书成于汉和帝永元十二年之新年，即公元 100 年。公元 121 年，农历九月初一，许慎之子许冲将此书献给朝廷。同月二十日，汉和帝亲自召见许冲，赐良布 40 匹以示嘉奖，并命其免礼。此书后世一直由皇家图书馆珍藏，以彰其学术贡献，代代相传至今。

今书之序言在古代常作为附录置于末尾，对书的主要内容和作者的写作目的作简要说明。故许慎之序言单成一卷，合主体之 14 卷，共 15 卷。全书收录 133 441 字，附详细注释和说明，由此，周代之"小"学至汉代俨然已成为一门"大"学问。正如后世学者所言，许慎之前汉字已存在成百上千年，他的解释虽然是基于当时之传统正学，亦难免有误，此当谨记。《说文解字》之评论众多，只须择出两位近代学者——段玉裁和桂馥。二人皆是大文字学家，生活于 18 世纪末至 19 世纪初期。后者以 40 年之心力治《说文解字》；前者亦用功 30 年有余。换言之，两位皆将毕生精力奉献于此研究。有趣的是，两人虽生活在同一时期，致力于同一研究，却素不相识，亦从未读过彼此的著作。这一点倒不难理解，桂馥生时多居于

---

8. 汉宣帝在位时间始于公元前 73 年。——编者注

西南之云南省，与主流的或中原的学术界多有隔绝。于今，两人的著作皆被采用，倒不必作高下之论。二人之成绩可谓同样卓著，略有不同之处在于，段玉裁之《说文解字注》偏重语音；桂馥之《说文义证》更广泛地关注字义。

此一时期，其他文字学家的作品也相继问世，如钮树玉、徐承庆、王筠、李富孙、苗夔，他们的著作亦有新发现，并修正了前人的一些错误，然而主要贡献仍是语音学——按韵律将古代的发音归类。顾亭林将发音分为 10 类，段玉裁由此发展至 17 类，后又逐渐扩大到 21 类，可谓分类日益精确和严谨。此 21 类发音至今沿用，但研究已延伸至所谓的"声势"，解释了某些段玉裁及其时人未释之古音现象。除此以外，过去 50 年该领域的研究成效甚微。

在许慎的语源学著作之外，本书还主要参考了另一资料——朱骏声（1788—1858）之《说文通训定声》，意即《语源学——广义的解释和标准的发音》。作者在序言中谈道，该书虽耗时十载，却仅为一初稿，有待进一步完善。1833 年，作者介绍了此书的大概框架，称书未成而先作序，实恐其不能完成。然而《说文通训定声》的命运未尝如此坎坷，根据朱骏声之传记，该书和其他著作终于 1851 年上呈皇帝御览。在语音学方面，朱骏声借鉴了段玉裁之《说文解字注》而自创一体系；在汉字的含义和构造方面，他亦有许多小的发现。与许慎不同，他将六书之组合单独分类列出，并依此六原则解释汉字，后面一节将详述。此外，他还阐明了诸多可疑和晦涩之处。至今，该词典多为大学者采用，初学者使用较少。

　　至此，不妨提出一普遍问题：既然学习汉语很困难，学生记忆大量词汇已不胜其力，又何须增加学习古体字之负担？于寻常人，古体字已极少使用，甚至几不可识。这里涉及语源学之功用问题，可从几个方面回答。首先，此处提到的小篆现在并未完全废用，而是随处可见，尤其是在私人印章上。如同古代之巴比伦人，中国人皆有一私章，印于文件上替代签名，因为签名易仿而印章难摹。这是从实用的角度看。其次，若不通晓六原则（参见第二节）——尤其是第五和第六原则，应稍后学习——则古文几不可读，更无从理解。

　　一般而论，学术领域已有知识体系的任何分支，皆有其存在和使用的价值。但随着知识的不断细化与发展，到了难以掌控的地步，就应当适度简化，于是对于某些学科或子学科之价值便产生了质疑。实际上，专治古代文字学的各学科就常被看作是多余的，然而语源学于文化史之贡献是不容置疑的。以目前的情形看，语源学日益丰富的知识不仅有助于阐明所学之语言，而且在相当程度上有助于理解记忆。

　　下文以英文单词的词源为例加以说明。单词"omnibus"（公交车）由拉丁文"omnis"（表示"所有的"），以及常用后缀"ibus"构成。该词在现代英语中表示马路上行驶的车辆，可缩写为"bus"（公交车）。如若知晓此拉丁词源，学习者就能明白"为所有人用"之意，并领会该词用来表示公共汽车的妙处，记忆起来也会很轻松。另一例是单词"restive"（倔强的，难驾驭的），常被误用作"restless"（焦躁不安的，好动的）。这是怎么一回事呢？如若学习者知道该词通常与马有关，则"refractory"（倔强）和

"rejecting control"（难以驾驭）之意自明，故而在用法上可以互换。此外，为了理解现代社会许多以 -logies（表言语、学科）、-sophies（表知识、学问）、-graphies（表写法）、-pathies（表感情、疾病）为后缀的词，必须略通拉丁文和希腊文。深入学习一些古汉语的词根、词干或起源，以及汉字的构造，可以用更理性的方法巩固学到的知识，何乐而不为呢？解决一个难题常带来巨大的学术成就感，思维也随之受到启发，又何必死记硬背呢？

至若学习词源会增加负担，此另当别论。在学习"Christ"（基督）之余，增加拉丁文的"Christus"和希腊语的"chreo-"及"christos"，真的感觉是负担吗？本书给出的例子都是汉语中同一字的古体形式。可惜，今之汉字不是皆能追溯其源头的。诸多非正统的解释皆出自臆想，实当摒弃。[9]

本书于小篆之侧又给出现在常用的书写体。他们的来源都是小篆，但更直接的来源是隶书，其写法鲜有变化，亦常称作"通俗体"。正如口语中有俗语，书面体中亦有不雅之体。对此，多是无从解释的。此外，还有一种动态的字体，叫"草书"，今人亦常使用，然极少用于印刷；若非经过专门训练，该字体极难辨认和识别。草书应当另有来源，很可能是隶书，然并无定论，其书写规范大致成于汉代初年。日语有两种书写体，其一与草书极为相似，必是受其启发。其实，古代之日本文化几乎整个源自中国。今之日本多有草书大家，其书法作品尤可欣赏和玩味，然这已入乎艺术领域，此处不予讨论。这里不妨谈谈小篆和楷书，二者今多用于书写和印刷，但最早必追溯至汉代，即耶稣诞生前两个世纪。

二

汉字的组成要素有三：一形，二音，三义。从传统角度看，汉字追求形美，音悦，义深，且能传达最精妙的思想和情感，使精神和心灵皆感到愉快。较之汉语，第一要素字形于印欧语系不甚倚重，因为其书写体仅限于字母形式和书写风格的变化，而汉语的每个字都有严格准确的形式，若不遵此法书写，往往会出错。其余两个要素在所有语言中的作用基本相同。

.

9. 在英译本 *Satapatha-Brahmana* 前言中，作者从词源学角度将汉字"宿"（表"停歇"），解释为"一间能住一百人的房子"。该解释的出处不得而知。"宿"字的古体与现代体不同，其下半部分仅表声，是"夙"字的古体形式，可参见许慎《说文解字》。亦可参见《经义述闻》十九下。而"宿"的右下部表示"一个人"睡在一张"垫子"上，是一种现代解释。参见本书"拓片 3"第 13 项。

许慎曾在书中给出周代讲授汉语的六原则（即六书），其定义和阐释如下：

（一）指事："视而可识，察而见意"。

（二）象形："画成其物，随体诘诎"。

（三）形声："以事为名，取譬相成"。

（四）会意："比类合谊，以见指㧑"。

（五）转注："建类一首，同意相受"。

（六）假借[10]："本无其字，依声托事"。

应当注意，以上术语的英文翻译与汉语的原意虽相近，实则不同，亦不可能相同。自17世纪以来，欧洲学者一直在研究汉语，对此类术语的翻译略有差异。然而其基本内容是一致的，因为源头是同一的。

简括言之，若以柏拉图式的纯理性观汉字之"意"，则所有汉字皆入乎"会意"；或可说所有汉字都是"指事"字，因为任何汉字皆表达一定的意思，遂有所指示。此处不宜深究哲学和语源学问题，可留出余地以待进一步修正，因为术语常常是陈旧和模糊的，而东西方语言的构造又差异悬殊。[11]

首先，不妨从字面上看六书的分类。通常认为，指事先于象形，主要是因其字形简单。然而以人类学角度观之，最早形成之文字必然是象形。因为图形皆是以不同角度对自然之物的摹绘，或复杂，或简略。其次是指事，因为从某种意义上说，它对所指和被指有了更进一步的区分。儿童常涂涂画画，却并无具体所指。象形与指事合二为一——所造之字多数为会意字。符号也是文字，但从语源学看又有所区别。符号通常很简洁，具有象征意义，是复杂字的组成部分。上述三类字已可构成大量词汇，但仍不胜所需，必须创出新的文字来。于是，又取三类文字之读音，以各种复杂叠加的方式与不同的字形结合，于是形声字产生了，并占据汉字总数的十分之九。至此，造字方法乃止。通常认为，音在形之后，故形声字被列为第三类，然而如严格遵循文字发展的脉络，则应排第四。此外，由汉字之用法又生出两类：转注（第五），用以引介新思想，以及假借（第六），用以完善字音变化。至此，汉语得以克服词汇不足和使用不便。

六书各自独立存在，然在某种程度上又彼此关联，通过搭配，复合的独体字不断增加，我们发现

指事之外，还有

象形并指事，

会意并指事[12]；

形声之外，还有

形声并指事；

.

10. "假借"的英文术语在原文中是"borrowed word"，或许应该是"loan word"，一般指从其他语言借用的"外来语"。但此处是指同一语言内部的假借。

11. 现在，学者对于某些汉字如何归类仍存在分歧，但对于六书的定义是一致认可的。

12. 本文将此类文字归入会意字。

象形之外，还有

形声并象形（象声），

会意并象形，以及

会意并形声并象形；

会意当中，还有

形声并会意。

六书的前四类十分明晰，下文将分类论述并给出范例。但对第五类文字，学者仍存有争议。最早由许慎给出的定义十分含糊，所举的两个例字"考"和"老"，皆表示"年老的"，而无进一步阐释。"转注"在英文中没有对等的词，姑且译作"transmisive"。此术语为复合词，由两个字组成："转"表"转变"；"注"表"流水"或"以水注入"。然而何以为"类"？又何以为一汇"（部）首"呢？此"（部）首"即是许慎词典中所谓的"（部）首"吗？周代人怎么会使用一千年后字典中才出现的部首呢？要之，"相受"究竟何指呢？

有一种解释使问题变得更复杂。它将部首分为两类：一是以声音归类，一是以字义归类。此外又出现一组"互体别声转注"和"互体别义转注"。该学说显然缺少依据，又与后来的"俗体字"相混淆，使得谜团愈加费解。郑樵（1104—1162）甚为推举此法，尽管如此，他仍不失为一位杰出的百科全书编撰者。

另一种解释将转注之"相受"释为"互训"。古代词典《尔雅》有言，同一含义能以40字表之，谓之"转注"。由此，异义同字为"假借"，异字同义为"转注"。换言之，"转注"即同义字。此说较为合理，且具有独创性，然其缺点是，两字若互为同义词，则可理解为"互训"，而不必另立一类。而从构词法看，许多同义词都不能归入一汇（部）首。况且，多义词之间若只有某一含义可互训，又该如何把他们归入一汇"（部）首"呢？这好比是两个或几个多边形，碰巧有一边互相吻合，却很难归入一类。如若将《尔雅》仅仅作为解释"转述"的专著，那么许多"假借字"也当归入"转注"，如此，这两类汉字就无从区别了。然而这正是戴震（1723[13]—1777）创出的理论。

还有一说以前者为基础而略有修改，认为"转注"仅限于字义（而不考虑字形和字音），且只有字义可以转化。此说采用的部类和部首都与许慎的相同。先设一字为部首，如"老"，则其他表示"老"的字皆归入其下。此说似乎更切合实际，是由著名语音学家江声（1721—1799）提出的。

对于第五和第六类汉字，在此略微展开讨论，下文将不再赘述。推而可知，在许慎生活的汉代，六书之本义已经陈旧，并有所删改，故许慎的释义或有偏差。朱骏声（上文提及）对此有一简单的解释：转注者，体不改造，引意相受。换言之：一个字的本义有所引申，而另成他义，而不是将几个字强作一义而归为同义词，即谓之"转注"。"假借"与本义无关，皆因读音类似而借用。同义异字，即"转注"；同音异字而取一义，即"假借"。换言之，"转注"是字根相同，本义相同，经"转变"或"转化"而

---

13. 戴震生于 1724 年。——编者注

表另一义，然字形不变。"假借"是字根不同，本义不同，未经"转化"而替代其他汉字，然字音不变。正是由"假借"出发，今人可对古代语音系统进行研究，因假借是将多个同音或近音字作一字使用。"转注"是字形不变，字义有所引申——故曰"转化"，可能是一些无形之字，而省去创造新字之力。后来，所谓的俗体字，即不遵循六书原则的汉字，逐渐被取代。

此说澄清了古时的诸多困惑，然亦不必作为定论。现代学者章太炎（1869—1936），著名的作家、历史学家和语音学家，亦是大汉学家，给出另一理论，认为六书的最后两类仍属"造字"范畴。在"转化"和引申过程中用头韵和叠韵创出新字，即为"转注"。随着汉字数量的增多，人们用同音近义字相互替代，以限制新字的创造，此为"假借"。该理论不甚完善，因其会无限制地扩大这两个术语的范畴，使语言中各种突发或自然的增长、变化、形成以及重塑，遂变得相当的任意和随机，从而与事实不符。即便第五类文字可用此说解释，第六类文字却不然，这在章氏自己的释义中是很明显的。

在许慎的字典中，第五类给出的例字甚少，第六类的相对较多。下文将推演出几条假借的规则：

（a）同音字而借用，或曰，同音异体字而互借。

（b）同韵而借用，或由单音节字之元音或双元音相同而借用。

（c）押头韵或首辅音相同而借用——此规则最为费解。

（d）由合并而借用，或根据读音将两字合二为一。

大体而言，对古汉语须有较丰富的知识，或者至少掌握了相当数量的汉字，方能对六书最后两类文字有较清晰的了解。故下文只择六书中前四类文字分别说明，对第五类文字偶尔也稍作阐述。

总之，上文所述之理论以及下文所举之例字皆为汉语之基础，没有这些知识便不可能了解这门语言。唯有掌握此基础知识，方可开展进一步的研究。汉语的学习方法一直是科学的，而此科学的研究方法是对所有人开放的，无论是西方人还是东方人。

后续各章将列举各类汉字。每组汉字之首为现代印刷体，用于各种印刷品——如报纸、期刊、书籍等。其次是小篆体，本章多有论述。其三为现代书写体。第四，每个汉字皆标注汉语注音符号，及其拉丁化转写，并给出简要的英文释义。

有的汉字给出了不同的古代书体，上可追溯至中华文明之初，下至约公元前 3 世纪中叶。部分汉字参考了学者闵寓五的《六书通》（撰于 1661 年，出版于 1720 年）。其中某些汉字或以古体，或以大篆体书写，还有同一汉字兼有多种书体的情况。另有一些所谓的"生僻字"则取其古体。上述各种书体列于汉字下方，以 a、b、c 等编号。书中所收字体，来源包括古代青铜器、竹简、古文献（如《老子》）、印章等，不一而足，或有利于展现汉字演化，或显示出汉字演变的可能性抑或历史发展。一个汉字可能有 10 种、20 种甚至更多古体；本书仅择其最能呈现演变之可能性者收录。释义存疑或来源不详的古体字，均未收录。汉代印章上的古体，亦未收录，因之虽非完全臆造，但极可能是以艺术之名而出自当时人的想象。每个汉字的编号，仅为检索方便，别无深意。

HISTORY OF THE CHINESE LANGUAGE

I

Chinese antique script can be traced to a time when tying knots in ropes or strings was used to make records in daily life, a nice reminiscence of which we see even today in the alphabets of certain languages written from a horizontal line downward, such as Sanskrit. It is also possible that the ancient Greek alphabets were derived from the same custom. This method of making records must have been a common practice among early civilizations, and it can still be found among some aboriginal tribes in South America. Ages passed and sank into oblivion and we do not know much about this development. It was not until the time when the Assyrians were busy building their separate towns or town-states and the Egyptians their pyramids (thus circa 3,000 B.C.), that the Chinese began to use a written language, marking the dawn of a new culture in the world—the entrance into the historic period. In a broader sense, the archaic signs, symbols, designs, pictograms, etc. can all be taken as the foundation and original source of the written language. As the Chinese tradition goes, it was the sage-king or culture-hero Bau Hsi 庖牺 , later called Fu Hsi 宓牺 , (because there was no light explosive labial sound in ancient Chinese), who first designed the eight trigrams. By placing one trigram above another, sixty-four hexagrams came into existence. It is highly probable that these designs had in the primitive society certain social usages also, and hence possessed a sociological value, although this still remains a hypothesis. But we fail to understand why any relation of the eight trigrams with the primeval language should be ruled out. The very first trigram Ch'ien 乾 , meaning 'Heaven', written in a slightly slanting position is the character Ch'i 气[1] meaning 'air' or 'breath', with the same pronunciation just a little inflected, and the trigram Kan 坎 [2] is the word for 'water' in the ancient script written horizontally, as in the word Yi 益 , meaning 'to pour water into a vessel'. That these forms of the archaic script later developed into a special mystic or metaphysical system for the purpose of oracle consultations, and thus fell away from their ordinary linguistic or social usages, is a theory

.

1. See II. 4.
2. See II. 9.

quite tenable.[3]

The reputed inventor of Chinese writing was a sage named Ts'ang Chieh 苍颉 . Of him we know only that as an officer or the history recorder in the court of Huang Ti 黄帝 , the first king in China (about 2698–2598 B.C.), he coded the whole language. Yet it can hardly be supposed that one man, be he a sage or however otherwise endowed, could have invented or shaped by himself alone an entire written language and then had it printed (since printing had not yet been dreamt of) and issued for public use. To invent an alphabet for the spoken language, which has in fact been done by one or two men in the history of certain races, is another thing. It was rather perhaps that many words invented in the ancient society were already in use when a certain learned master Ts'ang Chieh came forth and brought them to a certain standardization. Henceforth they became fixed types and perhaps caused less confusion in public writing. The collection or codification of this man was then regarded as a final authority. Further speculations we need not make, since the traditional legend ends there.

Ever since then historians have generally agreed that China stepped into its historical period about 2698 B.C. Again ages and ages, dynasties and dynasties passed without many vestiges being left to posterity. Among the most ancient relics of the language found in recent times, inscriptions on tortoise shells must be mentioned. (Plate I) Batches of tortoise shells have been unearthed since 1899 in Honan, a province in the central part of China, and they were found to bear inscriptions which were oracle records. This opened a new field of research in philology as well as in ancient history. Among the many pamphlets written on this subject by modern researchers, the collected work entitled *Oracle Records from the Waste of Yin* by the famous Canadian preacher and scholar Menzies is the most noteworthy. So far about five thousand words have been discovered, but nearly half of them remain unidentified. Words well recognized and generally agreed upon by scholars count less than one thousand. A renowned scholar of the Academica Sinica recently reconstructed certain chronological tables of a Calendar of the Yin Dynasty (1766–1122 B.C.) from the materials so far available. This was a task of tremendous difficulty and laborious effort, with the aim of shedding new light on ancient history. It was not entirely successful. Next to the inscriptions on tortoise shells must be mentioned the inscriptions on bronze vases and tripods, etc., of the Chow Dynasty (1122–256 B.C.), which are very well known. (Plates IV, V)

In the Chow Dynasty children of eight years of age were sent to grammar schools or "schools of small learning" and taught by tutors the signs and words of the six categories, which will be treated presently;

.

3. I beg to note that I do not know from which authentic source the erudite German Sinologue Richard Wilhelm has taken the notion that 'Yes' was indicated by a simple unbroken line, and 'No' by a broken one, and also his conclusion about the archaic characters in connection with the trigrams. —Vide *I Ging*, Diederichs Taschenausgabe, S. 11, 18. *Book of Changes*, trl. by C. F. Baynes, Ldn. ed. 1951, pp. xxix, xxx, xxxviii, xxxix.

this "small learning" meant in later ages a great branch of knowledge now called philology. These signs and words were supposed to be the traditional writings handed down from Ts'ang Chieh. Between 827 and 781 B.C. an officer or historian in the imperial court formed another style of writing, known afterwards as Ch'ou Shu 籀书 (either because his name was Ch'ou 籀, or because it was meant 'to be read', taking the word Ch'ou in its verbal sense), a very elegant and complicated calligraphy which was also taught to pupils. This newly formulated written language codified and compiled into a lexicon of fifteen chapters was also called Ta Ch'uan 大篆 in contrast to the Hsiao Ch'uan 小篆 of the Ch'in Dynasty (246–207 B.C.), signifying 'Major' and 'Minor' scripts respectively.⁴ Up to the Ch'in Dynasty there were at least three different scripts in vogue:

1) The Ku Wen 古文, or Archaic Script, said to have descended from Ts'ang Chieh, and used down to that period in which many of the Confucian classical works—discovered about a hundred years after the Ch'in Dynasty—were written;

2) The Ch'ou Shu 籀书 or Ta Ch'uan 大篆 of the Chow Dynasty which we still see on bronzes; and

3) The Hsiao Ch'uan 小篆 or 'Minor Script' used in the Ch'in Dynasty which was derived from the 'Major'.

These three scripts differed to a greater or lesser extent from each other, and a general tendency toward simplification can be clearly seen in the course of development of nearly three thousand years.

In the short-lived Ch'in Dynasty, Chinese culture suffered a great change because, under the absolute power of a tyrant, books were burned and scholars were persecuted in a way no less severe perhaps than the religious inquisitions in mediaeval Europe. Another form of writing in plain square shape known as Li Shu 隶书 was forced into use among the people by the government. Compared to any of the former scripts, it was even more abbreviated and convenient to write. Its original purpose was to save time in offices so as to meet the extraordinary exigencies of the state in marshalling great masses of the population into public services and to control great numbers of forced labourers, etc. By this time, the Archaic Script which we designated as "1" above had gradually fallen into disuse.

In studying the several ancient histories of China, along with which the Five Classics must also be taken into consideration, we find that the Chow Dynasty exceeded its two previous dynasties in cultural development, particularly in a very well cultivated propriety. The latter is called Li 礼 in Chinese and has no exact equivalent in English. It is variously translated as "mores" or "rites". It is something like a gentleman's code but much more than that, the cultivation of a godly behaviour, good, beautiful and exuberantly rich both in form and content. The same high aesthetic sense and taste can be seen in

.

4. These are also called "Large" and "Small" Seal Scripts because they are used on seals even today.

the artistic geometrical designs, decorative motives and written words on bronze vessels and musical instruments commonly exhibited in museums of the world today. That the script, Ta Ch'uan ("2" above) could not be suited to ordinary practical purposes is beyond doubt, but the Hsiao Ch'uan ("3" above), though much reduced in complexity, was still a very cumbersome though elegant handwriting, one that required no less time in its practice than the others. The chief minister of the Ch'in Dynasty, Li Sse 李斯 , who suggested the burning of books and other tyrannical measures, was himself a good scholar and calligrapher in this script, and many stone inscriptions written by him are left to us. He also compiled a lexicon giving only three thousand words in their standardized forms and he called it *The Book of Ts'ang Chieh*. Two other scholars, also high officials of the court, did the same thing; one compiled a dictionary of six chapters and the other, of seven chapters, both making broad references to the Ch'ou Shu. In the beginning of the Han Dynasty (206 B.C.–220 A.D.) certain unknown schoolmasters combined these three books into a work of fifty-five chapters of sixty words each, calling it also *The Book of Ts'ang Chieh*. This collected edition was later called *The Three Ts'angs Book* 三苍 .

Here we need not go into much detail about the ancient lexicography. New dictionaries were compiled thereafter, so that up to the first century B.C. two more volumes were added to that collected work, bringing the total number of words to 7,380. It was edited as a single volume and also called *The Three Ts'angs Book*. Other scattered works existed with new words not included therein.

Coming back to the scripts we find that there were eight kinds at the beginning of the Han Dynasty, as follows:

1) Ta Ch'uan 大篆 or Major Script, mentioned above, many of which are given in this book as examples of antique scripts.

2) Hsiao Ch'uan 小篆 or Minor Script, in which nearly all the words in the second place in the illustrative pages are written.

3) Ke Fu 刻符 or the script for engraving on tallies, which were usually made of bamboo and used in the army.

4) Ch'ung Shu 虫书 or Worm Script, used especially for writing on banners.

5) Mu Yin 摹印 or the script for seals.

6) Shu Shu 署书 or Title Script, usually used for writing on envelopes or large title boards.

7) Shu Shu 殳书 or the script written and moulded on weapons only.

8) Li Shu 隶书 , mentioned above.

It is understood that each word could be written in any of these eight styles, each suited to its purpose. The word is the same though the style may be different. Among these the eighth and the second are still very common nowadays, the first and the fifth are used and studied, but the other four are rarely seen.

It should be noted in passing that the sixth and seventh categories given above are not false repetitions or misprints. In Chinese these two names are written differently and pronounced in different tones though with the same sound, thus causing no confusion. But to any one unfamiliar with this language, these words "shu... shu... shu... shu..." must sound like someone heaving repeated sighs of despair! Be that as it may, here we meet the tremendous obstacle in latinizing the language, because there are too many words with the same sound and the same tone but with different meanings. They can only be understood without confusion in context and in their written forms. It is a special feature of the Chinese language that different tones are given to a sound, usually a word, in order to enrich the vocabulary, because ultimately the number of linguistic sounds is limited. Since the words are written in a square form, it is easy to put a semicircle at any of the four corners to denote the tone. (These are written counter-clockwise.) A word without any such mark at a corner is read in its normal tone as it is pronounced. This method is undoubtedly unsuitable and impracticable in latinization.

Since the tone of every word must be learned along with its pronunciation, some device had to be invented to denote it. The method generally used in the past was to put the number 1, 2, 3, 4, or 5 below the word, as is done in this book, a method which can only be used in a dictionary without causing confusion. A comparatively new method employs a straight line, a curve, a downward dash to the left or right placed above the vowel to denote the tones respectively. This is more convenient provided the reader does not confuse these signs with the long or short phonetic marks in English or the *l'accent aigu* and *l'accent grave* in French. On the whole latinization cannot be said to be a complete failure in China, as it helps the student in learning to speak Mandarin and prepares him for learning a European language. Nevertheless, even an expert finds deciphering these latinized words puzzling; and even if one has mastered this system one still remains illiterate in the language. This situation explains also the necessity of the special methods of training mentioned in the Introduction. It must be noted here that in spite of the failure of this movement of latinization, the other movement of abbreviation had a certain success. Ordinary words are written in their abbreviated forms with a lesser number of strokes, and that saves some time in writing. It has given to the written language almost a new physiognomy. However, history shows that oversimplification or abbreviation tends to cause uncertainties or perplexities (especially with regard to the words denoting numbers, which could easily be changed in legal documents) which always necessitated a return to the more complex forms. Perhaps this will prove to be the case in the future.

In a sense Chinese is a language that appeals more to the visual than to the auditory faculty. Those who have sharp eyes or a natural inclination towards visual forms will find the language easier than those particularly developed in their sense of hearing. Perhaps in Sanskrit the reverse is the case.

In the beginning of the Han Dynasty, there was a law that anyone above the age of seventeen wishing to enter the government service as an official scribe or clerk must be subjected to an examination on 9,000 words of Ch'ou Shu, and tested in the correct recognition of words in those eight styles. The best ones were given high offices, but officials who subsequently made mistakes in the words written on public documents and despatches, etc. were censured and impeached by the government. Gradually that law was not so strictly enforced and such examinations were no longer held after about 128 B.C. It was perhaps due to a general decline in the knowledge of the ancient scripts, which was natural since Li Shu (the 8th above) was so commonly used that there was no longer the necessity of such a profound learning. However, a knowledge so intimately connected with the education of the individual as well as the culture of the race was not to be lost, and two Emperors, Hsuan Ti 宣帝 (79–49 B.C.) and Ping Ti 平帝 (1–5 A.D.), both made encouraging revivals of the much degenerated study of etymology. Learned men, official scholars or private savants of fame were summoned from all over the land to the palace to lecture on this subject, and the best were given prizes. Much lost was recovered and hence *The Three Ts'angs Book* came into being.

Time advanced, studies progressed and knowledge increased. Here we meet the first great master in Chinese philology, Hsu Shên 许慎, who made an invaluable contribution to the culture of the race by compiling a comprehensive etymological dictionary called *Shou Wen Chiai Tsu*《说文解字》, which means "Analysis and Explanation of Signs and Words"; henceforth this was held as an authoritative work and it is still used today. Researches in later ages were necessarily based upon this work. Hsu Shên was a highly reputed scholar "whose knowledge in the Five Classics was unequalled", as the slogan of his time claimed. His biography, a brief one, is found in the *History of the Later Han Dynasty* by Fan Yeh (fasc. 69 b.) 范晔《后汉书》. This work, containing 9,353 words with 1,143 duplicated forms in fourteen chapters under 540 headings, was finished, as written in its appendix, on New Year's Day in the twelveth year of Yun Yuan 永元 under the reign of Ho Ti 和帝, corresponding to 100 A.D. It was offered to the imperial court by his son Hsu Chun 许冲 on the first of the ninth month, according to the Chinese calendar, in 121 A.D. Hsu Chun was granted an audience with the Emperor Ho Ti on the 20th of the same month, and as a token of appreciation for the offering he was rewarded with forty bundles of fine cloth with the order that no further expression of gratitude need be made. This work was then preserved in the Imperial Library, an act of great honour to the scholar, and handed down through generations and generations to the present day.

What we call the introduction to a book was normally placed at the end in ancient times as the appendix, usually summarizing in brief what was contained in the book along with the intention and purpose of the author. Thus Hsu Shên's Introduction stands separately as one fascicle and so, with the main work of fourteen chapters, the book is considered to consist of fifteen chapters. The main work, including annotations and explanations, contains 133,441 words, so a "small" learning in the Chow Dynasty had become a "great" learning by the time of the Han Dynasty. But we must not forget that before Hsu's time many centuries had passed, and his interpretations, though based upon the traditional orthodox learning of his time, could not be entirely free from error, as brought to light by scholars in later generations. Among the many commentaries on his work, we need only take the two latest into consideration: one by Tuan Yue Tsai 段玉裁, and the other by Kuei Fu 桂馥, both brilliant philologists who lived from the end of the 18th to the beginning of the 19th century. The latter devoted nearly forty years to this work and the former more than thirty; in other words, each spent his whole life's energy on it. It is interesting to note that although both lived in the same period and worked on the same subject, they neither knew each other nor did they ever see each other's work. This is understandable because Kuei Fu spent most of his lifetime in the southwestern province of Yunan, thus somewhat isolated from the general or central academic field. Both works are now being used, and it would be unwise to try to judge which is more valuable. We can only say that both are equally great, and if any difference is to be found, it is only that Tuan's *Annotations* placed more emphasis on phonetics, while Kuei's *Elucidations* gave a comparatively broader treatment to meaning.

In about the same period works of other philologists followed, such as those of Nyu Hsu Yue, 钮树玉 ; Hsu Cheng Ching, 徐承庆 ;

Wang Yuen, 王筠; Li Fu Sen, 李富孙; Miao Kuei, 苗夔, in which new discoveries were made, and the mistakes of their forerunners corrected; but their main contribution was in the field of phonology, in categorizing the ancient sounds according to different rhymes. The seventeen categories formulated by Tuan, based upon Ku Ting Ling's ten categories, were gradually enlarged and developed into twenty-one; that is to say, the division became more and more exact and precise. These twenty-one categories still stand as they were and studies have extended to the so-called "tendency of sound" 声势, explaining certain facts in ancient phonology which Tuan and his contemporaries could not explain. Apart from this not much progress has been made in this field during the past fifty years.

Besides these works on Hsu's etymology there is another major reference book to be consulted, upon which the present book is based. It is *Shou Wen T'ung Hsun Ting Sheng* 《说文通训定声》 or *Etymology— Generalized Explanations and Standardized Pronunciations* by Chu Tsun Sheng 朱骏声 (1788–1858 A.D.). In the preface to this book the author stated that ten years had been spent and as yet it was still only a draft to be finished. In 1833 he gave a general idea of the framework of the book, saying that he wrote the preface previous to its completion lest it could never be finished. However, its fate was not so tragic, for we find in his biography that this book together with his other works was offered to the king in 1851. In phonetics he followed T'uan's *Annotations*, yet he formed a special system of his own, and in the meaning and formation of words he also made numerous minor discoveries. In the order of arrangement by separate combinations of the six categories and in the explanations of words according to the six principles, which will be treated in the next chapter, he differed from Hsu Shên, and he elucidated many doubts and obscurities. This dictionary is still commonly used nowadays by advanced scholars, and less often by beginners.

Now a general question may be asked: Since the Chinese language is so difficult, and students have already enough to do in memorizing so much of its vocabulary, why should they be burdened with ancient forms of the same words, not commonly used or even recognized by the common people? This involves the question of the usefulness of etymology in general. The answer to this can be given from diverse viewpoints. First of all, the so-called Minor Scripts given here have not entirely fallen out of use today, as they are found everywhere and especially on personal seals. Every citizen in China carries a seal with him as did the ancient Babylonians, and a seal impressed on any document takes the place of one's signature, for a signature can easily be simulated, while a seal cannot. This is from a practical point of view. In the second place, without having a right knowledge of these principles (*vide* Chapter II) —especially the fifth and the sixth which must be learned afterwards—ancient texts can scarcely be read, let alone understood.

Generally speaking, the use or necessity of any branch of established knowledge in the academic field is never questioned. But when knowledge has ramified and grown to such unmanageable proportions that it has somehow to be curtailed, then doubts arise as to the use of certain specific divisions or subdivisions. Indeed, special studies in diverse subjects of ancient philology have often been considered excessive, but the contributions of etymology to cultural history can never be disputed. In the present case this much increased knowledge helps not only to illuminate the language learned, but to a great extent it helps one to commit it to memory in a more rational way.

This can be illustrated by tracing the derivation of a few English words. The word 'omnibus' is a combined form of the Latin 'omnis', meaning 'all', with the usual ending 'ibus'. In modern English it denotes a vehicle on the streets and it is further abbreviated into 'bus'. If the Latin original is learned, the meaning 'for all' is very clear to the student. He would appreciate the ingenuity of taking this word to denote such an object, and to commit it to memory would be effortless. Another example may be found in the word 'restive' which is often used incorrectly in place of 'restless'. How did it come into being? When it is understood that this word usually refers to horses, then its sense of 'refractory' or 'rejecting control' becomes clear, hence the interchange in the usage. Moreover, to understand the endless -logies, -sophies, -graphies, -pathies etc., in the modern world, one must know some Latin and Greek. Why should we not penetrate deep into the roots or stems or radicals of the old forms and constructions of Chinese, in order to secure some assured knowledge in a more rationalized way? When a puzzle has been solved, there will be a great intellectual satisfaction, and the mind will in that case be instantly enlightened; what then is the need of cramming and hard work in memorization?

With regard to the question of being burdensome, it is a different thing. Do we actually feel a burden when we learn, in addition to the word 'Christ' its Latin form 'Christus' and the Greek forms 'chreo-' and 'christos'? Yet the examples given in this book are only the antique forms of the same words of the same language. Unfortunately not every word now used can be traced to its origin so satisfactorily. Many non-orthodox explanations have arisen out of imagination, and they must be discarded.[5]

Next to the column of Minor Script in this book are the words of the written language now daily used. They had this as their common source, but they were more directly derived from Li Shu, a style showing only slight variations, in which there were many so-called "vulgar forms". Just as there are colloquial expressions in the spoken language, so there are also unrefined forms in the written language. Most of them we cannot explain. Apart from these, there is another running style of writing called Ts'ao Shu 草书, also commonly used nowadays but rarely printed; it is still more difficult to recognize or to decipher unless one has undergone training in this script. It must have had another origin, probably Li Shu, which we cannot definitely ascertain, and it also took its standardized shape from the beginning of the Han Dynasty. One of the two styles of Japanese letters must have taken its inspiration from this source, since it shows a great resemblance to it, just as Japanese culture was almost entirely derived from its Chinese source in ancient times. Japan has now many fine calligraphists of this style whose writings we highly appreciate and admire, but since this is included in the field of art, we need not bring it into discussion. We shall discuss only the Hsiao Ch'uan, and the Proper Script 楷书 now used in writing and printing which must have originated in the Han Dynasty at about the same time, viz., in the second century before Christ.

5. In the introduction to an English translation of *Satapatha-Brahmana*, a Chinese word 宿 meaning 'to dwell' was etymologically explained as 'a house capable of accommodating a hundred persons'. The writer must have taken it from a source unknown to us. In the ancient script it was written differently. The lower portion of the word indicates only the sound and it is the Archaic form of the word 凤, which is to be found in Hsu's Dictionary. See also 经义述闻十九下 That its lower right portion shows a 'mattress' with 'a man' sleeping on it is a modern explanation, cf. Pl. III. No. 13.

II

Three elements constitute the formation of Chinese words: first the form, next the sound, and third the meaning. From the traditional point of view, the form must be pleasing to the eyes, the sound must be pleasant to the ears, and the meaning must be expressive of the most subtle ideas and feelings that can appeal delightfully both to mind and heart. In the Indo-European languages the first element does not play so important a part as in Chinese, for the possibilities of variation in penmanship are still limited to the forming of letters and the style of writing them, while in Chinese each word has its proper and exact form and if not written precisely in that definite form, it is usually a mistake. The other two elements are more or less the same in all languages.

In Hsu Shên's work, six principles used in the Chow Dynasty for teaching the language were given, defined and elucidated as follows:

1) Indicatives:

defined as "words recognizable at the first glance and the idea understood upon observation".

2) Pictographs:

defined as "words formed by drawing the object, and curved lines are made according to the thing itself".

3) Harmonics:

defined as "words formed with the fact taken as an appellation, and the sound harmonized in a similitude".

4) Ideatives:

defined as "words formed through a combination of diverse elements of different categories with the meaning seen in the compound".

5) Transmissives:

defined as "by the establishment of groups under one heading, words in the same idea are mutually receptive".

6) Borrowed Words:[6]

defined as "words taken in accord with the sound, entrusted with the meaning where the original word is lacking".

It must be noted here that these terms are close to the originals but not identical, since that can never be. Since the seventeenth century European scholars have been studying Chinese and they might have

.

6. The term. tech. for "borrowed word" is perhaps "loan word", which denotes a word taken from another language, but this means a word taken from the same language.

translated these technical terms differently. However, the substance must be the same because all have been taken from the same source.

Generally speaking, all Chinese words can be defined as "ideatives" if we take the word "idea" in the Platonic sense, or all as "indicatives", since each word must mean something and thus indicate something. But here we need not delve so much into philosophy as into etymology, leaving a broad margin for further corrections because of the antiquated, cryptic terminology and also because of the discrepancy between the construction of the western languages and this oriental one. [7]

Let us first look superficially into the arrangement of these six groups or categories. We must suppose that the indicatives preceded the pictographs mainly because of their simplicity. But from the anthropological point of view, pictographs must have been formed first, since the figures were simply drawn or designed from the natural objects, in either complicated or abbreviated forms, in whatever perspective. Indicatives must have come next, because in a sense they were a step advanced, for there must have been the thing indicated and the indicator. Every child draws pictures, but he does not make an indication of anything. Combining the signs of these two categories together, words—mostly ideatives—were formed. A sign is also a word but, etymologically speaking, there is a difference, as signs are mostly simple and symbolic, serving as elements of complicated words. Yet even with the large vocabulary formed by these three groups there was still an insufficiency of words, and new words had to be formed.

So the sounds of all these three categories were taken and combined with the different forms in a great complexity and multiplication, and from this the harmonic words came into existence, amounting to nine-tenths of all Chinese words. The method of making words ended there. It is generally understood that sound comes after form or shape, and so the harmonics occupy the third place, even though, if we followed strictly this line of development, they would be placed in the fourth. Furthermore, in the usage of words, two more devices were employed: transmission (5th), in order to bring forth new ideas, and borrowing (6th) in order to consummate the changes of sound. Hence there was no longer any shortage of words or any inconvenience in usage.

These principles stand separately but are also to a certain extent related to each other; by correlation, the richness of compounded single words is increased. We find apart from

> pure indicatives, also
>
> pictographs cum indicatives,
>
> ideatives cum indicatives,[8] and
>
> pure harmonics, and
>
> harmonics cum indicatives, and apart from
>
> pure pictographs, there were also

.

7. Nowadays certain scholars disagree as to the classification of some words in these six categories, but they do not dispute the definitions of those words.

8. This item is merged into Ideatives in this book.

harmonics cum pictographs,

ideatives cum pictographs, and

ideatives cum harmonics cum pictographs, and among

ideatives, there were also

harmonics cum ideatives.

The first four categories of the six are clear enough and their examples will be given as they are treated separately afterwards, but with regard to the fifth, scholars are not agreed in their explanations. The original definition given by Hsu Shên remains very obscure, nor do the two words given as examples, K'ao 考 and Lao 老, both meaning 'old' enlighten us further. The term "transmissive" is used here simply because there is no better; the exact English equivalent is lacking. The term is a compound of two words: Chuan 转 meaning "to turn around", and Chu 注, meaning "water flowing" or "to pour water into". But what is meant by "group" and "one heading"? Does the "heading" mean the heading in Hsu Shên's Dictionary? Could the people of the Chow dynasty have used the headings of a dictionary one thousand years later? And above all, what is meant by "mutually receptive"?

One explanation makes the thing more complicated. It divides the "headings" into two groups: one group of words taking sound as its basis and another taking meaning as its basis. Besides, there arises another group of "exchangeable words with special sounds", and another group of "exchangeable words with special meanings". This theory utterly lacks support; and mixed with "vulgar words" of later styles, it brings this enigma into greater confusion. Yet this was advocated by Cheng Ts'iao 郑樵 (1104–1162 A.D.), otherwise a great compiler of an encyclopaedia.

Another explanation takes the idea of "transmissive" as "mutually receptive", meaning simply "mutually explicative". In Erh Ya 《尔雅》, an ancient dictionary, one meaning could be represented by as many as forty words, showing the way of "transmission". Thus one word used in diverse senses is a "borrowed word", while diverse words used in one sense are "transmissives"; in other words, "transmissives" are synonyms. This theory by itself is a sound one, not mentioned by anyone precedent to its author. But its weak point is that if one word is taught as synonymous with another, or vice versa, they are understood as "mutually explicative" indeed, but they need not form a separate category. Many synonyms cannot be grouped under one heading from the viewpoint of word construction. Furthermore, if words having more than one meaning can be mutually explicative only in one meaning, just as two or more polygons can only coincide with each other on one of their sides, how can they be successfully grouped under one "heading"? If Erh Ya is taken merely as a book of "transmissives", then many "borrowed words" included therein must be taken as the same, and there will be no distinction between these two categories. Yet this was the theory founded by Tai Chen 戴震 (1723–1777 A.D.).

Another explanation based on the previous one but more or less modified confines "transmissives" merely to the field of meaning (with the form and sound excluded) and holds that it is only the meaning that can be transmitted. The headings and groupings must be taken as those found in Hsu Shên's Dictionary. By establishing one word as a heading, e.g. Lao 老 "old", other words meaning "old" are grouped under it. This explanation seems to be nearer to the truth and is made by Chiang Shêng 江声 (1721–1799 A.D.), a noted phonologist.

It is worthwhile to treat these two categories here a bit more broadly, since they will not be discussed afterwards. We must admit that during the Han Dynasty, in Hsu Shên's time, the original idea of those six principles had already become antiquated and somewhat obliterated, and it is no wonder that Hsu shên should have somehow misunderstood it. According to Chu Tsun Sheng (mentioned above) it can be briefly explained in this way: a word without changing its form yet with its meaning extended for another application is called a "transmissive", or to express this in another way, if a word has its meaning extended and is so changed into another sense—but not many words are forced into one meaning and grouped as synonyms—the term "transmissive" is used. "Borrowed words" then have nothing to do with the original meaning, but they are adopted because of the identity of pronunciation. If one idea can go through several words, these are "transmissive"; if due to the sameness of one sound several words are used in a certain sense, these are "borrowed words". A "transmissive" is the original word with its original meaning, yet by "turning" or "going around" it is used in another sense with the word unchanged. A "borrowed word" is a different original word with a different original meaning, but without any extension of "turning around" it is used as a substitute for another word with the sound unchanged. It is through the "borrowed words" that ancient phonology can be studied because several words were used as one, owing to the sameness or likeness of the sound. By "transmissive", in which the word remained unchanged, yet the meaning was extended—so to say "turned around" —there could be unformed or unshaped words, saving the trouble of coding new words. In later ages the so-called "vulgar words" were substituted, viz., words formed without being based upon these six principles.

This explanation clarifies much of the ancient obscurity; even then, we need not take it as final. Our modern scholar Chang Tai Yen 章太炎 (died in 1936), a famous writer, historian, phonologist and a great master in Sinology in general, formulated another theory; he held that the last two categories pertained also to the field of the "formation of words". By both alliteration and repeated rhyme in "turning around" or extension new words were formed, and these were the "transmissives". When words had become too numerous, restrictions were made by using words of identical sound and similar idea to substitute for each other without forming new words; these were then the "borrowed" ones. This theory is not entirely satisfactory in so far as it would enlarge both items to an unlimited extent, and the multiple ramifications and spontaneous growth, change, shaping and re-shaping of the language would be seen as quite arbitrary and controlled, which could not be the fact. Even if the fifth category could be explained in this way, the sixth could not, as can obviously be seen from his own explanation.

In Hsu Shên's Dictionary, not many words of the fifth group were given, words of the sixth group being much more numerous. Among the latter, several rules could be deduced:

a) Words were borrowed through the identity in sound or, to put it another way, words of different forms with the same pronunciation could be substituted.

b) Words were borrowed through the identity of rhyme, or monosyllables with the same vowels or diphthongs were capable of being borrowed.

c) Words were borrowed because of alliteration or identity in consonants at the beginning; this is the least understood one.

d) Words were borrowed through combination, or two words were written as one in accordance with the sound.

On the whole, a clear understanding of these last two principles presupposes a fairly good knowledge of ancient Chinese texts or, at any rate, the mastery of a good number of words. So among the six principles only the first four are illustrated below with subdivisions, though occasionally here and there something of the fifth category is explained.

In conclusion it can be said that all that has been mentioned above and the words given below are among the essentials of the Chinese language, and, without this basic knowledge it would be impossible to understand the language at all. Only equipped with such a basic knowledge can one proceed with the general research work. The method of studying the Chinese language has always been a scientific one, and the same way of scientific research is open to all, whether Westerners or Easterners.

In the following chapters various categories of words are presented. The first word in each group is the modern typescript, which is used in all printing work—for newspapers, journals, books, etc. The second one is the form of the word in the Minor Script (Hsiao Ch'uan), discussed in Chapter 2. The third is the word as it is written today. The pronunciation of each word has been denoted both by the Chinese phonetic signs, which constitute the fourth item, and by the latinized transliteration. A brief explanation in English is also given.

Some antique forms of the same word, dating from the dawn of Chinese civilisation to about the middle of the third century B.C., as given in the book, *A Comprehensive Study of the Six Principles* by the scholar Ming Yue Wu (written in 1661 A.D. and edited and published in 1720 A.D.) are also added in some cases. Some of these words are written in the Archaic style and some are in the Major Script; in both several different forms of the same word might exist. Others have been taken from the category in the Archaic style which was called the "Peculiar Words". These various forms are placed below some words and numbered a, b, c, etc. They were gathered from diverse sources, such as old bronze pieces, bamboo slips, ancient texts (like that of Lao-tse), seals etc. Only those forms which help clarify the evolution of the written word, which illustrate the possibilities in the change of a word or its historical development, are shown here. A word may have ten or twenty or more different antique forms; only the ones that best show the possibilities of variation have been chosen. Antique forms with dubious interpretations, or those which are of other origins, have been discarded. The antique forms that were gathered from seals of the Han Dynasty which, though not entirely baseless, could have been created out of the imagination of the people of that period, and which were mainly done for artistic purposes, have not been adopted. The serial number of each word has no special significance; it is given merely for the convenience of reference.

I.

Indicatives

指 事

许慎对此类汉字的定义是

"视而可识，察而见意"。

指事的字面含义为"言其事"。

字所指为一抽象概念，一特征或一没有特定客观形态之运动。许慎列出两个例字，"上"和"下"，予以说明。此二字彼此关联，长横表界限，"上"和"下"之意一目了然。

此处须注意，某些没有释义的简单汉字也归入指事，如基本的数字四到十。某一符号，通常较为简单，用以标记数字，而没有其他特殊含义。后来较晚时期有一理论认为"同音则近义"，其解释不甚可信，此处不论。除上述情况外，每个汉字皆给出传统的释义。本节共收录 25 个纯指事字。

Hsu Shên's definition of this category is

> Words "recognizable at first glance and the idea understandable upon observation".

The term literally means "to point to the fact".

What is indicated is an abstraction, a feature or movement without any definite objective form. The two words given as examples by Hsu Shên, meaning "above" and "below", clearly show this idea. Since both are relative to each other, a horizontal line of demarcation is drawn, and the idea of "above" or "below" is understood.

It must be noted here that simple signs that have no explanations are included in this category, such as the cardinal numbers from four to ten. A certain sign, usually a very simple one, was used to indicate a certain number, with no other significance. Artificial explanations based upon a theory of "words harmonic in sound may be analogous in meaning" which arose at a much later date are here discarded; otherwise the traditional explanation is given here for every word. We note here only 25 pure indicatives.

一

1

yī/*I*₅

一；统一，一致；使统一，联合；第一，相同的，一致的
One;
unity, unification; to unify, to unite;
first, same, uniform

二

2

èr/*Êrh*₃

二；重复，一分为二，修复；第二，双重的
Two;
to repeat, to divide into two, to repair;
second, double

作为符号标于字下方，通常在右边，表示重复该字。

Marked below a word, usually on the right side, it denotes the repetition of the word.

三

3

sān/*San*₂

三 ; 三 重 的 ; 三 倍
Three; to treble; thrice

这三个古体更为复杂。右边的部首"弋"是后增的（参见 II. 94），以便在简单抽象的笔画之上添显分量和意义。该部首虽只表第一个字"弍"的读音，但后面两个字在造字时仍如法炮制。现代书体中，此三字仍在使用，但主要是在金融领域。

The three antique forms are more complicated. The sign on the right is a later addition (see II. 94) which serves to add weight and importance to the all too simple abstract line. Although it indicates the sound of the first word only, its use in the formation of the second and third words followed naturally. These three forms are found today in the modern written script, and used most commonly in the commercial field.

上

4

上

二　上　尸
　　　　尢

shàng/*Shang*₄

在……上，上升，最好的，尊敬，提升

Above, to ascend,

best, to esteem, to exalt

∪ ⊥ ⊥

在古体中，下面的长横表地平线，上面的短横表其上之物，故有"在……上"之意。有时下长横写成曲线，上短横也写成一竖或一点，如图所示。

In the Archaic script, the longer line below is the horizon, and the shorter line above indicates anything above it, hence the idea of "above". The bottom line was sometimes written as a curve; the top line was sometimes written vertically or as a dot, as illustrated here.

5

下

xià/*Hsia*₃, ₄

在……下，下面的，次等的；下降，放下，降低

Beneath, below, inferior;

to descend, to put down, to lower

其释义及各种书体与"上"相反。

The explanation for this word and its variations is the reverse of the one for the word above.

6

王

wáng/*Wang*₂, ₄

王子或国王

A prince or king

三横表天、地及中间的人。德行能通达三者的即王。在古体中亦横向书写。

The three lines represent Heaven, Earth, and Man in between. The one whose virtue pierces through these three planes is the king. The word was also written sideways in antique script.

7

shì/*Shih*₄

显示，说明；与神祇相关的事

To manifest, to show;
things connected with God

三竖笔代表日、月、星之光芒自"上"照耀下来。有时也少写一横。

The three downward strokes represent the rays of the sun, the moon and the stars radiating from "above". It was also written using one less stroke.

工

8

gōng/*Kung*₁

工作，工艺，技术
Work, craft, technique

三笔代表工程制图所用三角尺的三边。当时人们很可能已开始使用 T 形
（矩）尺。

The three lines represent the sides of the triangle used in technical drawing. It is highly
probable that the T-square was also used then.

土

9

tǔ/*T'u*₃

土地，土壤
Earth, soil

两横表土地和土壤，一竖表植物破土而出。上面一横有时写作一点或两斜横。

The ground and the soil are indicated by two lines with a plant springing forth in a vertical line. The top line was also written as a dot or as two sloping lines.

入

10

rù/*Ju*$_5$ (*ruh*)

进入，插入

To enter, to put in

象一植物，入土生根。

A plant striking roots in the soil is shown.

干

11

gān/*Kan*₁

反对，阻塞，冒犯

To oppose, to obstruct, to offend

倒"入"字，短横表阻碍或插入之物。

This is an inversion of the previous word. The short line indicates the obstruction or the thing entered into.

四

12

sì/*Ssu*₄

四

Four

a ≡　b ⩘

"a"为大篆体。四横亦可写作向下的斜线。

The pictograph in "a" shows how the word was written in the Major Script. The lines were also drawn sloping downwards.

五 **13**

wǔ/*Wu*~3~

五
Five

宇宙中起支配作用的五种运动（常误解为五种要素）——金、木、火、水和土。这些运动在阴、阳两个基本原则的共同作用下产生，由两条交叉的线表示。故而表示五。这是汉代许慎的传统释义，然而笔者认为这些笔画最早仅仅表示四个方位及中心点，故为五。传统之释义稍显牵强。

There are five cosmic movements governing the universe (wrongly understood as the five elements)— metal, wood, fire, water, and earth. They are created by the conjunction of the two basic principles, Yin and Yang, represented here by two lines crossing. From this came the idea of five. This was the orthodox explanation given by Hsu shên in the Han Dynasty. However, in the opinion of the present writer, the lines originally indicated simply the four directions plus the central point, hence five. The traditional explanation seems a bit contrived.

六

14

六   ㄌㄨ

liù/*Lu*₅

六

Six

七 15

ㄑㄧ

qī/*Ch'i*$_5$

七

Seven

八 16

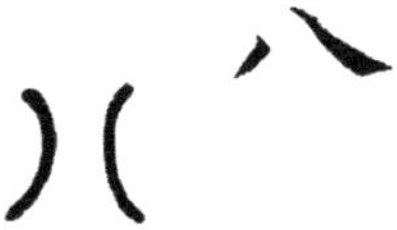

ㄅㄚ

bā/*Pa*$_5$

八

Eight

高上的意思指“分开”，因其字有分背之形。

In a higher sense, it means “to divide” because the sign shows a separation.

九

17

jiǔ/*Chiu*₃

九
Nine

九 ㄐ
   又

十

18

shí/*Shih*₅

十
Ten

传统释义是，横竖笔画表示八个方位，加上"顶端"和"底部"，共为十。

The traditional explanation is that the lines indicate the eight directions plus the directions "top" and "bottom" — hence ten.

丿

19

丿　丿　夊

piě/*Pi*₃

向左弯曲
A twist to the left

20

乀　乀　乄

fú/*Fu*₅

向右弯曲
A twist to the right

21

yì/*Yih*$_4$

（横着）牵引，拖
To draw, to pull

22

yí/*Yih*$_5$

流动
To flow

*反"厂"（上文21）。

丂

23

kǎo/*Kao*₁

抑 制

To check

一股气欲向上舒出而为某物所阻碍。

A current of air going upward checked by something above is shown.

ζ

24

hē/*Ho*₁,₂

呼气，呼出

To exhale, to breathe out

反"丂"（上文 23），表意也相反——气行舒畅，无阻碍。

The form is the reverse of No. 23, and the meaning is the opposite—the exhalation is unhampered.

25

yǐn/*Yin*₃

隐 藏
To hide

象一角落以藏身。

The corner denotes a hiding place.

II.

Pictographs

象　形

象形的造字原则极简单，许慎的定义也不难理解，如下：

"画成其物，随体诘诎"的汉字。

换而言之，以最少的笔画，画出物体最基本的形状。"鸟"字象鸟的样子，"鱼"字象鱼的模样，诸如此类，但有时字形所画的是物体从上方或后面或侧面所见之形。在古体字中，物体更接近真实的模样。

在此列出最常见的象形字，方便汉语初学者使用，其排列顺序与许慎的字典有所不同。本章仅收录 160 个象形字。

The principle of the formation of pictographs is a very simple one. The definition given by Hsu Shên is easily understandable; a direct and literal translation of it runs as follows:

> Words are formed "by drawing the object, and curved lines are made according to the thing itself".

In other words, objects are pictured as they are, giving the most essential form in the minimum number of strokes. A word for "bird" is drawn in the form of a bird, and a word for "fish" is in the form of a fish, etc. But the picture sketched is sometimes the appearance as seen from above or from behind or from the side. In antique scripts, the objects are more realistically represented.

The words given as examples here are the most common ones but the order, for the convenience of beginners, is arranged in a different manner from that of Hsu Shên's Dictionary. Only 160 words are presented here.

日 **1**

rì/*Jih*₅

太阳

Sun

该字的古体类似婆罗米字母的"tha"——圆圈中加一点,如同"a"所示;另一种字体"d",(圆圈周围的)四画表示太阳之光芒;字体"b"和"c"的来源有待研究。

In Archaic Script this word is like the ancient Brahmi letter "tha", a circle with a dot in the center, as shown in "a". In another form ("d"), four lines are drawn representing the rays of the sun. The origin of the forms in "b" and "c" requires research.

月 2

yuè/*Yüeh*₅

月 亮
Moon

各种古体表示出月亮满阙之形，（后来的）字体源于"b"。"d"是"b"的简写形式。

The antique forms show the full moon and the crescent moon. The form given above comes from "b". "d" is an abbreviated version of "b".

云 ［雲］ 3

yún/*Yün*₂

云 层
Clouds

"云"的古体更为写实。"a"取自古体。"b"中的"二"("上"的古体）是后来增加的。[ ] 中的字为现代繁体，显而易见，"云"字上面加个"雨"字。

In the antique forms the "cloud" is drawn more realistically. "a" is from the Archaic Script. In "b" one sees how the word for "above" was added later. In the modern written word given in parentheses the word for "rain" is added on top of the word for "cloud".

气

4

qì/*Ch'i*₄

呼吸，空气

Breath, air

气象之流动。

Currents of moving air are shown.

雨

5

*yǔ/Yü*₃

下 雨
Rain

最上一横表天，雨滴自云中降下。古体字非常形象。

The top line indicates the sky, with drops of rain falling from the cloud. In the antique script the picture is very clear.

6

*quǎn/Ch'üen*₃

田 间 的 小 水 沟
A small drain between fields

象水流动之形态。

A picture of water flowing is given.

*据《考工记》今本，古时修筑田间沟渠，宽一尺，深一尺，谓之く；
宽二尺，深二尺，谓之遂；宽四尺，深四尺，谓之沟；
宽八尺，深八尺，谓之洫；宽一丈六尺，深一丈六尺，谓之巜。

7

kuài/*Kuai*₄

小水沟，水流之汇聚

A small stream, a drain enlarged

叠"く"为"巜"，水流加倍。

The current of water is doubled.

川

8

川 川 𠇇

chuān/*Ch'uan*₂

较大的水流，河川
A large stream, a river

三 "巜" 为 "川"，水流变为三倍。
The current is tripled.

水

9

水 水

shuǐ/*Shui*₃

水
Water

a ≋ ， b 𝇊

复象水流动之形态。"a"的字形相同，但为横向书写。"b"与"川"（上文 8）字形相似。

Again, a picture of flowing water. "a" is the same form drawn horizontally. "b" is very similar to 8 above.

氷 （冰）

10

bīng/*Ping*₂

冰，冰锥

Ice, icicles

"a"是另一古体，上面部分与前文给出的字形相同，表冰之裂纹。下部的起源不明。

"a" is another antique form, the upper portion retaining the same form as given above, which represents the cracks of ice. The origin of the lower portion is unknown.

*《段注》："以冰代仌，用别制凝字"。邵英《群经正字》："冰冻作仌，坚凝本字作冰。俗以冰代仌，凝代冰字，而仌字遂废不用。"

永

11

yǒng/*Yung*₃

永久的 ， 长 的 ， 永恒的

Perpetual, long, eternal

a b c

"永恒"之意源于河水长流不息。古体象水流自悬崖流下或落下。注意"b"的中间部分为空，它与前文字形相同，但中间的一笔省去。

The idea of "eternal" was drawn from the everflowing water of a river. In the antique forms, water is shown flowing or falling from a cliff. In "b" the empty portion is to be read. It is the same as the form given above, with the central line omitted.

泉

12

quán/*Ts'uan*$_2$

ㄑㄩㄢ

水源或泉水
A fountain or spring

a   b

象水自高处落下。"b"的上部为"水"。"a"字形更为抽象，但意思相同。

This is the picture of water flowing from a height. In "b" the word for "water" is written on top. "a" is a more abstract representation of the same idea.

火

13

huǒ/*Huo*$_3$

ㄏㄨㄛ

火
Fire

象火焰之上行。"a"中可见烟由火中升起。

Fire flaming upwards is pictured. In "a" the smoke coming out of the fire is added.

14

shān/*Shan*₂

山脉，山丘

A mountain, a hill

"a"和"b"的山形明晰。"b"的竖画表山峰或极顶。

In "a" and "b" the picture is clear. The vertical lines in "b" represent pinnacles or great height.

厂

15

hǎn/*Han*₂

山之崖岩，人可居于其下
A mountain cliff under which men could live

石

16

shí/*Shih*₅

石头，岩石
Stone, rock

象崖下之石。"a"为竹简所书之古体。本书所引之竹简字均取自宋代郭忠恕编撰的《汗简》。

A "stone" is drawn under the cliff. "a" is an antique form found on bamboo slips. The words from the bamboo slips have all been taken from the book *Bamboo Tablets*, compiled by Ko Chung Shu of the Sung Dynasty.

*《汗简》是北宋初年郭忠恕汇集的一部古文字书。
书名取自《后汉书》"杀青简以写经书",谓之"杀青",亦谓"汗简",
借以说明"古文"是源于古人在竹简上所写经书的文字。

白 [堆]

17

duī/*Tui*₁

一群,一堆,一团,堆积

A heap, a pile, a mass, to heap up

象崖下之土堆或小土丘,17 和 18 中的文字皆为侧面图。

Heaps of earth under a cliff or a small hill are pictured. In both 17 and 18 the pictures are to be viewed from the side.

阜

18

fù/*Fiu*₄

土堆；大量的；累积

A mound; abundant; to accumulate

象崖下之土堆或大片土地。

Earth mounds or a large piece of land overshadowed by a cliff are shown.

垒

19

lěi/*Lei*₂

堆积

To heap up

象累土筑墙之形。

Heaps of earth for building are shown.

田

20

tián/*T'ien*₂

稻 田 ， 种 粮 食 的 土 地

A rice field, a grain field

a 　 b

字形的意思是田地中的阡陌之道。"a"和"b"字形相同，有稻谷长于田间。

The crosspaths within the field indicate the meaning of the form. In "a" and "b" the same form is given with the addition of the growing rice plant.

口

21

wéi/*Wei*₁

围 场 ， 圆 周 ； 围 绕

An enclosure, circumference; to surround

回

22

huí/*Hui*₁

回来，回旋
To return, to recoil

"a"中回旋之意更为明显。"a"及上文字体均为古代青铜器上之回纹。

In "a" the recoil is better seen. Both this one and the form above are common designs on ancient bronzes.

大

23

dà/*Ta*₄

伟大的，大的，成熟的
Great, big, full-grown

象成人之正面像。

The frontal view of a full-grown man is shown.

人

24

rén/*Jên*₁

人
Man

a ᵇ

古体象人曲体之侧影。

The antique forms show the side view of a man bending.

目

25

mù/*Mu*₅

眼 睛
The eyes

上文字体为纵向书写。"a"为大篆体，眼睛的自然形态尤可见。"b"亦为侧面图。

The word above is drawn vertically. "a", from the Major Script, shows the eye still in its natural form. "b" is to be also viewed from the side.

儿

26

*ěr/ Êrh*₃

耳朵

The ear

"a"和"b"均为耳朵的简化图形，并表示出发际线和下颚骨。

"a" and "b" are both simple drawings of the ear, with the hairline and the line of the jawbone indicated.

囟

27

xìn/*Hsin*~4~

头顶 ， 头盖骨

The top of the head, the skull

一丛头发见于头顶上。

A tuft of hair is seen on top of the head.

自

28

zì/*Tsû*~4~

自 己

Self

字形起初象鼻子的形状，（因为）人们称呼自己时常指着鼻子。"a"和"b"字形相似。

This word was originally a picture of the nose. People usually point to their noses when they refer to themselves. "a" and "b" are similar drawings.

口 **29**

kǒu/*K'ou*₃

嘴，开口

The mouth, an opening

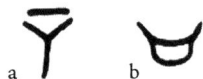

"a"更为抽象，竖笔象下巴之裂纹。"b"更为写实。

"a" is more abstract, the vertical line being the cleft of the chin. "b" is more realistic.

牙

30

yá/*Ya*₂

牙　丫

牙 齿 ， 臼 齿
A tooth or teeth, the molars

a 　　 b

"b" 有两部分组成——上部象一颗牙齿，下部象嘴里长满牙齿。"a" 和 "b"
均为古体。

In "b" there is a double picture—one of a tooth, on top, and one of the mouth with teeth,

below. Both "a" and "b" are from the Archaic Script.

亦

31

亦 -

yì/*I*₅

和，也，同样的
And, also, likewise

a 亦 b 亦

现用作虚词。原指人的腋窝，用两竖或"b"中的两点表示。

This word is now used as an expletive. Originally it meant "armpits", which are indicated by two lines or as in "b" by two dots.

首

32

首 尸又

shǒu/*Shou*₃

头；首领
The head; chief

象头发长于头顶上。"a"字形相同，而无头发。

Hair is seen on top of the head. "a" is the same form without the hair.

面

33

miàn/*Mien*₄

脸

The face

象人的正面。

A frontal view of the face is shown.

而 **34**

而　而　儿

ér/*Êrh*₁

和，然而，但是
And, and yet, but

a 而

现用作虚词。原指颊须，象形字。"a"为另一写法。

This word is now used as an expletive. Originally it meant "mustaches", as drawn. "a" is another version.

冄（冉）　**35**

冄　冄

rǎn/*Nien*₂

腮须
Whiskers

臣（颐）

36

yí/*I*₁

下巴，下颌
The chin, the jaws

象下巴的下部；为左侧图。
The lower part is drawn; the picture is to be viewed from the left side.

尸

37

shī/*Shih*₁

人卧于桌上，扮作祭祀中的亡灵；尸体
A man leaning on a table who
impersonates the dead at a sacrifice; a corpse

心

38

xīn/*Hsin*₂

心脏
The heart

注意"b"和"c"中，字形从圆形逐渐演变为竖形，现用作部首。"a"为古体。

Notice how in "b" and "c" the round form gradually changed into the long form, now used as a classifier. "a" is from the Archaic Script.

手

39

shǒu/*Shou*₃

手
The hand

又 ［有］

39a

yòu [yǒu]/*Yu*₃,₄

和 ， 也 ， 再 ， 除 …… 以 外

（ 用 作 虚 词 ）

And, also, again, in addition to

(used as an expletive)

"又"的古体原指"手"，是手的简化形式，用以造字。又也指"右边"。[ ]
中的"有"在古典作品中常用来代替"又"。

The form for Yu in the Archaic Script originally meant "the hand". It was the abbreviated
form of Shou and was used in the formation of other words. Yu also meant "the right side".
The modern printed form of Yu given in parentheses is always used in the classics instead of
the first form given.

叉

40

chā/*Ch'a*$_2$

手指交叉；叉子

To interlace the fingers; a fork

a

"a"中，双手交叉之形清晰可见。

In "a" the picture of two hands interlacing is very clear.

爪

41

zhǎo/*Ts'ao*$_3$

手指的指甲和脚趾的趾甲；抓

The nails on the fingers and toes;

to scratch

*《段注》：“仰手曰掌，覆手曰爪”。

动词的意义后来写作“抓”。参见下文107。

42

lǚ/*Lü*~3~

脊　柱　，　脊　椎　骨

The spine, the vertebrae

a

"a"为古体，象两节脊椎骨之形。

"a" is from the Archaic Script, a drawing of two vertebrae.

要 ［腰］

43

yào [yāo]/*Yao*$_{2,4}$

腰，腰部，中间
The waist, the loins, the middle

象两手置于腰间，双手叉腰之形。

The picture shows the hands resting on the waist, arms akimbo.

力

44

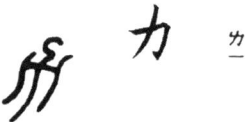

lì/*Li*$_5$

力量，精力，权力
Strength, energy, power

a

象肌肉拉紧，故表力量。"a" 为古体。

This is a picture of the muscles in tension, thus strength. "a" is from the Archaic Script.

女　　　　　　　　　　　　　　　　　　　　　45

nǚ/*Nü*₃

女孩 ，女儿 ，女人

A girl, a daughter, a woman

a　　　b

"a" 和 "b" 均象女人跪坐之侧影。

"a" and "b" show the side view of a woman kneeling.

母

46

mǔ/*Mu*$_3$

母亲

A mother

a   b

由"女"字加两笔表乳房。古体"a"和"b"字形相似。

Two lines indicating the two breasts are added to the form for "Nü". The antique forms shown in "a" and "b" are similar.

兒（儿）

47

ér/*Êrh*$_1$

儿子，儿童

A son, a child

字上部的开口，表示头顶的囟门尚未长合。下部为古体的"人"。

The open space in the upper portion of the word indicates that the fontanel of the head has not yet grown together. The lower portion is the word for "man" in Archaic Script.

48

mào/*Mao*$_4$

外貌，举止

Appearance, bearing

上部象人的头和脸，下部为"人"。

The head and face are indicated on top of the word for "man".

子

49

子 卩

zǐ/*Tzu*₃

孩子，儿子

A child, a son

最初象襁褓中的婴儿，露出头和双手，上文"a"和"c"均可见其形。"d"
为侧影。"a"和"b"上部的曲线表头发。其余均为简单的象形。

The original picture was of a baby wrapped in cloth, with the head and two arms shown. This
can be seen above and in "a" and "c". "d" is in profile. The wavy lines above the figure in "a"
and "b" represent the hair. The others are simple pictographs.

乃

50

nǎi/*Nai*₃

那么，并且（用作连词和反义连词）

Then, and also

(used as a conjunctive and disjunctive particle)

向下的曲线表示呼吸不畅，故指说话困难。

The lines curved downward represent difficulty in exhalation; this indicates a difficulty in speech.

彳

51

chì/*Ch'ih*₅

迈出（左脚）

To step (with the left foot)

象大腿、小腿和脚的动作。

The thigh, leg and foot in motion are shown.

止

52

止 止 止

zhǐ/*Chih*₃

停止；基础

To stop; foundation

象脚趾的形状，三笔表示五，在"左"和"右"字中亦然。

This is a picture of the toes. Three lines mean five as in the words for "left" and "right".

交

53

jiāo/*Chiao*₂

相 交 ， 交 付 ， 递 送 ， 交 给
To join, to commit to,
to deliver, to hand to

a

象人两腿交叉之形，故有"相交"之意，其他意思由此引申而来。"a"为生僻字。

The picture of the crossed legs of a man gives the idea of "being joined"; the other meanings followed from this. "a" is a Peculiar Word.

文

54

wén/Wen₁

装饰；纹饰；图案，文字

To decorate;

Ornamental signs; designs, literature

字形中的交叉线表一种装饰图案。后逐渐用以指宇宙间人或神创造所有美的形式，包括表现为秩序与和谐的方方面面。

The pictograph shows crosslines, a type of decorative design. This word gradually came to mean every beautiful manifestation in the universe, to include all aspects of manifested order and harmony, created either by man or by God.

包

55

包 ㄅ
ㄠ

bāo/*Pao*₂

包裹；打包，包括
A parcel; to wrap, to include

象人怀抱一物

This is a picture of a man embracing something.

贯（贯）

56

guàn/*Kuan*₄

贯穿，串起
To go through, to string on

a

长横表穿过宝石之线。"a" 为相似的古体。现代书体的上部源于前文字体。

The long horizontal line is the string piercing a precious gem. "a" is a similar Archaic form.

The upper portion of the modern written word is derived from the form above.

串

串

chuàn/*Ch'uan*

串连， 连接

To string together, to connect

串原读作 guàn， 今已独立成字， 意思相同。

Ch'uan was originally pronounced as Kuan, but it is now a separate word with the same

meaning.

弗

57

chǎn/*Ch'an*$_3$

烤肉的叉子

Forks for roasting meat

起源于"串"字（上文 56），竖线表叉子，方形表叉上之肉。

This word is derived from 56, Ch'uan. In this case the lines represent the fork and the squares the meat it holds.

丰

58

jiè/*Chiai*₃,₅

上 古 时 代 创 造 文 字 之 前 ，

在 其 上 刻 画 以 记 事 的 木 牍 或 竹 简

A piece of wood or bamboo on which

cuts were made for recording things before

the invention of words in primitive times

长竖表示木牍或竹简（许慎之释义不可取）。

The long vertical line represents the wood or bamboo. (Hsu's explanation has been discarded.)

*《说文》："丰，艸蔡也。象艸生之散乱也。"

"上古未有书契，刻齿于竹木以记事。"

卜

59

bǔ/*Pu*₅

卜　　卜　　ㄅ
　　　　　　　ㄨ

（用龟壳）占卜

To divine (by means of a tortoise shell)

竖笔表龟壳，右边短横表灼烧龟壳局部的小火。以龟壳之裂纹行占卜，壳裂开之声似"bu"。

The vertical line represents the shell, and the short line on the right the tiny flame with which a small portion of the shell was scorched. The cracks were read for augurs. The sound of the shell cracking was like "Pu".

丁

60

dīng/*Ting*₂

个　　丁　　ㄉ
　　　　　　　ㄥ

个人

An individual

象一钉子的形状。

This is the picture of a nail.

61

fāng/*Fang*₂

容 器

A container

容器底部向左侧。"a"为大篆体。

The bottom of the container is to the left. "a" is from the Major Script.

曲

62

qū/*Ch'ü*₅

弯曲的，弯的
Crooked, bent

a

象一空容器。"a"取自古体。

A hollow container is shown. "a" is from the Archaic Script.

米

63

mǐ/*Mi*₃

脱壳的稻谷，生米
Hulled rice, uncooked rice

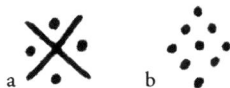

"a" 用作贵族服装的纹饰，表示"米"。

"a" is a design which was used on the robes of the noble classes, meaning "rice".

禾

64

hé/Q_2

生 长 的 谷 物

Growing grain

象带穗的庄稼向左弯曲。"a"和"b"取自古代青铜器上的金文，表示生长的庄稼。

The plant is shown with an ear bending to the left. "a" and "b" are antique forms taken from ancient bronzes, showing the growing plants.

斗

65

dǒu/*Tou*₃

旧时一种干货的度量器，
316 英寸见方为标准的 1 斗

A dry measure,
Standardized at 316 cubic inches

a

上文字体与"a"均象一个带把的度量器。

The form above and "a" both show the measure with a handle.

*约可量 12 斤粮食。

升

66

shēng/*Sheng*₂

31.6 英寸见方为 1 升, 10 升为 1 斗
A measure of 31.6 cubic inches,
1/10 of a "Tou"

臼

67

jiù/*Chiu*₄

研砵
A mortar

a

象简单的研砵之形，里面装有米。"a"为生僻字，字形相似。

The form above shows a simple picture of a mortar with rice inside. "a" is a Peculiar Word, a similar picture.

皿

68

mǐn/*Ming*₃

器皿，（盛饭食等的）用器

A utensil, a vessel (for rice, etc.)

豆

69

dòu/*Tou*₄

祭祀时盛放肉的器皿，用木、铜或陶制成

A sacrificial vessel made of wood, bronze, or porcelain, for holding meat

上横表器皿的盖子。

The line on top in the form above is the cover of the vessel.

70

fǒu/*Hou*₃

盛液体的容器

A vessel for containing liquid

a

上文字形近乎一带顶盖的器皿。"a"象更为原始的器皿形状，无颈无盖。

The exact shape of the vessel with the lid on top is drawn in the form above. "a" is the picture of a more primitive vessel, without a neck or cover.

鬲　　　　　　　　　　　　　　　**71**

鬲　鬲　力

大锅

A large cauldron

lì/Li₅

a 高　b 鬲　c 鬲　d 鬲

上文字形象一有纹饰的三足大锅。下部象器皿烧于火上，并非器皿的足。"c"
为生僻字。"c"和"d"表不同类型的器皿。

The form above shows a cauldron with decorative designs and three legs. The lower portion
does not represent legs but a container for the fire. "c" is a Peculiar Word. "c" and "d" show
a different type of vessel.

72

chàng/*Ch'ang*₄

祭祀的烈酒，

以黑黍（或米，如图置于器皿内）和香料酿成

Sacrificial spirits made by fermenting millet

(or rice, as seen in the vessel) and fragrant herbs

a   b

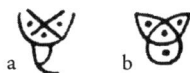

下部的"匕"象取酒的短勺。"b"为大篆体。

The short ladle used is drawn on the bottom of the word. "b" is from the Major Script.

壺（壷）

73

hú/*Hu*₁

壺，水壶

A pot, a jug

象带顶盖的壶。"a"为古体，"b"取自大篆体，所列字形皆为简化体。

The exact shape of the pot with a lid on top is drawn. "a" is Archaic Script and "b" is from the Major Script. All are simple pictures of the word.

鼎 74

dǐng/*Ting*₃

三足两耳的青铜器；大锅

A tripod of bronze with two ears;
a cauldron

"a"和"b"为更古旧的字体。

Forms "a" and "b" seem to be the more primitive ones.

兀

兀 兀 ﹤

75

jī/*Ch'i*₁

长椅，基础，支撑
A bench, a base, a support

几

几 几 凵

76

jǐ/*Chi*₃

短足的小桌
A small table with short legs

户 **77**

hù/*Hu*₄

门 的 一半 为 户 ， 小 的 门
A leaf of a door, a small door

門 （门） **78**

mén/*Mên*₁

大 门 ， 门 口
A door, a gate

两个 （上文的）"户" 组成 "门"。

This is the previous word doubled.

窻 (窗)

79

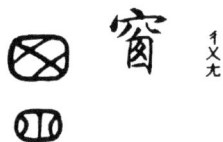

chuāng/*Ch'uang*₁

带 横 档 的 窗 户

A transom window

"a" 为古体，窗户的形状尤见。

"a" is an Archaic form, a very clear picture.

囧

80

jiǒng/*Chiung*₂

墙 上 的 窗 户； 敞 亮

A window on the wall; light

井

81

jǐng/*Tsing*₃

井

A well

上文字形象俯视井时四周的栏杆和中间的水桶。

A bird's eye view of the railings with a pail in the middle is drawn in the form above.

丹

82

dān/*Tan*₁

丹药；朱砂

A pill; cinnabar

a

象采掘矿石的矿井。"a"取自竹简。

The mine pit where the mineral stone is found is pictured. "a" was taken from the bamboo slips.

弓

83

gōng/*Kung*₁

弓 箭

A bow

"a"象满弦之弓；"b"为生僻字，象未满弦之弓。

"a" shows the strung bow; in "b", a Peculiar Word, the bow is not yet strung.

矢

84

shǐ/*Shih*₃

矢 尸

箭
An arrow

a

"a" 取自古体。
"a" is from the Archaic Script.

刀

85

dāo/*Tao*₂

刀 勾

刀 ， 剑
A knife, a sword

仅勾勒出刀柄及上部的刀刃。

Only the handle and the upper portion have been sketched out.

斤

斤　斤　ㄐㄣ

86

jīn/*Chin*₁

斧子
An axe

同上，仅象征性表示出斧柄。

Again, the handle only has been indicated.

舟

舟　舟　ㄓㄡ

87

zhōu/*Chou*₂

船
A boat

象纵向的船。"a"取自古体，箭头可能表示水面。"b"象俯视的船形。

The boat is drawn vertically. In "a", from the Archaic Script, the arrow perhaps shows the surface of the water. "b" is a view from the top.

方

88

fāng/*Fang*₂

方形

A square

字形原本象两条并行的船，仅船头微微可见。

The drawing originally showed two boats proceeding side by side with only the prows seen.

車（车）

89

che/*Ch'ê*₂

车辆，手推车

A cart, a barrow

字形纵向画出车的后视图，长竖表车轴，两横表车轮。"a"和"b"中，车轭位于车轮之上。"a"为生僻字。

The picture, drawn vertically, shows the cart from behind, the long vertical line being the axis and the two horizontal lines the wheels. In "a" and "b" the yoke is drawn above the wheels. "a" is a Peculiar Word.

盾

90

dùn/*Tun*₃

保护头和眼睛的头盔，盾牌
A helment to protect the head and eyes,
a buckler

"a" 取自古体。
"a" is from the Archaic Script.

勺

91

sháo/*Sho*₅

用勺舀取；勺子
To ladle out with a spoon; a spoon

象勺子的纵向图；短横表示液体。

The picture is drawn vertically; the short line indicates the liquid.

爵

92

jué/Tsio$_5$

酒杯或高脚杯；贵族的头衔

A cup or goblet; a title of nobility

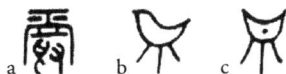

上部象带顶盖的酒杯，下部为"鬯"（酒）和"又"（手），即手握酒杯。（参见 II. 39a，72）"a"是更为简化的字体。"b"和"c"象早期简化的酒杯。

In the upper portion of the form above a cup is drawn with a lid on top, and the words for "spirit" and "hand" are drawn below it; i.e., a wine cup held in the hand. (See II. 39a, 72) "a" is a more abbreviated version of the same form. "b" and "c" are simpler drawings of the object, of an earlier date.

角

93

jiǎo/*Chio*₅

兽角，角落，角度

A horn, a corner, an angle

字形象禽兽的角。后来指角形的酒杯，通常为铜制，三足。

The word is in the form of a horn. Later on, Chio came to mean a wine cup made in the same form, usually of bronze, with three legs.

弋

94

yì/*I*₅

尖锐的木桩；猎取

A sharpened stake; to arrest

a

竖笔表木桩；两短横表支撑物或系于桩上之物。"a"取自古体。

The vertical line is the stake; the two shorter lines indicate a support or something hanging

on the stake. "a" is from the Archaic Script.

戈   **95**

$g\bar{e}/Ko_2$

长 矛；戟 枪

A lance; a spear

古代的一种兵器，可刺可钩。"c"为生僻字。"a""b"和"d"见于古青铜器。

This was a certain type of ancient weapon which could pierce as well as hook. "c" is a

Peculiar Word. "a", "b", and "d" appeared on ancient bronzes.

矛

96

máo/*Mou*₂

长 矛 ， 戟

A lance, a spear

一种类似斧子的长形兵器，用于战车上。"a"取自古体，左边象矛的顶端，右边加上"戈"（95）字。

This was a long axelike weapon used on a war chariot. In "a", from the Archaic Script, the exact form of the end of the weapon is drawn, with the word Ko (95) added on the right.

卟

97

hàn/*Han*₂

植 物 的 花 苞

The bud of a plant

垂

98

chuí/*Ch'ui*

垂下，使……落下

To hang down, to let fall

象植物的枝叶垂下之形。"a"字形更为明晰。

The word is a picture of the leaves of a plant hanging down. "a" is a clearer drawing.

瓜

99

guā/*Kua*₂

瓜类，葫芦

Melons, gourds

象瓜之形，两端生有藤蔓。

This is a picture of a melon with vines extended on both sides.

竹

100

zhú/*Chuh*₅

竹子
Bamboo

象竹叶之形；"a"和"b"更为形象。

Bamboo leaves are pictured; "a" and "b" are more graphic.

來（来）

101

lái/*Lai*₁

过来
To come

原指"小麦"或"大麦"，如字形所示，指上天赐予或送"来"的，故有来之意。

This word originally meant "wheat" or "barley", as drawn here, which were regarded as something that has been given or "come" from Heaven, hence the current meaning.

出

102

chū/*Ch'u*₅

出 来

To come out

字形象草木破土而出。"c"亦为生僻字，可见早期汉字的象形更为直观。

A picture of the plants growing out of the soil was used for this word. Again, "c", which is a Peculiar Word, illustrates how the older forms tended to represent the object more straightforwardly.

勿 **103**

wù/*Fu*₅

旗帜，旗；匆忙
A banner, a flag; in a hurry

a 　 b

亦用作否定词，表"不"，或作虚词，表"不要"。本意指匆忙，可能与下文 104"㱃"意思相同。

Fu is used also as a negative particle meaning "not" or "do not", an expletive. The origin of the meaning "in a hurry" is probably the same as that of Yen, 104 below.

㱃 **104**

yǎn/*Yen*₃

结束，停止
To cease, to desist from

字形象一挂起的旌旗。"a"中旗与杆相连，右边竖画表示高高的旗杆。古代，以升旗为信号召集大家发布公告或劳作，故必须先"停止"日常的事务。在紧急情况下升旗，就有了上文 103 "勿"字"匆忙"之意。

This word is a picture of a hanging banner. In "a" the connection with the post is not broken; one should think of the line on the right as a very high post. In ancient times banners were hung to summon the people together for proclamations or work, therefore they had to "desist from" their ordinary occupations. Their use in emergencies would explain the sense of "in a hurry" for Fu, 103 above.

105

máo/*Mao*$_2$

人 的 头 发 或 眉 毛 ； 动 物 的 毛 ， 毛 皮 ， 绒 毛

The hair or the eyebrows of a man;

the hair of an animal, fur, down

肉

106

ròu/*Ju*₅

肉体，肉（食物）

Flesh, meat

爪

107

zhǎo, zhuǎ/*Tsao*₃

鸟或动物的爪子；人的指甲或手指

The claws of birds or animals;

the nails or fingers of a man

革

108

gé/Kê$_5$

革

《古》

革新；除去毛的兽皮，皮革
To renovate;
hides deprived of hair, leather

a   b

"a" 和 "b" 均为古体字，象剥去皮毛、露出肋骨的动物。"革新" 之意由本意引申而来。

In "a" and "b", both Archaic Script, the picture of the animal shorn of its hair with its ribs exposed is drawn. The sense "to renovate" was derived from this original use of the word.

109

gōu/*Keo*₂

堆架木材，以修建房屋
Logs piled up
for the building of a house

110

yǔ, yú/*Yü*₁,₃

给予
To give

抽象地表示给出和收到。

Giving and taking are represented abstractly.

高

111

gāo/*Kao*₂

高的，崇高的，高大的，高贵的
High, exalted, tall, noble

象高耸的建筑之顶层，故表高之意。"a"为大篆体；"b"为生僻字。
The picture of the top story of an elevated structure conveys the idea. "a" is Major Script; "b" is a Peculiar Word.

克

112

kè/*K'eh*₅

攻克，有能力；胜任的
To conquer, to be able to; competent

上部为简化的"高";下部象人的肩。如果人能用肩高高扛起某物,则谓之"有能力"或"胜任"的。"a"取自古体,"b"取自大篆体。

An abbreviated form of the word for "high" is on top; below is the form of a man's shoulder. If one shoulders something high he must be "able" or "competent" to do it. "a" is from the Archaic Script and "b" is from the Major Script.

系

113

xì/*Hsi*₄

系列,系统;系在一起

A series, a system; to tie together

字形象下端垂悬的束丝。

The picture drawn is of a silk skein with the ends hanging.

衣

114

yī/*I*₁

衣服，外套，服装
Clothing, overcoat, garment

象一简化的长袍的上部。

This is a brief picture of the upper part of a robe.

琴

115

qín/*Ch'in*₂

中式的琴（一种乐器）
A Chinese lute

象琴的一端及琴轸。

The picture shows the end of the instrument and the tuning pegs.

*伏羲、神农等制作的乐器，用来禁止淫邪，端正人心。

册

116

cè/Ts'ê₅

注册，记录

Registers, records

竖笔表纸发明之前用来记录的竹简。两横表串连竹简的皮绳。"b"为生僻字。

The vertical lines are the bamboo slips used for writing before the invention of paper. The horizontal lines represent the two leather strips binding them together. "b" is a Peculiar Word.

网   **117**

wǎng/*Wang*₃

网状物，网子，网络
Network, a net, a web

字形象一张渔网。"a"为古体，"b"为大篆体。
The drawings represent a fish net. "a" is Archaic Script and "b" is Major Script.

率   **118**

shuài/*Suai*₅

收集，率领
To collect, to lead

字形象一捕鸟的网，上下两端的竖线表用来挂鸟网的杆子。

This is the picture of a net for catching birds. The poles on which it is hung are indicated by the vertical lines on the top and the bottom of the sketch.

119

bān/Po_4

（农民用以）运垃圾的篮子，带有长推杆

A basket for collecting refuse,
pushed by a long handle (used by farmers)

a

"a" 为相似字形。

"a" is a similar picture.

畢（毕）

120

畢　畢　ㄅ
　　　　　一

完毕，结束

To finish, to conclude

象捕野兔和野鸡的网子。

A hunting net for catching rabbits and pheasants is drawn.

牛

121

牛　牛　广
　　　　　又

niú/*Niu*₂

公牛，奶牛

An ox, a cow

象牛的后视图，抽象表示出牛的角、头、背和尾巴。

This is an abstract sketch of the horns, head, hump, and tail of a cow as it appears from behind.

羊

122

*yáng/Yang*₂

绵羊，山羊
A sheep, a goat

象羊的耳朵、角、四足和尾巴。

The ears and horns, the four feet and tail are sketched.

犬

123

*quǎn/Ch'üen*₃

狗
A dog

a　b　c

象狗竖立之形。"a"和"b"取自古体，"c"取自大篆体。

The drawing is made vertically. "a" and "b" are from the Archaic Script and "c" is from the Major Script.

124

shǐ/*Shih*₃

猪，阉猪
A pig, a hog

125

tù/*T'u*₄

野兔，兔子
A hare, a rabbit

a

"a"取自大篆体。

"a" is from the Major Script.

126

sì/*Ssi*₃

犀牛

A rhinoceros

a　b　c

现代印刷体源于古体字"a"。

The modern printed word comes from "a", which is from the Archaic Script.

鼠

127

鼠　尸ㄨ

shǔ/*Shu*₃

鼠，老鼠

A rat, a mouse

a

"a" 取自古体，象鼠的立面图。

"a" is from the Archaic Script, drawn vertically.

采

128

采　夕ㄢˊ

biàn/*Pang*₄

辨别

To distinguish

象动物脚趾展开时的爪形，以表字义。

The picture of the paw of an animal when the toes are spread out expresses the meaning of the word.

129

zhì/*Ch'ih*₄

无足之爬行动物

Reptiles without feet

a   b

字形原象长脊椎动物向前爬行之态。"b"为生僻字。

Originally this was a picture of an animal with long vertebrae moving forward. "b" is a Peculiar Word.

130

lù/*Lu*₅

鹿，雄鹿

A deer, a stag

"a" 取自竹简，象抽象地画出鹿形。

"a" is from the bamboo slips, an abstract picture of the animal.

馬（马）

131

mǎ/*Ma*₃

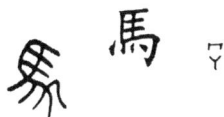

马

A horse

亦为马的纵向图，可见其鬃毛自上垂下。每种字体均可见马的头、身子、四足和尾巴。"c"为生僻字。

Again, the animal is drawn vertically. The mane can be seen flowing out from the upper part of the horse. The head, body, feet and tail are shown in every picture. "c" is a Peculiar Word.

爲（为） 132

為 ㄨㄟˊ

wéi/*Wei*₁

干，做，行动

To do, to make, to act out

字形原象"一只母猴"，此意后来废弃。"b"和"c"均为古体。

Originally this word meant "a female monkey", and gives this picture, but this meaning has become obsolete. "b" and "c" are Archaic Script.

象 133

xiàng/*Siang*₄

ㄒㄧ ㄤˋ

大象，象牙

An elephant, ivory

"a"字形极为写实；"b"为大篆体，象的纵向图。以长鼻子表大象。

"a" is a very clear picture; "b", Major Script, is drawn vertically. The long trunk indicates the animal.

134

yǔ/*Yü*₃

猴 类 动 物

A monkey-like animal

著名夏朝（建于公元前 2205 年）开国君王。"a"和"b"均为生僻字。

This is the name of the famous founder of the Hsia dynasty, 2205 B.C. "a" and "b" are Peculiar Words.

佳 **135**

zhuī/*Wei*₁

和，仅有（虚词）

And, only (expletive)

字形原象一种短尾鸟。"b"和"c"见于商代青铜器上。

This was originally a picture of a short-tailed bird. "b" and "c" appeared on Shang Dynasty bronzes.

乌（乌） **136**

wū/*Wu*₁

乌鸦或白嘴鸦

A crow or rook

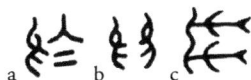

亦用作虚词。所列古体字均取自大篆体。"b"象并立的两只鸟，"c"象双飞的两只鸟。

This word is also used as an expletive. All the antique forms are from the Archaic Script. "b" shows two birds sitting and "c" two birds flying together.

鳥（鸟）

137

niǎo/*Niao*$_3$

鳥 广
　 幺

鸟 儿

A bird

"a"取自竹简。

"a" is from the bamboo slips.

*鸟字点睛，乌则不。因其纯黑，不见其睛也。

鳥

138

què/*Hsi*₃

喜鹊
A magpie

a   b

"a" 为古体，象喜鹊之形；"b" 取自古青铜器。

"a" is Archaic Script, a clear picture; "b" is from the old bronze vessels.

焉

139

yān/*Yen*₂

如何，为什么，哪里？—— 句末助词
How, why, where?
—a final particle

原意指"黄色的焉鸟"。现字义源自其读音。"a"取自古体。

Originally the word meant "a bird of yellow colour". Its present meaning came from the sound. "a" is from the Archaic Script.

140

yàn/*Yen*₄

燕子

The swallow

"a"为古体；"b"取自竹简。所列字体均象燕子特有的尾巴。

"a" is Archaic Script; "b" is a form taken from the bamboo slips. The typical tail is shown in all the drawings.

羽

141

yǔ/*Yü*₃

羽毛，羽翼
Feathers, wings

飛（飞）

142

fēi/*Fei*₁

飞行
To fly

a b

象展翅飞翔之态。"a"和"b"更为生动写实。

This is a picture of the wings spread out in flight. "a" and "b" are more expressive pictures.

迅

143

xùn/*Hsin*₄

ㄒㄩㄣ

快 的 ， 疾 速 的
Quick, swift

象鸟疾飞而不见其羽。该字属指事。

The bird is flying so quickly that the feathers can no longer be seen. This word belongs to the indicatives.

虫 ［蟲］

144

chóng/*Ch'ung*₁

ㄔㄨㄥ

蠕 虫
A worm

原意指"毒蛇",读作"huǐ"。三"虫"即"蟲",[ ] 中的蟲为现代印刷繁体。今取上部的虫代之,以简化书写。

Originally this word meant "a poisonous snake" and was pronounced as "Fei". The word for "worm" was this form tripled, as shown in the modern printed word given in parentheses. Today the word on top is used in general for its simplicity in writing.

*《说文》:"有足谓之蟲,无足谓之豸。"(参见上文 129)

魚(鱼) **145**

yú/*Yü*₂

鱼

A fish

"a"为古体;"b"取自周代的石鼓文。

"a" is Archaic Script; "b" is a Stone Drum Inscription, from the Chou Dynasty.

它

146

tā/*T'o*$_2$

那， 另 一 个

That, another

该字原象蛇形，很可能是眼镜蛇。

Originally the word was the picture of a snake, probably a cobra.

巴

147

bā/*Pa*$_1$

大 蟒 蛇

A boa constrictor

a　b

"a" 取自古体; "b" 为生僻字。

"a" is from the Archaic Script; "b" is a Peculiar Word.

龜（龟）

148

guī/*Kuei*₁

乌 龟

A tortoise

"a"和"b"均取自古体，象龟的俯视图。

"a" and "b" are from the Archaic Script, showing the appearance of the animal from above.

易

149

yì/*I*₅

容 易 的 ， 仁 慈 的 ； 变 化

Easy, lenient; to change

象蜥蜴之形。"a"为古体。

This word is the picture of a lizard. "a" is Archaic Script.

黽 （黾）

*měng/Ming*₃

蟾蜍，树蛙

A toad, a tree-frog

"a"和"b"取自古体，"c和"d"为生僻字。

"a" and "b" are from the Archaic Script and "c" and "d" are Peculiar Words.

蜀

151

shǔ/*Shu*~5~

ㄕ
ㄨ

蜀虫

A caterpillar

＊桑树上形状像蚕的害虫。

萬（万）

152

wàn/*Wan*~4~

ㄨㄢ

一万

Ten thousand

a　b　c

原象蝎子之形。"b"为大篆体，"c"取自生僻字，字形非常精简。

Originally this word was the picture of a scorpion. "b" is Major Script and "c" is from the Peculiar Script, a very simplified form.

153

鼠

liè/Le₅

马 的 鬃 毛

A horse's mane

154

以

yǐ/I₃

由 ， 通 过 ， 以 …… 方 式

By, through, by means of

已 **154a**

原象薏仁或薏苡的种子。用作转注字时，表上文之意。"a" 取自小篆体。

Originally the word was a picture of the seeds of Job's tears, or "coix lachryma". Used as a transmissive it has the meaning given above. "a" is from the Minor Script.

巳 **155**

*sì/Ssu*₄

停止，使平静；类似的

To stop, to be quiet; similar

a

该字现有两种不同的读音、意思和书体。在隋代之前，154，154a 和 155 的字形并不区分，可相互替换，读作"sì"，指地支的第六个数，表示一天或一年的某一时段。"a" 是巳字的古体。154a 的"已"字今读作"yǐ"，表上文之意。

This word now has two different sounds, two different meanings and two written forms. Up to the Sui Dynasty there was no distinction between the forms given in 154, 154a, and 155, and the usages were interchangeable. Pronounced as "Ssu", it means the sixth number of the "earthly branches", denoting periods of the day or the year. "a" is an Archaic form of Ssu. The word in 154a now pronounced "I" has the meaning given above.

己

己　己　₄

156

jǐ/Chi₃

自 己

Self

ₐ 正

"a" 为古体，与现代书体非常接近。字形象横向和纵向分丝成线。本意指"时代"或"历史上的时期"。作假借字，表示"自己"。亦用来表示"天干"的第六个数字；因此，也作数词。

The Archaic Script in "a" is very close to the modern written word. The word depicts the separation of silk into threads in horizontal and vertical lines. Its original meaning was that of "era", "a period of history". As a borrowed word it means "self". It is used to denote the sixth number of the "heavenly stems"; thus it is also a numeral.

宀

宀　宀　冖
宀

157

mián/*Mien*₂

屋子，屋顶
House, roof

穴

穴　穴　穴
穴

158

xué/*Hsüeh*₅

洞穴，洞孔
Cave, holes

未采用许慎之释义。字形简单表示屋顶有两个开口。（参见上文 157）

Hsu Shên's explanation has not been adopted. The word is a simple pictograph showing two

openings in a roof. (See 157)

夂

及

159

suī/*Sui*~1~

蹒 跚

To stagger

玉

王 玉

160

yù/*Yü*~4~

玉石, 宝石

Jade, a gem

a

字形象饰带或缎带从中串连起三块玉石。"a"取自古体。

The drawing shows three pieces of jade joined by a lace or ribbon in the middle. "a" is from the Archaic Script.

III.

Pictographs cum Indicatives

象形并指事

中

1

zhōng/*Chung*₁

中 中

中间，中心
The middle, centre

a

竖笔表示一箭射中目标，并从中间刺穿。"a"取自大篆体，左右的两横表示四支箭。

An arrow represented by the vertical line strikes the target and pierces it through the middle. In "a", from the Major Script, the two strokes on the left and the right indicate four arrows.

正

2

zhèng/*Chëng*₄

正 正

正直的，正确的，公正的
Upright, true, just

a

该字常写于布上作为靶子，根据周代的度量衡，布为两尺（44cm）见方。其他的字义皆由"正中目标"而出。"a"为古体，上部增加一横笔组成"上"字。

The word is drawn in the form of a target usually designed on cloth, which was two Chinese feet (44 cm.) square, according to the measurements of the Chow Dynasty. All the meanings of the word are derived from this sense, — "hit at the right point". In "a", which is Archaic Script, the addition of one more line forms the word "above" on the top.

本

3

běn/*Pên*₃

根 ， 起 源 ， 根 源 （也指主要的或首要的）

Root, origin, source

(also the idea of principal or capital)

a

字的下部表树木的根。"a"中的树根更为明晰。

The root of a tree is indicated by the lower half of the word. In "a" the roots are more clearly seen.

末

4

mò/Mo₅

末尾
The end

上文 3 "本"的反形——反本为末。横笔表树冠，顶部。"a"取自竹简。

This is the opposite of 3 above. The horizontal line indicates the top of the tree, the limit. "a" is from the bamboo slips.

旦

5

日　旦　勹

dàn/*Tan*₄

早晨，黎明

The morning, the dawn

象太阳升出地平线。参见 II. 1 "日"字。

In the picture the sun is appearing above the horizon. See II. 1.

夕

6

夕　夕　厶

xī/*Hsi*₅

傍晚，黄昏

Evening, dusk

ɑ 夕

象月亮露出一半之形，如黄昏时。参见 II. 2。

The moon is drawn just at the time when it is half-seen, i.e., dusk. See II. 2.

父

7

父

fù, fǔ/*Fu*_{3, 4}

父亲，长辈

A father, an elder

a   b

象人手举一杖；很可能是一火把，因家中通常由年长者照看火堆。参见 II. 39a。"b"字形相同，但多为曲线。

The picture represents one who holds a stick in his hand; most probably a torch is meant, as the elders of a family usually kept the fire. See II. 39a. "b" shows the same in a more cursive style.

尹

8

$\text{yǐn}/Yin_3$

尹

治理，统治，指挥

To govern, to rule, to direct

象右手持仗。参见 II. 39a。

In this drawing a stick is held in the right hand. See II. 39a.

寸

9

$\text{cùn}/Ts\,'un_4$

寸，10 寸为 1 尺

An inch, 1/10 of a Chinese foot

短横表手腕附近摸脉之处。距离手腕约 1/10 尺。参见 II. 39a。该字引申意指"尺度"。

The short horizontal line indicates the place near the hand where the pulse can be felt. The distance of this place from the hand is the measure of 1/10 of a Chinese foot. See II. 39a. In a higher sense, this word means "measurement".

主

10

zhǔ/*Chu₃*

主公，主人，所有者

A lord, a master, an owner

原象灯盏之形，顶部长点表火焰。假借字，读音同"壴"（zhù），指"演奏一种远而可见的大型乐器"。参见 IX. 68。作转注字，指"地位高而受人尊敬或敬仰的人"；故表"主公"等意。

The picture was originally of a lamp with its flame indicated by the long dot on top. This is a borrowed word which has the same sound as "Shu", meaning "the display of tall musical instruments visible at a distance". See IX. 68. As a transmissive it means "men of high position respected or looked up to"; hence the idea of "a lord", etc.

朱

11

zhū/*Chu*₁

朱红色，朱砂

Red, vermilion

中间横笔表树心呈红色。"a"取自青铜器，用点代替横笔。

The horizontal line in the middle indicates the interior of a tree, which is red. In "a", which ·is a form taken from the bronzes, the straight line is replaced by a dot.

片

12

piàn/*P'ien*₄

一 片 ， 碎 片 ， 薄 片

A piece, a splinter, a slice

半"木"为片。

This is half of the word for "wood".

刃

13

rèn/*Jên*₄

刀 或 剑 锐 利 的 锋 刃

The sharp edge of a knife or a sword

短笔指向剑的刀刃。参见 II. 85。

The short stroke points to the edge of the sword. See II. 85.

刃

14

刅   刃

chuāng/*Ch'uang*₂

创 伤 ， 切 ； 被 锋 利 的 武 器 割 伤 ；

伤 口 ， 伤 疤

To wound, to cut;

wounded by edged weapons;

a sore, a scar

右短横表示武器留下的伤口。

The short line on the right indicates the wound made by the weapon.

夫

15

夫   夫

fū/*Fu*₁

男 子 ， 丈 夫

A man, a husband

横笔表插于发髻上的长簪，此为成人（男子）的装束。

The horizontal line represents the long hairpin worn through the topknot, an adult fashion.

立

16

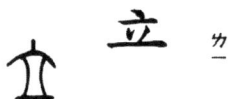

lì/*Lih*~5~

站立，建立

To stand up, to establish

象立于地上之人，下横表地面。

This is a drawing of a man standing on the ground, indicated by the horizontal line on the bottom.

乏

17

fá/*Fah*₅

缺乏

To be in want

反"正"（III. 2）为乏，字义也相反。原意指方形的兽皮，用以挡箭。

The form is the reverse of Chëng, III. 2, and the meaning is the opposite. The original idea was a square piece of hide to protect one from arrows.

巾

18

jīn/*Chin*₁

毛巾，餐巾，方巾

A towel, napkin, or kerchief

竖笔表挂绳。

The vertical line shows the hanging string.

卒

交 卒 ㄗㄨˊ

19

zú/*Tsu*₅

士 卒
A soldier

字形象士卒的制服，下部短横表徽章。参见 II. 114。作假借字，表示"聚集""结束"等。

The uniform of a soldier is sketched with a badge indicated by the short horizontal line in the lower portion of the word. See II. 114. As a borrowed word, it means "to cluster", "to come to an end", etc.

广

广 广 一ㄢˇ

20

yǎn/*Yen*₃

遮盖物，屋顶
A covering, a roof

象远眺时高耸房屋的屋檐。

This is a sketch of the edge of the roof of a tall house seen from a distance.

21

tà/*Ta*₅

踏 步

To tread

反"止"（II. 52）为屮。

This is the reverse form of Chih, II. 52.

22

yǐn/*Yin*₃

继 续 前 行 ， 远 行

To move on, long walk

由"彳"字引申出来，指"蹒跚"或"迈出左脚"。参见 II. 51。

This is an extension of the word Ch'ih, "to stagger" or "to step with the left foot". See II. 51.

至

23

至　　屮

zhì/*Chih*₄

触 及 ， 达 到 ， 进 入

To reach, to arrive at, to enter

象鸟飞落到地面，下横表地面。

This is the picture of a bird swooping down onto the ground, indicated by the line on the bottom.

不

24

*bù/Pu*₅

不是

Not

顶部横笔表天空。鸟飞起来，而"不是"落下。

The horizontal line on top indicates the sky. A bird is flying up and **not** coming down.

血

25

*xuè/Hsüeh*₅

鲜血

Blood

短横表祭祀时盛于器具中祭牲的血。参见 II. 68。

The short horizontal line indicates the blood of the sacrificial animal contained in a vessel. See II. 68.

且

26

且 ㄑㄩˇ

qiě/*Tsu*₃

祭祀时盛放肉的器具
A stand for meat at sacrifices

a △ b ▢

象盛肉之俎。横笔表地面。"b"取自竹简。

The meat was placed on such a stand. The horizontal line represents the ground. "b" is from the bamboo slips.

甘

27

甘 ㄍㄢ

gān/*Kan*₂

甘甜的，愉快的
Sweet, pleasant

短横表口中所尝之味道。参见 II. 29。

The short line indicates the taste in the mouth. See II. 29.

28

mǎo/*Mao*₄

覆 盖
Covering

中间的短横表示被覆盖之物。

The short line inside the drawing indicates the thing covered.

29

mào/*Mao*₄

帽 子 ， 盖 子
Hat, cover

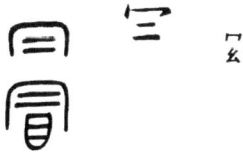

底下的横线表示头冠。

The bottom line indicates the crown of the head.

内

30

内 内

nèi/*Nui*~4, 5~

内部，里面

Within, inside

a b

在"入"字基础上（参见 I. 10）加上"遥远的边界"之意。"a"和"b"为生
僻字。

The form is based on the word "to enter" —see I. 10—with the addition of the idea of a
"remote boundary". "a" and "b" are Peculiar Words.

屯

屯 屯 古文

31

tún/*T'un*₁

艰难, 堆积, 营地

Difficulty, accumulation, camp

a

象芽在土中生长，积聚生命力，仅有一小嫩芽艰难地破土而出。

This is a picture of sprouts germinating in the soil, showing the accumulation of vital force, with only a little shoot coming out of the earth with difficulty.

之

业 之 业

32

zhī/*Chih*₁

达到, 去到

To arrive at, to go to

a

可用作代词，指"它，这"等，亦用作物主形容词和虚词。字形象草木自土中长出。"a"为商代古体。

This word is also used as a pronoun for "it, this", etc., and as a possessive and a particle. In the picture the plant has grown out of the earth. "a" is an Archaic form from the Shan Dynasty.

33

*zhé/Choeh*₄

草叶

A blade of grass

上面的曲线表弯曲的植物；下面的根尤可见。

The upper curve shows the bending plant; the root is seen underground.

卡 [菽]

34

尗   ㄕㄨ

shú [shū]/*Shu*₅

豆类或豆子
Pulse or beans

a   b   c

字形象叔豆生长的样子。下面有根。"a""b"和"c"表示豆类天性蔓枝。"c"为生僻字。

The sprout of the pulse grows out like the form pictured. The roots are underneath. "a", "b", and "c", show the creeping nature of this plant. "c" is a Peculiar Word.

才

35

才   ㄘㄞ

cái/*Ts'ai*₁

天才，才能，权力，力量
Talent, ability, power, force

象草木初生的样子。交叉线表新芽自土中长出，生命力之象征。"a"中的点表土地。

The drawing represents the beginning of the growth of plants. The cross indicates the sprout shooting forth from the soil, a sign of vitality. In "a" the soil is represented by a dot.

齊（齐）   **36**

   qí/Ts'i₂

平齐的，一致的，大致相同的

Even, uniform, all alike

象高度一致的麦穗。下面两横表耕作后的土地。"a"中仅表示出三个麦穗。

This is a picture of ears of wheat grown at the same height. The two lines on the bottom indicate the cultivated earth. In "a" only the three ears are shown.

IV.

Ideatives

会 意

此处"会意"是一纯词源学术语，不宜扩展到哲学层面。不难理解，造字继象形之后是指事，二者又相互组合成新字，表特定的意思。许慎称此类汉字为："比类合谊，以见指㧑。"这些表意的符号多源于人类自身及其活动，故极易识别而不易产生误解。能找到的会意字约有830个，但多数今已不用。有些字，因废弃已久，即便略明其意，其读音也不得而知，故不在此列出例字。

通常表达多层意思或强调，最惯用的方法是将字形或符号重复两次、三次，甚至四次叠加在一起。此类汉字约有50个，其中有14到15个常用字，其余的即便在古籍中也很少出现。

另须注意，一字多意的会意字，此处未收录。本章所举之例字仅为常用字，有正统释义，即标准字义的字；以及最典型的由旧字组合而成的新字。起初会意的造字或只是一权宜之策，后范围不断扩大而逐渐成为一造字原则。

本章共收录约270个会意字，考虑到释义方便，其排序未严格遵循古代的分类。

The term "ideative" used here is purely etymological, and must not be taken in any larger philosophical sense. It can easily be understood that after the pictographs and the indicatives were formed, a new combination of some of them into one word could give a certain specific idea. According to Hsu Shên, words of this category are those

> "formed through a combination of diverse elements of different categories with the meaning seen (or literally 'the aim expressed') in the compound".

The symbols used to represent these ideas are mostly derived from the human being himself and his activities, since they are the most easily discernable by all and can hardly be misunderstood. About 830 such words can be found, but many of them are now out of use. Some have become so obsolete that, even when we can somehow catch the idea of the word, we no longer know its pronunciation; these words are not given here as examples.

The most common method of expressing an idea of multiplicity or to show emphasis is to have the form or sign of a word doubled or tripled or even put in a fourfold combination. There are about fifty such words in existence, but we can count only fourteen or fifteen in ordinary usage and the rest are not found frequently even in ancient texts.

It must also be noted here that the ideatives which allow more than one explanation are not used here. The examples given in this chapter are only those words most commonly used, those which have an orthodox and hence somewhat standardized explanation, and those which most clearly show the ingenuity of shaping new words by grouping together the old forms. The creation of ideatives was perhaps of a makeshift nature in the beginning, but afterwards, its sphere having been enlarged and consolidated, it became an established principle.

For the convenience of explanation the order of these words, about 270 in total, is not strictly in accordance with ancient classifications.

1

niàn/*Yü*₅ (*Nien*₄)

二 十
Twenty

a

由两个"十"字会意。"a"取自古体。参见 I. 18。

This word is a combination of two "tens". "a" is in Archaic Script. See I. 18.

2

sà/*Sa*₅

三 十
Thirty

a 卅

由三个"十"字会意。"a"取自古体。

Here three "tens" are put together. "a" is from the Archaic Script.

世

古　世　尸

3

shì/*Shih*₄

一代

A generation

a 卋

底部的曲线表时间之延续；三十年为一代。"a"取自竹简。

The curved line on the bottom of the word indicates extension in time; a period of 30 years is one generation. "a" is from the bamboo slips.

士

4

士　　士　乙

shì/*Ssu*₄

学者，饱学之士

A scholar, a learned man

由"十"和"一"组成。古人云：能够在多中见到一（"十"表示多），又能在一中见到多，即为学者。

This is a combination of "ten" and "one". The old explanation runs: he who comprehends oneness in multiplicity, represented by "ten", and multiplicity in oneness, is a scholar.

仕

5

仕　仕　乙

shì/*Ssu*₄

学习；担任仕宦

To learn; to fill an office

由上文 4 "士"和 II. 24 "人"字组成。

This word is a combination of 4 above and II. 24, "man".

吉

6

吉 吉 _{斗一}

ji/Chi₅

吉祥的，幸福的，吉利的

Lucky, happy, auspicious

"士"之"言"谓之"吉"。参见上文 4 和 II. 29。

The "sayings" of a "scholar" are of this nature. See 4 above and II. 29.

告

7

告 告 _{巛幺}

gào/Kao_{4, 5}

告诉，通知，宣告

To tell, to inform, to announce to

许慎认为，该字表示将横木系于牛角上，以警示牛顶撞人的危险。但更确切
的释义是"之"（走）和"口"合而为告。参见 II. 29 和 III. 32。

According to Hsü Shên this word means "the wood tied to the horns of an ox to warn people
of the danger of being butted". It seems more accurate to explain it as a compound of "to
go" and "mouth". See II. 29 and III. 32.

好   8

好   厂
ㄠ   hǎo, hào/*Hao*_{3, 4}

好 的 ， 适 宜 的 ， 正 确 的 ， 优 秀 的
Good, well, right, excellent

由"女"和"子"组成。原意指"美好"。参见 II. 45，49。

This word is a combination of the words for "daughter" and "son". Originally it meant
"beautiful". See II. 45, 49.

各

9

各

$gè/Ko_5$

各自，每个，个人

Each, every, each person

由"口"和下文的象形字"夊"组成，表示：某人不顾他人阻碍继续前行；换言之，各人自行其道。

This is a combination of the word for "mouth" and the following pictograph: someone is going forward in spite of the fact that someone else is trying to stop him; i.e., each goes his own way.

夂

10

丮 夂 ㅂ

zhǐ/*Chih*₄

象人的两腿后有拖曳或阻碍的样子，故表"从后面"之意。

This is a pictograph of a man with his legs being touched or hindered by something from behind — hence the idea of "coming from behind".

＊参见 II. 159 夊（suī）。徐灏《段注笺》："戴氏侗曰：夂、夊特一字。

灏按：戴说是也。其斜画或出或否，乃用笔之小异。"

"从夊之字多在下面，从夂者多在上，故斜画或出或否，各取其美观耳。"

比

11

𠤎 比 ㄅ

bǐ/*Pi*₃

使联合，跟随，比较；亲密的，在旁边

To associate with, to follow, to compare;

intimate, close to

象两个并排倒立的矛，故表示"组合成对或按序排列"。"a"为古体，字形更清晰。依次排列各种事物供比较。

From the symbol of two inverted spears placed together comes the idea of "to combine or to arrange in pairs or in succession". The picture is more clear in "a", which is Archaic Script. There can be a comparison made between things arranged in this way.

此

12

$c\check{i}/Tz'u_3$

这 个 ， 它 ， 这 里

This, it, here

由上文 11 "比"的一半加上"止"组成。在连续或依次排列的事物中的一处停住，故表示"这个""这里"。参见 II. 52。

Half of the word Pi in 11 above has been taken and combined with the word for "to stop". To stop at something which is in a serial arrangement or successive order and thereby to indicate it means "this", "here". See II. 52.

眾（众）   **13**

                                                                zhòng/*Ch'ung*₄

                                                                众 多 ， 群 众
                                                                A multitude, a crowd

由"目"下面三个"人"——即许多人——而会意。"a"中以"口"代替"目"。
参见 II. 24，25。

Three "men"— that is, many persons — are drawn below the word for "eye". In "a" a mouth
is drawn instead of an eye. See II. 24, 25.

老   **14**

                                                                lǎo/*Lao*₃

                                                                老 的 ， 年 长 的 ， 尊 长 的
                                                                Old, aged, venerable

a 老

由"毛""人"和"匕"（huà，变化）三个字组成，表示人的头发变成灰色或白色，以头发颜色的"变化"表示年老。"a"为古体，上面象人的头上有发，下面的"匕"字表变化。参见 II. 24，105。

Three words — "hair", "man", and "change" — are combined. This means that when the hair of a man turns grey or white, its colour has "changed", showing old age. In "a", Archaic Script, the head of a man with the hair depicted is drawn over the word for change. See II. 24, 105.

周

15

周 zhōu/*Chou*₂

周围，周全的

All around, comprehensive

a 周

原意指"秘密的，平静的，谨慎的"，由下文 16 "用"字和"口"字组成。"a"
常见于青铜器上。

The original sense of this word was "secret, peaceful, cautious", by a combination of
"use"— see 16 below —of "words" (the mouth). "a" is often seen on bronze vessels.

用

16

用 用 ɔ

yòng/Yung₄

使 用 ， 雇 用
To use, to employ

a 用

"卜"（表占卜）与"中"（表中间）合而为用。采纳切中要点的推测或计划，
故有"可用"之意。"a"取自青铜器。参见 II. 59 和 III. 1。

This word is formed by the combination of the word Pu, "to divine", and Chung, "middle".
The conjecture or scheme that hits the right point can be employed, hence the idea of
"practicable". "a" is from the bronze vessels. See II. 59 and III. 1.

公

17

公

gōng/*Kung*₁

公共的，公开的，公正的；

公爵，最高的贵族头衔（仅次于帝王）

Public, open to all, impartial;

a duke, the highest rank of nobility (next to the emperor)

上面两笔为"八"字（I. 16），表示"分开"，"相反"或"背对着"。下面"厶"字（下文 18）表"隐私"或"自私"。与自私相对即公共的或公正的。为公爵者必然品性高贵。

The two strokes on top, I. 16, mean "to divide", "opposed to", or "with the back turned to". The lower part is the word for "privacy" or "selfishness"— see 18 below. What is opposed to selfishness is that which is public or impartial. The duke must have a character of such nobility.

厶

18

sī/*Ssu*₁

隐私，自私
Privacy, selfishness

仁

19

rén/*Jên*₁

仁爱，美德，仁慈，善良
The Divine's love,
virtue, benevolence, goodness

原指两人之间的关系；"仁"是儒家思想的核心，在英文中无完全对应之翻译。参见 I. 2，II. 24。

Originally denoting the relation between two men, this word stands for the central principle of Confucianism. There is no exact equivalent for it in English. See I. 2 ; II. 24.

信

20

信　信　ㄐㄧㄣ

xìn/*Hsin*₄

信任；诚实，信息

To trust;

sincerity, a message

a　b　c

字形表人言出必信。许慎将该字列为会意字典型。"a"用"口"字表示人所说的话。"b"由"言"字和"心"字组成。"c"为古体，右边为"言"字。参见 II. 24 和 VII. 4。

The idea of the word form is that what is spoken by a man must be trustworthy. This was given by Hsu shên as an example of the ideative category. In "a", what was spoken is represented by the mouth only. "b" shows the word for "words" and the word for "mind-heart" combined. In "c", which is Archaic Script, the form on the right side represents "words". See II. 24 and VII. 4.

位

21

wèi/*Wei*₄

位 置 ， 情 形 ， 等 级 或 程 度

A position, a situation, rank or degree

a b

原意指朝堂左右两侧大臣的站位。由"人"和"立"组成。参见 II. 24 和 III. 16。"a"与"b"字形相同。

The original sense of the word indicated the standing positions of the nobles on the left and right sides of the king's court. "A man" and "to stand" are combined. See II. 24 and III. 16. "a" and "b" are the same.

休

22

xiū/*Hsiu*₂

休 T
 ㄧ
 ㄡ

休息

To rest

由"人"依傍着"木"而会意；表示休息。参见 II. 24 和 V. 6。

The word shows a "man" leaning on a "tree"; he is at rest. See II. 24 and V. 6.

伐

23

fá/*Fah*₅

伐 ㄈ
 ㄚ

公然袭击；对他国频繁发动有组织的进攻

To attack openly;

a regularly organized attack on a country

戍

由"人"挥"戈"会意。参见 II. 24，95。"a"象人将戈扛于肩上。

The idea shown is that of a "man" using a "weapon". See II. 24, 95. In "a" the man is carrying the weapon on his shoulder.

24

shù/*Shu*₄

驻军；驻守边境的士兵

Garrison; soldier on guard at the frontier

由"人"持"戈"会意，故指卫兵。参见上文 23。

The idea shown is that of a "man" shouldering his "weapon"; he must be a guard. See 23 above.

夾（夹）

25

夾 夾 ㄐㄧㄚ

jiā/Chia₅

用手臂夹住
To clasp under the arm

象"成年人"两臂下各挟一"人"。参见 II. 23，24。

A "full-grown man" is pictured carrying a "man" under each arm. See II. 23, 24.

夷

26

夷 夷

yí/I₁

东部的蛮夷
Barbarians on the east

象蛮夷常持弓箭之形。参见 II. 23，83。

The people meant usually carried a bow. See II. 23, 83.

従（从）　　　　　　　　　　　　　　　　　　**27**

cóng/*Ts'ong*$_1$

跟 从

To follow

象两人朝同一方向行进。亦属于指事。"a"为变体，表示两人的"彳"与
"止"。参见下文 47a。

Two persons are pictured going in the same direction. This word could also be an indicative.

"a" is a variation. Their "walking" or "stopping" is indicated. See 47a below.

北

28

běi/*Pê*₅

北方；（故对的）
North; (antagonistic)

由两个"人"背面相向而会意。人通常向光而坐，故背面也为北面。该字亦属指事。

Two persons are drawn with their backs turned towards each other. Usually a man sits facing the light, so the back side is also taken as the northern side. This is also an indicative.

囚

29

qiú/*Ts'iu*₂

囚　禁；囚　犯

To imprison; a prisoner

由"口"和"人"两个字合而会意。参见 II. 21。

Two words — "encircling" and "man" — express the idea. See II. 21.

及

30

jí/*Chi*₅

到　达，追　上，延　伸

To reach to, to come up to, to extend

由"手"从后面伸向某人而会意。参见 II. 24，39a。

The "hand" is pictured reaching towards someone from behind. See II. 24, 39a.

困

31

kùn/*K'un*₄

围困；困扰

Surrounded by; distress

原意指"老旧的房屋"——由"木"在"口"中而会意。参见 II. 21 和 V. 6。

Originally the meaning of this word was "an old house" — "wood" in an "enclosure". See II. 21 and V. 6.

囷

32

qūn/*T'un*₁

存放米的仓库或桶

A barn or bin for rice

由"禾"在"口"中而会意。参见 II. 21，64。

The word for "rice" is in an "enclosure". See II. 21, 64.

粟

33

粟　粟　含

sù/*Su*₅

谷 粒 ， 小 米 ， 玉 米

Grain, millet, maize

桌
a

上部为象形，表果实压弯草木；下部为"米"字（参见 II. 63）。"a"中果实更为清晰。

The word on top is a pictograph showing the "bending of fruit on any plant"; beneath it is the word for "rice". See II. 63. "a" shows the fruit more clearly.

昌

34

昌　昌

chāng/*Ch'ang*₂

美言；光荣的，灿烂的，昌盛的

Nice saying;

glorious, brilliant, prosperous

"日"（表光辉）与"曰"（表说话或语言）合而为昌。参见 II. 1 和 V. 1。"a"
取自竹简，其下部表示口。

This is a combination of the word for "sun", meaning brilliancy, and the word for "to speak
or speech". See II. 1 and V. 1. In "a", which is from the bamboo slips, the lower part of the
word represents the mouth.

頃（顷）

35

qīng, qǐng/*Ch'ing*₂, ₃

倾斜；倾向

Leaning; to incline

左边"匕"表弯曲；合而表右边的"头"偏向一侧。参见 II. 32。"a"为生僻字，"头"的写法稍有不同。

The sign on the left shows "bending"; this indicates that the "head" on the right is bent towards one side. See II. 32. "a" is Peculiar Script. The head is given with a slight variation.

亡

36

wáng/*Wang*₂

逃亡，离开，死亡，迷惘

To escape, to go away, to die, to be lost

由进"入"隐秘的角落（由右部"乚"表示）而会意。参见 I. 10，25。

The idea pictured is that of "entering" into some hidden place, indicated by the right angle.
See I. 10, 25.

艹

37

gǒng/*Gung*₃

双 手 相 握 ， 举 手

Hands joined, hands raised

亦表示"提供"或"举起"某物。参见 II. 39，39a。

This word can also have the sense of "offering" or "elevating" something. See II. 39, 39a.

弄

38

nòng/*Lung*₄

玩弄

To play

由双手把玩一块玉石而会意。参见 II. 160。

Two hands are pictured playing with a piece of jade. See II. 160.

共

39

gòng/*Gung*₃, ₄

共事；共同地；全体

To work together;

collectively; all

a　　b

字形源于古体"a","a"中其字义表示得更明确。该字亦指"拱手致意"。

The form above is derived from the Archaic Script pictured in "a", which shows the idea more clearly. It means also "to salute with both hands folded".

左 **40**

zuǒ/*Tso*₃

左边；协助工作

The left side; to help in the work

a 丁 b 𢓅

由左手协助右手工作而会意。参见 I. 8。"a"简单表示左边。

The left hand, shown, is meant to help the right hand in any work. See I. 8. "a" simply indicates the direction.

右

司 右 又

41

yòu/*Yu*₄

右边；帮助

The right side; to help

由"手"和"口"合而会意，即一起说话、工作。

The idea of the picture is that the "hand" and the "mouth", i.e. speech, work together.

舂

舂 春 彳ㄨㄥ

42

chōng/*Ch'ung*₁

舂捣谷物以去壳

To pound grain

in order to remove the husk

由"艸"（双手）持握"午"（杵）于"臼"上而会意。参见 II. 67。

The picture is of two hands holding a pestle over a mortar. See II. 67.

奠

43

diàn/*Tien*₄

以 酒 祭 奠

To offer libations

由双手拱献一樽酒而会意。上面两点为"水"字的简写，表示酒。"a"的下部为放酒樽的凳子。这种情况下该字只可表示酒。

Two hands are shown offering a goblet of wine. The two curves on top are an abbreviated form of the word for water and indicate the liquid. In "a" the lower part of the word is the stool on which the goblet is placed. In this case the word would simply mean "libation".

仄

44

zè/Ts'ê₅

倾 斜，偏 向

Inclined, slanting

由人低头进入崖下的洞穴而会意。原意指"狭窄"或"局限"，描摹出人在洞穴之态。参见 II. 15，24。"a"取自大篆体，字形中人的头偏向身体左侧。"b"为指事，简单表示出头偏向右边。

The picture shows a man bending his head in order to enter a hollow in a cliff. The original sense of this word was "narrow" or "confined", depicting a man in a cave. See II. 15, 24. In "a", which is from the Major Script, the man's head is inclined towards his left side. "b" is an indicative simply showing the head bent towards the right.

思

45

思 ム

思

$s\bar{\imath}/Ssu_1$

思考，沉思，思虑

To think, to contemplate, to consider

ᵃ 串

由两个字组成："囟"（头顶）位于"心"之上而会意。表示心思的整全作用。参见 II. 27，38。"a"的字义相同。

This is a combination of two words: the "crown of the head" above the "heart". The whole of the function of the mental being is meant. See II. 27, 38. "a" has the same idea.

異（异）

46

異

yì/I_4

另 外 的 ; 奇 怪 的 , 非 凡 的 , 不 同 的

The other; strange, extraordinary, different

a　　b

原意指"分开"或"分离"，由用双手将置于下方"丌"上的所"给"之物分开而会意。参见 II. 75 和上文 37。

The original sense of this word was "to divide" or "to separate", showing two hands dividing what has been "given", which is placed on a "stand" below these forms. See II. 75 and 37 above.

步

47

$bù/Pu_4$

脚步，步伐；步行

A step, a pace; to walk

由连续的脚步而会意。参见 II. 52 和 III. 21。

This is a picture of footsteps in succession. See II. 52 and III. 21.

走

47a

$chuò/Ch'o_5$

由"彳"和"止"组成。参见 II. 51，52。

This is a combination of "to step" and "to stop". See II. 51, 52.

竝（并）

48

bìng/*Ping*₄

联 合 ， 一 起
United, together with

由两个人肩并肩站立而会意。参见 III. 16。

Two persons are pictured standing shoulder to shoulder. See III. 16.

行

49

xíng/*Hsing*₂

步 行
To walk

由左脚和右脚的动态而会意。参见 II. 51。

This is an indication of the left and right legs moving. See II. 51.

延，延

50

延 延 延

yán (chān)/*Yen*₂ (*Chen*)

平缓地步行
To pace placidly

ₐ 延

由"止"和"廴"字组成。参见 II. 52 和 III. 22。第一个印刷体"延"读作
"chān"，今已废用。"延"由"延"加上一撇构成。参见 I. 21，"厂"是其字源。
"延"字原指长途步行，今更着重延续之意，包括时间和空间的延伸。"a"为
古体，尤可见这一变化。

This word is formed by a combination of the words for "footstep" and "extension". See II.
52 and III. 22. The first printed form, pronounced "Chen", is now obsolete. Yen was formed
by the addition of a dash to Chen, above. See I. 21 for its origin. Its original meaning was "a
long distance walk". Now the emphasis is placed on the idea of extension, both in time and
in space. This development can be seen in "a", which is from the Archaic Script.

衍   **51**

                                                                        yǎn/*Yen*₃

                                                                        溢 出
                                                                        To overflow

由水向外蔓延或流淌而会意。参见上文 49 和 II. 9。

Water spreading or flowing forth is pictured. See 49 above and II. 9.

前   **52**

                                                                        qián/*Ts'ien*₂

                        前 行 ； 之 前 ， 在 …… 前 面 ， 以 前 ， 领 先
                                                                        To proceed;
                                        before, in front of, formerly, ahead

由人立于舟上，不行而前进会意。参见 II. 52，87。

The idea of the word form is that when standing on a boat, one proceeds forward without

walking. See II. 52, 87.

後（后）　　　53

後　厂ㄡ

hòu/Hou[4]

后面，背部，随后；后裔

Behind, the back of, to come after;
posterity

由三个字组成——"彳"（表蹒跚），"幺"（表最后），和"夂"（表腿后有阻力）。
参见上文 10，II. 51 和 IV. 185。

This is a combination of three signs — "to stagger"; "the least", meaning the last; and
"hindered at the feet from behind". See 10 above, II. 51, and IV. 185.

匊（掬）　　　54

匊　ㄐㄩ

jū/Chü[5]

满满一捧；用手捧握

A handful; to grasp with the hand

由手"抓"或"抱"("包")着"米"而会意。参见 II. 55，63。

Some "rice" is drawn within the "grasp" or "fold". See II. 55, 63.

争（争）   55

zhēng/*Tzêng*₂

争论，争夺，抗争；扭（绳子）

To wrangle, to contend, to strive,

to twist (as a rope)

由指事字"厂"和"爭"（下文 56）组成。参见 I. 21。"a"和"b"均为较早期的字体，争夺之意更明显——四只手同时争抢一物（由竖笔表示）。

This word is a combination of the indicative "to draw" and the word in 56 below. See I. 21. "a" and "b", both older forms, show better the contention — the hands are fighting for something, indicated by the vertical line.

受

56

受

ㄆ
一
ㄠ

biào/*P'iao*₃

给 ， 拿 ， 交给

To give, to take, to hand to

由上面的"爪"（手指）和下面的"又"（手）会意。表示交给的动作。

"Fingers" are drawn on top and a "hand" is beneath. An action is meant.

送

57

送

ㄙ
ㄨ
ㄥ

sòng/*Sung*₄

陪同 ， 护送 ， 发送

To accompany, to escort, to send

由左边的"辶"（上文 47a）表行走，和"夅"（下文 59）组成。

This is a combination of Ch'o, meaning "walking", on the left, 47a above, and 59 below.

媵

58

腾 媵 乙

yìng/*Ying*₄

陪同新娘出嫁的女仆；派送

A maid who accompanies a bride
to her new home; to send

左边为"亻"旁，右边为"夅"（下文 59）。该字现已很少使用。

The classifier for "man" is on the left and 59 below is on the right. This word is rarely used.

祭

燊 弜 ㄗㄨㄢ

59

zhuàn/*Tsin*₄

提供
To offer

字形表示祭祀中双手持"火"，如火炬等。该字未收入许慎的字典，而是取自其他材料作为补充。今已废用。

This picture shows a "fire", for example a torch, held by both hands in an offering. This word is not found in Hsu shěn's Dictionary, but is a supplement taken from other sources. It is now obsolete.

章

章 ㄓㄤ

60

zhāng/*Chang*₂

章节，一个部分或段落
A chapter, a section or paragraph

由"十"字（参见 I. 18）和"音"字（参见 VII. 3）组成，表示一曲音乐到了"第十"或"最后"部分。"a"也指音乐（由字的上部表示）已接近尾声。

By the combination of the words for "ten", see I. 18, and "music", see VII. 3, the idea is given of a musical performance coming to its "tenth" or last part. "a" also gives the idea of music (in the upper portion of the word) coming to a stop.

61

mù/*Mu*$_5$

放牧；牧人，放牛郎

To tend cattle; a herdsman, a cowherd

左边为"牛"字，右边表示驱赶牛的手。参见拓片 2. 5，II. 121 和 IX. 6。

The left portion of the word is the "cattle", and the right is a hand driving them. See Plate II.5, II.121, and IX. 6.

敖

62

敖　兀幺

áo/*Ngao₂*

闲逛，遨游
To ramble, to travel

由"放"字——表"放开"或"放松"，和左上部的"出"字组成。参见 II. 102。

This is a combination of the word meaning "to let go" or "to loosen", and the word for "out" in the upper left portion of the word. See II. 102.

敫

63

敫　⼄

jiǎo/*Yo₂*

光线流散
The flashing of light

左上为"白"，左下及右部为"放"，二者合而为敫。

This is a combination of the word for "white", in the upper left portion of the picture, and the word for "to let go" in the lower left half and the entire right half.

般   **64**

舟殳   般 ㄅ

pán/*Pan*₁

盘 旋

To go round and round

由手划动船旋转而会意。参见 II. 87 和 IX. 6。

The picture is of a boat being wheeled around by hand. See II. 87 and IX. 6.

*今读作 bān。

解

65

解 解 ㄐㄧㄝ

jiě/*Chiai*₃

解 开 ， 放 松 ， 释 放

To untie, to loosen, to release

由"刀"（右上）分解"牛"（右下）"角"（左部）而会意。 参见 II. 85，
93，121。

In this word a "knife", in the upper right half, is shown being used to divide a "horn", on the
left side, of an "ox", lower right. See II. 85, 93, 121.

*亦读作 xiè。

制

66

制 制 ㄓ

zhì/*Chih*₄

切 割 ， 木 工 活 ， 塑 造 ， 制 造 ， 创 造

To cut, to work on wood,

to shape, to make, to create

上部两个"木"字，表示一棵大树；右边为一把"刀"。参见 II. 85 和 V. 6。
"a"和"b"所表示的意思相似。

Here the word for "wood" is doubled at the top, indicating a large tree; a "knife" is on the right. See II. 85 and V. 6. "a" and "b" have a very similar idea.

匠

67

jiàng/*Tsiang*₄

木工，工匠

A carpenter, an artisan

外面的"匚"表示一种测量仪器，里面的"斤"表示切割工具。两种工具既象征工匠，也象征其从事的工作。参见 II. 86。

The outer portion of the word represents an instrument for measuring, and the tool for cutting is inside. Tools signify the worker as well as the work. See II. 86.

小

68

xiǎo/*Siao*₃

小 的 ， 微 小 的 ， 不 重 要 的
Small, petty, insignificant

两边的曲线为"八"字，原指"分开"，竖笔表示某物自中间分开。将物体分开即使之变小。

The two outer curves are the sign for "eight", which originally meant "to divide", and the vertical line indicates something divided in the middle. To divide a thing means to make it smaller.

少

69

shǎo/*Shao*₃, ₄

少 量 的 ， 较 少 的 ， 缺 少
Few, less, short of

由"小"（上文 68）加一撇，表示已切分之物继而被割裂，故更少了。

The line added to the form in 68 above indicates that the thing divided has been further portioned off, thus it is less.

分

70

fēn/*Fên*₁, ₄

分 开

To divide

由下部的"刀"切分物体会意。

The division is being made by the "knife" in the lower portion of the word.

劣

71

liè/*Lüeh*₅

较 差 的 ， 恶 劣 的

Inferior, vile

由"少"和"力"组成，合而表缺乏力量之意，故为较差的。参见 II. 44 和上文 69。

The words for "less" and "strength" are combined here to give the idea of a lack of energy and thus inferiority. See II. 44 and 69 above.

與 （与）　　　　　　　　　　　72

$yǔ/Yü_{3,1}$

给予

To give

由"一""勺"被倾倒出来或给予某人而会意。参见 I. 1 和 II. 91。

Here "one" "ladle" is being poured out or given to someone. See I. 1 and II. 91.

支

73

zhī/*Chih*₁

支 止

树 枝

A branch

由手持握或摘下一半的"竹"（表树枝）而会意。参见 II. 100。

In the drawing a hand is holding or plucking half of the word for "bamboo", indicating a branch. See II. 100.

長（长）

74

cháng/*Ch'ang*₂

長 尤

长久的（既指时间，也指空间）

Long (referring both to time and space)

a 長 b 尕

人体最长之物为头发。中间的长横表示将头发束起。下面的"匕"表变化，因人到老年头发的颜色会发生变化。该字综合了象形，指事和会意。另有一解释，中间的横笔下可见一"人"字。由此表示人头发颜色的变化，暗示时间很长。"a"中亦可见头发，但"b"也许另有来源，其上部可能取自"匹"（表示一捆布或丝）字。参见 V. 25。

The longest thing on one's body is the hair. Hair is pictured here tied together by the long line in the middle. The lower sign means "to transform", because the hair finally changes colour in old age. This word is a pictograph, indicative and ideative combined. Another explanation is that one can see the word for "man" under the line in the middle. From this comes the idea of the change in colour of a man's hair, implying a long period of time. In "a" we see the hair also, but "b" has probably another origin. The upper portion of the word could be taken from the word for "a bundle of cloth or silk". See V. 25.

多

75

duō/*To*$_2$

许多，很多，大量的

Many, much, numerous

由两个"夕"字组成。参见 III. 6。

This is the word for "evening" written twice. See III. 6.

叶

76

xié/*Hsieh*5

叶　叶　T|廿

和 谐 ， 协 同 ； 协 议

In harmony, united in; agreement

协（协）

a　　　　　　　　　　　　　　　　　　　　　b　c

字形表示十个声音同一调子，故有和谐之意。参见 I. 18 和 II. 29。"a"由三个重叠的"力"加上"十"字构成。参见 II. 44。"b"中没有"十"字。"c"取自青铜器，亦为合成字，其来源已无从考据。

The idea of the form is that ten voices united in one tune means harmony. See I. 18 and II. 29. In "a" three words for "strength" are combined and "ten" is retained. See II. 44. In "b" there is no "ten". "c" is also a combined form from the bronze vessels, the origin of which is obscure.

古

77

gǔ/Ku₃

古代的，古董的，古老的

Ancient, antique, old

由众口相传而会意，经由"十"张"口"传述之物，必定年代久远或古旧。参见 I. 18 和 II. 29。

The idea here is that what has been passed down orally, what has been told by "ten" "mouths", must be something very old, of antiquity. See I. 18 and II. 29.

君

君　君　ㄐㄩㄣ

78

*jūn/Chün*₁

首领，君主

A chief, a sovereign

字形表示掌握统治权并发号施令的人即为首领或君主。"口"表示命令。参见 II. 29 和 III. 8。

The idea of the picture is that he who holds the rule and gives commands is the chief or king. The "mouth" signifies the command. See II. 29 and III. 8.

元

79

元

yuán/*Yüan*₁

首先， 头部， 首领

The first, the head, the chief

由"上"和"人"两个字组成。人体的顶部即是头。参见 I. 4 和 II. 24b。"a" 的字义相同。

This is a combination of two words — "above" and "man". What is on top of a man is his head. See I. 4 and II. 24b. "a" has the same idea.

先

80

xiān/*Sien*₂

先 ㄙㄧㄢ

首先，先于，最初的
First, before, foremost

上部为"之"，下部为"人"。行于他人之前即表领先之意。参见 II. 24b 和 III. 32。"b"显然出自相同字源。

The word for "to go" is on top and a "man" is beneath. To go before a man means to precede him, hence the idea. See II. 24b and III. 32. "b" shows clearly the same origin.

名

81

míng/*Ming*₂

名 ㄇㄧㄥ

名字；命名
Name; to give one's own name

a

上部为"夕"，表傍晚或夜晚。下部为"口"，因在黑暗中碰到别人时，人会喊出自己的名字。参见 II. 29 和 III. 6。"a"的字义相同。

The word for "evening" is on top here, meaning dusk or darkness. The word for "mouth" is below it because when one meets someone in the darkness, one calls out one's name. See II. 29 and III. 6. "a" has the same idea.

合

合　合　厂己

82

hé/Ho₅

结 合 ， 集 合 ， 一 致 ， 联 合

Combine, congregate, agree, unite

上部的"亼"为指事，表"集中"，三笔组成三角形，指三个物件放在一起。下部为"口"，表声音。三人达成一致，故而联合起来。

The upper portion of the word is an indicative meaning "to gather", indicated by three things put together, the three lines placed in a triangular form. Beneath it is the "mouth" or voice. Three persons are in agreement, and so united.

僉 （佥）

83

qiān/*Ch'ien*₂

全部， 整体
All, the whole

上部的"亼"与"合"字（上文 82）相同，下部的"从"（上文 27）表"跟随"。中间为两个"口"字。各部分合而会意。

The upper portion of this word is the same as that of 82 above, and the lower portion is the word for "to follow", see 27 above. The middle portion is two "mouths". The combined idea gives the meaning.

邑

84

yì/*I*₅

区域， 城镇， 国家
A district, a town, a country

字形上部表分封的土地；下部的"巴"为皇权的象征。"a"中皇权符号重复
出现。

The form on top indicates an enclosed piece of land; beneath it is the imperial token of
authority. In "a" the token is repeated.

令

85

lìng/*Ling*₂, ₄

命 令 ， 发 出 指 令
To command, to give orders

由"亼"（表集中，参见上文 82，83）和"卩"（表皇权象征）合而会意。

Two signs, "to gather" — see 82, 83 above — and "the token of imperial authority", are
combined to represent the idea of the word.

命

86

mìng/*Ming*₄

命令，发出指令（特别是口头命令）

To command, to give orders,
especially oral commands

由"令"字（上文 85）加上"口"组成，表示口头的命令。

The word for "mouth" has been added to 85 above to show that oral commands are meant.

同

87

tóng/*T'ung*₁

共同，相同，同样的

Together, the same as, alike

由"口"和"亼"（表示"覆盖"或"所有当中"）而会意，指"异口同声"。参见 III. 28。

The word for "mouth" combined with the word for "covering" or "among all" implies the idea of "unanimous voice". See III. 28.

舌

88

shé/*Shê*₅

舌头

The tongue

a

上部的"干"表"对抗"或"干涉"；下部为"口"字。言从口出，食从口入，皆离不开舌头。参见 I. 11 和 II. 29。"a"与古体相似。

The upper portion of this word is the word for "to offend" or "to intervene"; the word for "mouth" is below it. For speech to come out of or for anything to be taken into the mouth the tongue must intervene. See I. 11 and II. 29. "a" is a similar form from the Archaic Script.

讷 （讷）   **89**

訥 𤔔   nè/Na₅ (Nui₅)

口 吃

To stammer

由言语堵在口"内"而会意；由此表"口吃"之意。参见 III. 30。

The picture shows that words are held "within" the mouth; from this comes the idea of "to stammer". See III. 30.

號 （号）   **90**

号 號   háo, hào/Hao₂,₄

号啕大哭，哀号

To call out aloud, to wail

由气息或声音自口中发出而会意。参见 I. 23。

This is a picture of the breath or rather the sound going upwards out of the mouth. See I. 23.

品

91

品 品 ㄆㄧㄣ

众 多 ， 阶 层 ， 等 级

A multitude, classes, grades

由三个"口"表示众多。"a"取自古体，"口"由圆形变为三角形。

Three "mouths" indicate a multitude. "a" is from the Archaic Script, the rounded form changed to a triangular one.

聑

92

聑 聑 ㄊㄧ

qì/*Ch'i*₅

耳 语

To whisper

由"口"贴近"耳"说话而会意。参见 II. 26。

The idea here is given by showing a "mouth" speaking near an "ear". See II. 26.

吹

93

chuī/*Ch'ui*₁

吹 送 ， 吐 气

To blow, to breathe out

右边由两个字组成："人"和向上的"气"，表示"哈欠"。参见下文 160。该字由"欠"字左边加上"口"旁。

The right half of the word is a combination of two signs: a "man" and the "breath" going upwards, meaning "to yawn". See 160 below. The word for "mouth" is added on the left.

占

94

zhàn/Chan~2,4~

占 占 㞢

占卜；预言
To divine; prognostication

由"卜"（表"占卜"）在"口"上而会意。参见 II. 59。
On top of "mouth" is Pu, "to divine". See II. 59.

知

95

zhī/Chih~1~

知 知 㞢

知道，理解
To know, to comprehend

左边的"矢"指箭 ，表迅速之意。人心中有所领会，并能很快用言语表达出来，可谓知道或理解。参见 II. 84。"a"取自生僻字。

On the left is the word for "arrow", representing swiftness. What is understood in the mind and can be swiftly expressed by words is something known or comprehended. See II. 84. "a" is from the Peculiar Script.

吠

96

吠　吠　匕

fèi/*Fei*₄

狗 叫

To bark

由"口"和"犬"字组成。参见 II. 123。

This is a combination of the words for "mouth" and "dog". See II. 123.

尨（龙）

97

máng/*Mang*₂

多毛的狗
A shaggy dog

由"犬"字加上长毛而会意。参见 II. 123。

The long hairs are pictured on the word for "dog" to give the meaning. See II. 123.

98

biāo/*Piao*₂

狗奔跑之态；疾速，冲动
The running of dogs;
swiftness, impetuosity

由三只"犬"奔跑而会意。

Three "dogs" running are combined to form this word.

戾 **99**

$l\hat{\imath}/Li_4$

戾 戾 ㄌㄧ

弯 曲 ， 扭 曲 ； 倔 强 的

To bend, to twist; perverse

由犬必须曲体从门下爬出而会意。参见 II. 77。

The idea of the picture is that a dog going out of a door from underneath it must bend and twist his body. See II. 77.

100

chán/*Tsan*$_2$

（最为敏捷的）狡兔

The species of the most swift rabbit

由两个重叠的"兔"字（II. 125）组成。

The is the word for "rabbit", II. 125, written twice.

101

yì/*I*$_5$

逃跑，退隐；安逸，闲暇

To escape, to retire; ease, leisure

左边的"辵"（上文 47a）表示右边的"兔"逃走了——即逃脱——由此会意。

The left half of the word, ch'o, 47a above, indicates that the "rabbit" on the right has run

off — i.e., escaped — giving the meaning of the word.

竄 （竄）   **102**

cuàn/*Ts'uan*₄

躲 藏 ， 隐 藏 ， 潜 伏

To hide, to sneak off, to skulk

由"鼠"跑回"穴"中而会意。参见 II. 127，158。"a"的字义相同。

The idea of the picture is that of "rats" running to their "holes". See II. 127. 158. "a" has

the same idea.

看

103

kān, kàn/*K'an*₁, ₄

看见，观看，观察

To see, to look at, to observe

由"手"放在"目"上遮挡光线以便观看而会意。参见 II. 25，39。

The idea of the word is expressed by a picture of the "hand" raised above the "eyes" to shade off the light in order to see. See II. 25, 39.

見（见）

104

jiàn/*Chien*₄

看见，看待；视力

To see, to perceive; vision

由"目"在"人"之上而会意。参见 II. 24，25。"a"取自古体，字形相差甚微。

The word for "eye" is on top of the word for "man". See II. 24, 25. "a", from the Archaic Script, is not very different.

直

直

105

zhí/Chih₅

直立的，笔直的，正直的

Upright, straight, just

由"十"（即许多）"目"（表眼睛）注视着"乚"（表隐蔽的角落）而会意，表示无处隐藏。参见 I. 18，25 和 II. 25。"a"字形相同。

The picture of "ten" — that is, many — "eyes" looking toward an "obscure corner" gives the idea that nothing can be hidden. See I.18, 25 and II. 25. "a" is the same picture.

規（规）

106

規 《X乀

規

*guī/Kuei*₁

圆规；规则，惯例

A pair of compasses;
regulation, custom

左边的"矢"指箭，表示一直线。右边为"见"（表看见）。由直尺生方形，由方形生圆周。"目"视一物是否为"直"，故指规则。参见上文 104 和 II. 84。

The word on the left means "arrow", representing a straight line. The word on the right means "to see". The square was said to come from the straight ruler and the circle to come from the square. To "see" whether something is "straight" implies regulation. See 104 above and II. 84.

相

107

xiāng, xiàng/*Siang*₂,₄

察看，看见
To look at, to see

右边的"目"看着或注视左边的"木"，而树木为地上甚可观者。参见 II. 25 和 V. 6。"a"字形相同。

The "eye" on the right sees or is looking at the "vegetation" on the left, which is deemed worth seeing on the earth. See II. 25 and V. 6. "a" is the same picture.

是

108

shì/*Shih*₄

是的，正直的；（动词）成为
Yes, right; the verb to be

a

由"正"（表正直的或正确的）在"日"下而会意。太阳被视为"正确"和简
易之原则；故表"是的"之意。参见 II. 1 和 III. 2 。"a"字义相同。

Here the word for "right" or "correct" is beneath the word for "sun". The sun is taken as a
standard of "correctness" and simplicity; hence the idea of "It is". See II. 1 and III. 2. "a" has
the same idea.

里

109

里　里　ㄌㄧ

lǐ/Li_3

小巷，街道，邻里

A lane, a street, a neighborhood

由"田"和"土"字组成。古语有言"五户为邻，五邻为里"。里今作为一长
度单位，约合 1890 英尺（500 米）。参见 I. 9 和 II. 20。

This is a combination of the words for "ground" and "field". The old saying was that "Five
houses constitute a neighborhood; five neighborhoods make a Li". Today the li is a measure
of length reckoned at about 1890 English feet. See I. 9 and II. 20.

坐

110

坐

ㄗㄨㄛˋ

zuò/*Tso*₄

坐下；座位

To sit; a seat

a 坐

上部表一关着的门，顶部上栓。下部为"土"字。"a"为古体，表示两人面
对面坐在地上。古人常席地而坐。现代字体由古体演化而来。参见 I. 9。

The upper portion of the word shows a door closed and barred at the top. The word for
"ground" is beneath it. "a", which is Archaic Script, is a picture of two men seated on the
earth facing each other. People used to sit on the ground in ancient times. The modern script
follows the Archaic form. See I. 9.

留

111

留 畱 *liú/Liu₂*

挽留，停留，款待

To detain, to remain, to entertain

字形与上文 110"坐"字相同，唯下部"土"替换为"田"字。表示农民在田间劳作时，家中大门紧闭。参见 II. 20。"a"取自古体。

This is the same form as in 110 above except that the word for "ground" has been changed into the word for "field". The idea is that while the farmers remained in the field the doors of their houses were closed. See II. 20. "a" is from the Archaic Script.

男

112

nán/*Nan*₂

男人，儿子，成年男子

Man, a son, an adult man

由人的"力"（表力气或精力）用于"田"（主要指农田）间而会意。参见 II.
20，44。

The combination of words here indicates someone whose "strength" or "energy" is
employed in the "field", referring mainly to the agricultural field. See II. 20, 44.

113

yì/*I*₄

割草

To mow

刈

113a

刈 刈

由简单的两画组成，象割草用的大剪刀或剪子之形。如"a"所示，有时在字左边加上"刀"。参见 II. 85。

This word is a simple combination of two strokes which symbolize a pair of large scissors or shears for cutting grass. The same word is sometimes written with the addition of the word for "knife", as illustrated in "a". See II. 85.

艸，草

114

cǎo/*Ts'ao*$_3$

屮屮 艸 草

草

小草，稻草，草药，野草
Grass, straw, herbs, weeds

由两个"屮"（下文 115）组成。

This is a double form of 115 below.

屮

115

chè/*Choe*₅

屮   屮   ₹

草 木 之 新 芽

The sprout of a plant

象植物发出新芽之形。

This is a simple picture of the sprout of any plant.

卉

116

huì/*Hui*₄

卉   ㄏㄨㄟˋ

花 卉 ， 植 物

Flowering plants, plants

由三个"屮"（上文 115）组成。开花的植物通常为丛生。

This is a triple form of 115 above. Usually flowering plants are grown in groups.

莽

117

mǎng/*Mang*₃

灌木，丛林，乡野
Undergrowth, jungle, rustic land

由四个"屮"（上文 115）组成，表示长满植物。

The form in 115 written four times indicates that vegetation is growing all around.

折

118

shé/*Chê*₅

摘（花），折断（枝条），弯曲
To pluck (as a flower),
to break (as a twig), to bend

象以"斤"（表斧子）砍树木之形。参见 II. 86。

The picture shows that the "axe" is being applied to the plant. See II. 86.

*亦读作 zhé。

生

119

shēng/*Sheng*$_2$

生长， 长出， 产生

To grow, to produce, to bring forth

象植物从"土"中长出。参见 I. 9。

In this picture the plant is growing from the "earth" beneath it. See I. 9.

苗

120

苗 苗 ⎡冖⎤
⎣幺⎦

新芽，禾之幼苗

Sprouts, the young rice plant

miáo/*Miao*₂

象"艸"（表禾之幼苗）生长于"田"间。参见上文 114 和 II. 20。

Here the word for "grass", which resembles the young rice plant, is shown growing in the "field". See 114 above and II. 20.

森

121

森 森 ㄕ

sēn/*Shen*₂

草木茂盛；阴森

Luxuriant vegetation; dark

由三个"木"（表树林）重叠而成。参见 V. 6。

This is the word for "wood", meaning here "trees", written in a triple form. See V. 6.

林

122

lín/*Lin*₂

森 林 ， 小 树 林

A forest, a grove

由两个 "木" 并列而成。参见 V. 6。

This is a double form of the word for "wood". See V. 6.

束

123

shù/*Shu*₅

捆 绑 ， 束 紧

To bind, to tie up

中间的圈指结；由此表一束东西之意。

The ring drawn in the middle of this word indicates a tie; from this comes the idea of anything in a bundle.

束

124

束　束　柬

jiǎn/*Chien*₃

选择，辨别

To select, to discriminate

由"束"（上文 123）中间的圈内加上"八"（表分开）而会意。故表从一束中选出之意。参见 I. 16。

This is the word in 123 above with the sign meaning "to divide" written inside the ring. This gives the idea of selecting something from a bundle. See I. 16.

析

125

析 析 厶

xī/*Hsi*₅

劈开木头，分割
To split wood, to divide

象以"斤"（表斧头）劈"木"之形。参见 II. 86 和 V. 6。
In the picture the "axe" is being applied to the "wood". See II. 86 and V. 6.

采

126

采 采 兂

cǎi/*Ts'ai*₃

摘取，挑选，采集
To pluck, to choose, to collect

釆

象以"爫"（表手）摘"木"。参见 II. 107。

This is a picture of "fingers" working on a "plant". See II. 107.

莫，暮　　　　　　　　　　　　**127**

mò, mù/*Mo*₅

傍晚；晚的

Evening; late

象日落时阳光由树林中透射出来。参见上文 117 和 II. 1。

In this picture the sun is setting and shining through the forest. See 117 above and II. 1.

葬

128

zàng/*Tsang*₄

埋葬

To bury

中间长横表板子，其上停放有"死"人。下葬时置于灌木或树林中。参见下文 197。

The long horizontal line in the middle represents a board upon which the "dead body", just above it, is placed. It was laid inside the shrub growth or the forest. See 197 below.

寒

129

hán/*Han*₁

寒冷的，冬天的

Cold, wintry

象"人"在"宀"（表屋子）中以"艸"（表草垫）覆体，其下有"仌"（表冰），故表寒冷之意。参见 II. 10，24，157 和上文 117。

In the picture here a "man" is inside a "house" under his "straw coverings", and below him is the "ice", indicating coldness. See II. 10, 24, 157 and 117 above.

東（东）

130

dōng/Tung₁

东方

East

象阳光从树林中透出来；其方位为东。参见 II. 1 和 V. 6。

The drawing here is of the sun shining through the trees; that direction is taken as the east. See II. 1 and V. 6.

131

gǎo/*Kao*₃

太阳照耀

The sun shining brightly

由日在木上而会意，表示太阳高高升起。

The sun is drawn on top of a tree, meaning that it is high in the sky.

132

yǎo/*Yao*₃

黑暗的，昏暗的，阴沉的，遥远的

Dark, obscure, sombre, far off

由日沉树根之下而会意。

In this picture the sun has sunk below the level of the roots of a tree.

隻（只）

隻 ㄓ

133

zhī/*Chih*₅

单 个 的 ， 二 者 之 一
Single, one of a pair

由手持"一只"鸟而会意。参见 II. 39a，135。

The idea of the picture is that the hand is holding *one* bird. See II. 39a, 135.

雙（双）

雙 ㄕㄨㄤ

134

shuāng/*Shuang*₁

两 个 ， 一 对 ， 一 双 ；
双 方 ， 偶 数 （ 与 奇 数 相 对 ）
A couple, a brace, a pair;
both, even (as opposed to odd)

由手持"一对"鸟而会意。

Here the hand is holding *two* birds.

135

秉

bǐng/*Ping*₃

抓住，持握
To grasp, to hold

由手持一禾苗而会意。参见 II. 39a，64。"a"字形相同。

This is the picture of a hand holding a rice plant. See II. 39a, 64. "a" is the same picture.

136

兼

jiān/*Chien*₂

二者兼备，和，一起；联合
**Both, and, together with;
to unite**

由手持"两"禾而会意。

In this picture the hand is holding *two* rice plants.

聿

137

yù/*Yü*₅

铅笔；叙述；于是

A pencil; to narrate; thereupon

下短横表书写之物——通常为竹简；手握铅笔或毛笔于其上书写。

The short horizontal line at the bottom of the word indicates the thing — usually a piece of bamboo — which was written upon; the pencil or brush is held in the hand.

史

138

shǐ/*Shih*₃

史   尸

历史，编年史，史学家，史料编纂者

History, chronicles, historian, historiographer

a

由"手"持握"中"（表正确的或正义的）而会意。参见 III. 1。"a"字义相同。

This is a picture of the hand holding "what is right or just". See III. 1. "a" has the same idea.

戒

139

jiè/*Chiai*₄

戒   ㄐ
     ㄧ
     ㄞ

警戒，警告；

戒律（佛教名词，合梵文尸罗［Sīla］）

To guard against, to warn;

precautions (in Buddhism, Shila)

a

由双手持握防卫的武器而会意。参见 II. 95。"a"字义相同。

Here two hands are drawn holding the weapon for guarding. See II. 95. "a" is the same.

雀

140

que/*Ts'io*₅

雀 雀 ㄊ一已

麻雀

A sparrow

由"小"和"鸟"两个字组成。参见上文 68 和 II. 135。

This is the combination of two words, "small" and "bird". See 68 above and II. 135.

枭（梟） **141**

xiāo/*Hsiao*₂

猫头鹰
An owl

象猫头鹰的头显露于树梢而会意。参见 II. 137 和 V. 6。

In this picture the head of an owl is conspicuous — it is seen on the top of a tree. See II. 137 and V. 6.

集 **142**

jí/*Tzi*₅

集合在一起，聚集
To gather together, to assemble

由"三"（表示多）鸟集聚在树上而会意。参见 II. 135 和 V. 6。

Here "three", meaning many, birds are assembled on a tree. See II. 135 and V. 6.

雋（隽） **143**

隽 juàn/*Ts'üan*₄

有肉的，胖的，肥美的

Fleshy, fat, delicious

由"弓"和"鸟"字组成——被射中的野生飞禽，其肉肥美。参见 II. 83，135。

The words for "bow" and "fowl" are combined in this word — the taste of a wild fowl shot down is delicious. See II. 83, 135.

144

噪

噪　噪　ㄙㄠ

鸟叫声；故表唧唧哼叫

The chirping of birds;
hence, the hum of voices

由三（表示多）"口"在树木上而会意，与上文 142 类似。参见 II. 29。

The idea is represented here by a picture of many "mouths" in a tree, similar to 142 above.
See II. 29.

145

兵

兵　兵　ㄅㄥ

兵器，士兵

Weapons, soldier

字形原本由双手持握"斤"（表武器）而会意；今意为"士兵"。参见 II. 39，86。

The original idea of the word and the picture was that of hands holding a "weapon"; today this word means "a soldier". See II. 39, 86.

戎

146

róng/*Jung*₁

打 仗 用 的 武 器

Weapons of war

由"戈"和"甲"字组成。参见 II. 95。"a"为另一种书体。

This is a combination of the words for "spear" and "helmet". See II. 95. "a" is another version of the same word.

武

147

武 x

wǔ/*Wu*₃

军 事 的 ， 战 争 的

Military, warlike

由"止"（表停止）和"戈"（表矛）组成；武者，可阻止他人用兵者也。"止"亦表示"步"或"走"之意。举"戈"上前即展示武力之意。参见 II. 52，95。许慎将其作为会意字的示例。

This word is formed by combining the words for "to stop" and "spear"; he who is able to prevent others from using weapons is "military". But the word for "stop" means also "step" or "to step". To step out with a "spear" can mean a display of military strength. See II. 52, 95. This word is an example given by Hsu shên of the ideative category.

射

148

射 尸 世

shè/Shê~4, 5~

发射，向……射击，瞄准

To shoot, to shoot at, to aim at

由"身"（表人）射出一"矢"（表箭）而会意，左边的"身"表人。参见 II. 84 和 X. 8。

In this picture an "arrow" has been shot off by a "man", the man being represented by the word for "body" on the left. See II. 84 and X. 8.

軍（军）

149

jūn/*Chün*₁

军事的，军队
Military, an army

由中间的"车"（表战车）和外部的"包"（表包围或环绕）组成。参见 II.
55，89。

The word for "war chariots" inside and "to surround or encircle" on the outside are combined to form this word. See II. 55, 89.

或 ［域］

150

huò [yù]/*Ho*₅ [*Yü*]

国家，王国，邦国
A country, a kingdom, a dukedom

左下短横表大地，圆圈表其范围或地界；"戈"字表自卫的军力。今作假借字，表"或者"，读作 huò。[ ] 中的"域"读作 yù，其上文之字义今已弃用。

The short horizontal line in the lower left half of the word indicates the earth, and the circle its compass or boundaries; the "spear" is its military strength for self-defence. Today as a borrowed word it means "or" is pronounced Hoh. The meaning given above, for the word pronounced as Yü (written in parentheses) is now obsolete.

151

jù/*Chü*₄

供给，装备，呈现

To supply, to equip with, to present

上部为简写的"贝"字，贝壳在古代用作钱币；下部为"廾"字（表给予）；
两部分合而会意。参见上文 37 和下文 152。

The word on top is an abbreviated form of the word for "shells", which were used in ancient
times as coins; below it is the sign for "offering"; this combination gives the sense of the
word. See 37 above and 152 below.

贝（贝）   **152**

bèi/*Pei*₄

贝 币 ， 贝 壳
Cowries, shells

简朴的象形字。

This is a simple pictograph.

買（买）

153

mǎi/Mai₃

购买，采购

To purchase, to buy

由"网"捕捞"贝"而会意，换言之，表示获利。参见 II. 117。

The idea of the form is "to net in" "shells", or, in other words, to make a profit. See II. 117.

貫（贯）

154

guàn/Kuan₄

用线串起

To string on a thread

象串连贝壳或钱币的绳索。参见 II. 56。

This is the picture of a string of shells or coins. See II. 56.

则（則） 155

zé/*Tsê*5

刻画图案；规则，标准

To pattern; a rule, a standard

原意指雕刻——右边的"刀"在"鼎"（此处仅给出简写）上刻画，由此雕刻出图案。参见 II. 74，85。

Originally this word meant "to carve" — the "knife" on the right is supposed to be cutting on a "tripod", which is given here only in its abbreviated form. Patterns are carved. See II. 74, 85.

赞（贊） 156

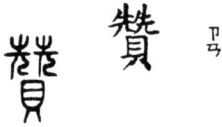

zàn/*Tsan*₄

赞助，支持

To assist, to second

原意指为了与他人、朋友或领主结盟而初次会面。上部为两个"先"字，表赠予，下部为"贝"字，表会面时赠送的贵重物品，这种会面是古代极正式的场合。参见上文 80 和 152。"a"是生僻字。

Originally this word meant "to meet for the first time for the purpose of forming a bond with someone, a friend or a master". The double form on top of the word means "offering" and the word for "shells" beneath it represents the precious things which were offered at this meeting, which was a very ceremonial occasion in ancient times. See 80 and 152 above. "a" is from the Peculiar Script.

殷   **157**

殷　殷　　ㄧㄣ

yīn/*Yin*₁

殷 实 的 ， 繁 茂 的 ， 极 好 的
Abundant, flourishing, great

原意指"在重要的演出中跳舞"。左部象"身体的扭转"，右部象手中持"斤"
（表武器）。参见 X. 8。

This word originally meant "dancing in a great presentation". The left portion of the word
pictures the "turning of the body" and the right the "weapons" held in the hand. See X. 8.

凶   **158**

凶　凶　　ㄒㄩㄥ

xiōng/*Hsiung*₁

不 祥 的 ， 灾 祸 ， 邪 恶 的
Unfortunate, disaster, evil

字形外部象一坑，有物相交陷入其中。此字亦为指事。

Here the outer form of the word represents a pit, and the crisscross a fall into it. This word is also an indicative.

159

㶲

yōng/Yung₁

妨碍，堵塞

To obstruct, to stop up

下部的"邑"表地区，上部的"川"表溪流，合而表示"溢出"或"积水成池"。"a"为大篆体，"b"为生僻字。

The combination of the word for "district", the lower half of the word, and "streams of water", above it, gives the idea of "overflow" or "forming a pond". "a" is the same in Major Script and "b" is a Peculiar Word.

欠   **160**

qiàn/*Ch'ien*₄

哈欠
To yawn

象"气"从口或"人"上部升散出去。参见 II. 4，24b 和上文 93。

This is a representation of the "breath" going upwards from the mouth or "man". See II. 4, 24b and 93 above.

涎 ［羨］   **161**

xián [xiàn]/*Hsien*₄, ₂

唾液，垂涎；强烈的愿望
Saliva, water running from the mouth;
expressive of intense desire

由"水"和"欠"合而会意。参见 II. 9 和上文 160。

In this word "water" and "yawning" are combined to give the meaning. See II. 9 and 160 above.

涉

162

shè/*Shê*₅

涉 水， 涉 及

To ford a stream, to involve

由右边的"步"涉入左边的"水"中而会意；即涉入水中或牵涉进去。参见 II. 9 和上文 47。

The idea is indicated here by the "footsteps", on the right, which are in the "water", left; i.e. to be involved in water and hence in any matter. See II. 9 and 47 above.

原

原　原　㘰

163

yuán/*Yüan*₁

源 头

A source

由"泉"自"厂"（表山崖）下涌出而会意。参见 II. 12，15。

This is the picture of a "spring" coming from under a "mountain cliff". See II. 12, 15.

州

州　州　㼌

164

zhōu/*Chou*₂

河 或 湖 中 小 岛

An islet in a river or lake

ₐ 州

由两个"川"字中间相连而成，亦属象形。参见 II. 8。"a"取自古体。

Two words for "stream" are joined in the middle to form this word, which could also be a pictograph. See II. 8. "a" is from the Archaic Script.

沓

165

沓　ㄊㄚ

tà/*T'a*₅

拖沓；喋喋不休

Dilatory; babbling flow of talk

"水"字下面一个"曰"字（表说话或言语），表示话（沓沓）如流水。参见 II. 9 和 V. 1。

The word for "to say" or "speech" is below the word for "water", indicating speeches flowing out like water. See II. 9 and V. 1.

益

益　益　一

166

yì/*I*₅

增 益 ， 溢 出 ， 有 益

To increase, to overflow, to profit

由 "水" 溢出器皿而会意。参见 II. 9，68。

This is a picture of "water" overflowing its container. See II. 9, 68.

盥

盥　盥　《乂ㅁ

167

guàn/*Kuan*₃

洗 手

To wash the hands

由上中部的"水"冲洗两侧的"手"，后下流至"皿"中而会意。参见 II. 9，68。

This picture represents "water", the upper middle portion of the word, being poured on the "hands" on either side and falling into the "basin" below. See II. 9, 68.

宗

168

zōng/*Tsung*₁

ㄗㄨㄥ

宗庙，宗族

The ancestral temple, a clan

由在"宀"（表屋子）中行"示"（表祭祀）而会意。参见 I. 7 和 II. 157。

This is the "house" in which "sacrifices" are made. See I. 7 and II. 157.

祝

169

祝 祝 ꟼ

zhù/Chu₅

祝 福 ， 祈 求

To bless, to invoke

原意指负责吟诵的祭司，由右下的"人"，右上的"口"和左部的"示"合而会意。参见 I. 7 和 II. 24b，29。

Originally this word represented the priest who chants, indicated by the word for "man" on the right with a "mouth" on top, in a "sacrifice", the left half of the word. See I. 7 and II. 24b, 29.

祭

170

祭 祭 ꟻ

jì/Tzi₄

祭 祀

To sacrifice

由右上的"手"、左上的"肉"和下部的"示"合而会意，表示在祭祀时手中持肉。参见 I. 7 和 II. 39，106。

The upper left half of this word is a piece of "meat", held by a "hand" on the right, in a "sacrifice", beneath. See I. 7 and II. 39, 106.

興（兴）

171

興

T
ㄥ

xīng/Hsing₂

兴起，上升，开始

To raise, to rise, to begin

a

上中部为"同"字；其他四部分合为"舁"字，表"提"或"拿"。故有"同"心协力提起某物之意。参见上文 87。"a"取自古体，字形更明晰。

The figure in the upper middle portion of the word is the word for "together"; the other four parts constitute the word for "to lift" or "to carry". The idea is of strengths combined "together" to lift something. See 87 above. "a", which is from the Archaic Script, is clearer.

典

172

diǎn/*Dien*₃

记录，文档，法典，准则，典籍

Records, documents,
a code, a canon, books

a

象写有文字记录的竹简置于台上。参见 II. 75，116。"a"中无台子。

This is a picture of the documents written on bamboo slabs placed on a support. See II. 75, 116. In "a" the support is not shown.

扁

173

扁　扁　ㄅㄧㄢ

碑 ， 牌 匾

A tablet, a signboard

象一块提署牌匾置于"户"（表门）上。参见 II. 77，116。

Here a written tablet is pictured placed on a "door". See II. 77, 116.

侖（仑）

174

侖　侖　ㄌㄨㄣ

思 考 ， 冥 想 ， 整 理

To think, to meditate, to arrange

侖

a

由"人"（表集中）起来的"册"（表书籍）而会意。参见 II. 116 和上文 82。"a"
为古体。

The idea of the picture is a "collection" of "books". See II. 116 and 82 above. "a" is Archaic
Script.

册   **175**

㸚 册   shān/*Hsan*₁

删除（书或稿子中的章节）

To delete

(passages from a book or scripture)

由简牍右边加上"刂"（表刀）而会意。写在竹简上的漆字只能用刀将其刮
去。参见 II. 85。

In this word the "knife" is shown on the right of the bamboo documents. Words written
with lacquer on bamboo could only be erased by scraping with a knife. See II. 85.

系

176

系 T一

xì/*Hsi*₄

联系，联结，连续，体系，宗谱
A connection, a link,
a succession, a system, a genealogy

字形象一束上端束结、下端垂悬的丝，故而会意。参见 II. 113。

The idea of the word is represented by a picture of a bundle of silk with the tie on top and the ends hanging down. See II. 113.

絲（丝）

177

絲 厶

sī/*Ssu*₁

蚕丝，丝线，金属丝
Silk, thread, wire

由两个"糸"（II. 113）组成。

This is a double form of II. 113.

终（終）

178

*zhōng/Chung*₁

终点；最终的

The end; final

右部为"冬"字，其上部表示一束丝，下部为"冫"，表示冰。一年之终即冬天。亦为形声字。参见 II. 113 和 IX. 113。

The right half is the word for "winter", which is comprised of the form of a tie for a bundle of silk, on the top, and the word for "ice" below it. Winter is the end of the year. This is also a harmonic word. See II. 113 and IX. 113.

縣［懸（悬）］

179

xuán/*Hsüan*₂

悬挂，延缓

To hang up, to suspend

左部为倒悬的"首"字；右部为"系"字。将物品悬于高处时，头部往往向后仰，仿佛倒着一样。参见 II. 32 和上文 176。

On the left is the word for "head" written in an inverted form; on the right is the word for "tie". When hanging somehing in a high place, the head must be bent backwards, as if inverted. See II. 32 and 176 above.

绵（绵）

180

mián/*Mien*₁

丝绵；绵绵不绝

Floss silk; continuous

左部表"织锦";丝缕"连绵"不断。参见下文 216，上文 176 和 III. 18。

The word on the left means "woven silk"; a length of silk is "continuous". See 216 below, 176 above, and III.18.

聯 （联）   181

lián/*Lien*₁

联 合 ， 连 接 ， 关 联

To unite, to connect, to associate

由两个字合而会意。左部为"耳"——字形象耳与下颌相连。右部为"丝"，表丝缕接连不断。参见上文 177 和 II. 26。

Two different words here give the meaning of the word. On the left is the word for "ear" — the ear is connected with the jaw, which is shown in the drawing. On the right is the word for "silk", which is long and continuous, unbroken and joined. See 177 above and II. 26.

戀

182

*luán/Luan*₃

絲乱
Confused

原意指言语紊乱不断。中间为"言"字表示说话。后也用以表示"联合"或"治理"。今已少于使用，只作为部首。参见 VII. 4 和上文 177。"a"取自古体，字义相同。字形象三缕凌乱的丝线，上有"爪"（表手指）欲将其捋顺。

This word originally meant "continuous talk in profusion". The middle word means "talk". Afterwards it came to mean also "to tie together" or "to manage". This word is seldom used today except as a radical. See VII. 4 and 177 above. "a", which is from the Archaic Script, has the same meaning. Three series of silk in confusion are pictured, with the "fingers" above them trying to bring them into order.

亂（乱）   **183**

亂   luàn/*Luan*₄

统治 ， 建立秩序 ； 混乱 ， 叛乱
To govern, to bring about order;
disorder, rebellion

象上面的"爪"（表手指）和下面的"又"（表手）在整理中间的"丝"，用一
马蹄形架子将其分开。该字既表"混乱"，亦表"秩序"。参见 II. 39，107。

In this picture the "fingers" on top and the "hands" on the bottom are working on the "silk"
in the middle, separating it on a horseshoe-like frame. Both "disorder" and "ordering" are
meant by this form. See II. 39, 107.

幼 **184**

幼 又

yòu/Yu₄

年幼的，幼稚的，柔弱的

Young, juvenile, delicate

由"幺"和"力"组成；未满 15 岁的男孩"年幼"而"力弱"。参见 II. 44 和下文 185。

This is a combination of the words for "small" and "strength"; a boy below the age of fifteen is "young" and of "small strength". See II. 44 and 185 below.

幺 **185**

幺 幺

yāo/Yao₂

小的，细微的

Small, subtle

象丝线之一半；此处未采用许慎之释义。

This is the picture of half of a silk thread; Hsü shěn's explanation has been discarded.

　＊《定声》："此字当从半糸，糸者丝之半，幺者糸之半。"

幺幺

186

幺幺　　丝　幺

yōu/*Yu*₂

小的，极细微的

Small, very subtle

由两个"幺"字（上文 185）组成，以强调其字义。

The doubling of the form in 185 above gives emphasis to the idea.

幽

187

幽　又

yōu/*Yu*₂

幽暗的，隐蔽的

Dark, secret

由"山"字上面加"𢆶"（上文 186）而会意，表山中一隐蔽之处。该字同为形声和会意字。参见 II. 14。

The word for "mountain" added to the form in 186 above gives the idea of a secluded spot in a mountain. This word is harmonic as well as ideative. See II. 14.

玄

188

玄　ㄒㄩㄢ

xuán/*Hsüan*₁

深黑色；幽暗的，深远的，玄妙的，深奥的

A dark colour;
sombre, deep, subtle, abstruse

原意指"玄妙的和隐蔽的"。上部为"入"字；下部表示丝。丝线六入红色染料而成暗黑色。"a"取自古体，字义相同，增加的两点表示黝黑。

The original idea of this word was "subtle and covered". The upper portion is the word for "entering"; the lower portion indicates the silk. When the silk has been immersed in the red dyeing solution and dried six times, it becomes this dark color. "a", from the Archaic Script, has the same meaning. Two dots were added to indicate the darkness.

幾（几）   **189**

jī/*Chi*₁

细微的，隐藏的；预兆，预言；
几乎，关于，大概的；少许，一些，几个
Subtle, recondite; an omen, a presage;
almost, about, approximate;
a few, some, several

由"戌"（上文24）和"丝"（上文186）组成。原意指"预见到细微的状况和危机"。

This is a combination of the word for "garrison" in 24 above and the word for "very subtle" in 186 above. The original sense of this word was "to foresee a delicate and dangerous situation".

計（计） 190

jì/Chi₄

计算，估计，计划；装置，计策
To calculate, to reckon, to plan;
a device, a strategem

右边为"十"，笼统地表示数字；右边为"言"字。谈论或涉及数字即表计算。参见 I. 18 和 VII. 4。

On the right side of this word is the number "ten", representing numbers in general; on the left is the word for "talk". To talk about or with regard to numbers means to calculate. See I. 18 and VII. 4.

討（讨）   **191**

討 _{ㄊㄠ}

tǎo/*T'ao*₃

统治，要求，镇压叛乱或骚乱
**To govern, to demand,
to suppress rebellion or disorder**

右部为"寸"，表度量、法律和规定。该字原意指"颁布法律或命令"。参见
III. 9 和 VII. 4。

The word for "inch" on the right means measurement and law and statute. "To promulgate
law and order" was the original sense of the word. See III. 9 and VII. 4.

設（设）   **192**

設 _{ㄕㄜ}

shè/*Shê*₅

安排，设计，设立
To arrange, to devise, to establish

右部为"殳"，表示"用手势驱遣他人做事"；用言语（左部为"言"）和手势指挥别人，即安排。参见 VII. 4 和 IX. 161。

The word in the right half of this word means "to direct someone with a hand movement to do a certain service"; to direct someone with both words (the left half of the word) and gestures means to make arrangements. See VII. 4 and IX. 161.

守

193

shǒu/*Shou*₃

守卫，看护，维持

To guard, to attend to, to maintain

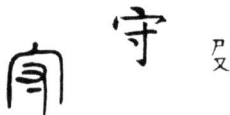

原意指"官吏的职守"，由"寸"（表法度）上面加"宀"（表屋子）而会意，指檐下一室之内，法度和官职均得以维持。参见 II. 157 和 III. 9。"a"为生僻字。

Originally this word meant "the responsibility of an office", the idea of which is represented by the "house" drawn over the word for "law and statute", meaning the house under the roof of which laws and offices were maintained. See II. 157 and III. 9. "a" is Peculiar Script.

肘

194

肘

zhǒu/*Chou*₃

肘 部

The elbow

据 III. 9 释义，"寸" 表手腕处的脉搏。左边的 "肉" 使字义延伸。参见 II. 106。

As explained in III. 9, the word for "inch" indicates the pulse spot near the wrist. The word for "flesh" on the left extends the meaning. See II. 106.

骨

195

gǔ/Ku₅

骨头

A bone

上部为象形字"凸"（表头骨）；下部为"肉"字。肉身的内部结构（即是骨架和骨骼）。参见 II. 106。"a"的字形更形象。

The upper portion of this word is a pictograph for "skull"; below it is the word for "flesh". That which forms the inner framework for the flesh is the skeleton, the bones. See II. 106. "a" is a more representative drawing.

習 （习）

196

xí/Si₅

练习，学习；实践，习惯

To practise, to study; practices, custom

上部为"羽"，表翅膀或羽毛，下部为"自"的另一种书体，由"鼻"和"口"字组成。后一种字体表示拍击，暗示须用力频繁而快速地扇动翅膀。此外，亦指小鸟频频试飞。参见 II. 28，141。

This word is formed by a combination of the word for "wings" or "feathers" on top of another form of the word for "self", in which the words for "nose" and "mouth" are combined. The idea of panting in the latter word suggests the great effort required by the rapid, frequent motion of the wings. Also, young birds are frequently seen practising how to fly. See II. 28, 141.

死

197

死 ₂

sǐ/*Ssu*₃

死亡；死的，无生命
To die; dead, inanimate

由右部的"人"和下文 198 的"歹"组成。参见 II. 24。

This picture is a combination of a word for "man", on the right, with the form in 198 below. See II. 24.

歹（歺）

198

è/*Wo*₅

骨骼残骸
The skeletal remains

属指事，下文 199 的简写。"a"取自古体；由"尸"字上面加象形字"冎"
组成。

This is an indicative which is an abbreviated form of 199 below. "a" is from the Archaic
Script; it is a combination of the pictograph for "bones" written on top of the word for
"corpse".

冎 ［剐］ 　　　　　　　　　　　　　　　　　　　　　　　**199**

guǎ/Kua₃

劈 成 碎 片

To hack to pieces

象剔除肉后的残骨。"a"为同一字右边加上" 刂"旁，是通俗写法。

This is a pictograph representing the skull after the flesh has been carved off. "a" is the same
with a word for "knife" added on the right. It is a vulgar form.

200

zhěn/*Chên*₃

浓密的；长长的黑发

Bushy; long black hair

a

由"人"字加上三撇（"彡"，表示长发）而会意。参见 II. 24。"a"中的三撇表小鸟新长的羽毛。不过在许慎的字典中，两种写法皆列为字源，与其他字合用时未加区分。

This is the word for "man" with the long hair represented by the three detached strokes. See II. 24. In "a" the three lines represent the newly-grown feathers of a young bird. However, in Hsu shên's dictionary both these forms were given as the origin of this word and not distinguished in their use in combination with other words.

走

201

走　走　⼫⼜

zǒu/*Tsou*₃

行走，疾行

To walk, to hasten

由"止"（表脚趾）上面加"夭"（表弯曲）组成。人疾行时会弯曲脚趾。参见 II. 23，52 和上文 44b。

The word for "bending" is written on top of the word for "toes". One bends his toes in swift walking. See II. 23, 52, and 44b above.

夭

202

夭　夭　一幺

yāo/*Yao*₂

气色好

Fresh-looking

象人的头偏向左侧，自得的样子。参见 II. 23 和上文 44b。

This is a picture of a man bending his head to the left in a pleased manner. See II. 23 and 44b above.

建

建 建 ㄐㄧㄢ

203

jiàn/*Chien*₄

建造，建立

To erect, to establish

原意指"建立或创建帝国法律或朝廷律令"。由下文 204 和 205 组成。

Originally this word meant "to set up or found an imperial law or order of the court". It is a combination of 204 and 205 below.

律

204

lǜ/*Lü*₅

律　律　力

法律，法令，规定

A law, a statute, a rule

属形声字，由"聿"（上文 137）和"彳"（II. 51）组成。

This is a harmonic word, a combination of 137 above and II. 51.

廷

205

tíng/*T'ing*₂

廷　廷　云乙

朝廷

The court of a palace

亦属形声字。国君或王侯立于殿门之内，召见候在露天庭院中的群臣。左部参见 III. 22。右部为下文 206。

This is also a harmonic word. The king or duke stood inside the gate of the palace to give audience while his ministers all stood in the courtyard in the open air. See III. 22 for the word on the left. The word on the right is given in 206 below.

206

rén/Jên$_2$

立正站直

To stand erectly at attention

由"人"和"土"字组成。

This word is a combination of the words for "man" and "ground".

半

207

半　半　𠬞

bàn/*Pan*₄

一半；对分

Half; to halve

此处用"牛"字，因牛体大，可分作两半。顶部左右两撇为"八"字，表分开。原意指将公文一分为二。今用另一字表此意，即由"半"字右边加上部首"刂"组成的"判"字。参见 I. 16 和 II. 121。

The word for "ox" is used here because an ox is large and can be divided into two halves. The two curves on both sides at the top form the word for "division". This is the original word denoting the official documents which were divided into two halves. Today another word is used in this sense. The classifier for "knife" is added on the right side of the form given here. See I. 16 and II. 121.

陽（阳）

208

yáng/Yang₂

打 开 ， 展 开 ； 明 亮 的
（《 易 经 》 中 的 " 阳 " 原 则 ）
To open out, to expand; bright
(the positive principle in the Book of Changes)

中间的横表示云；其上有"日"，其下为"勿"（表旗帜）。字义为云开而日出，犹如旗帜展开。亦属指事。参见 II. 1，103。

The horizontal line in the middle represents clouds; the "sun" is above it and a "flag" below it. The idea is that when the clouds have cleared the sun shines out like the opening of a flag. This is also an indicative word. See II. 1, 103.

明

209

míng/Ming₂

明 亮 的 ， 清 楚 的 ， 聪 明 的
Bright, clear, intelligent

象月光自窗棂照进来。"a"取自古体，由"日"和"月"字组成，二者皆表光明。"b"亦相同。参见 Ⅱ. 1，2，80。

The idea of the word is given by a picture of the moonlight shining through a transom window. "a", which is from the Archaic Script, is a combination of the words for "sun" and "moon", both brilliant. "b" is the same. See Ⅱ. 1, 2, 80.

晉 （晋）

210

jìn/*Tsin*4

进行，前进，长进

To proceed, to advance, to increase

下部为"日"字，表白天，万事万物来来往往——由上部两个"至"而会意。由此引申出长进之意。参见 Ⅱ. 1 和 Ⅲ. 23。

The form for "sun" in the lower portion of the word indicates the daytime, when everything comes and comes — the idea of the double form of the word on top — or goes and goes. From this comes the idea of progress. See Ⅱ. 1 and Ⅲ. 23.

晶

211

晶 <ruby>晶<rt>ㄐㄧㄥ</rt></ruby>

jīng/*Tsing*₂

明亮的，清澈的；水晶

Bright, clear; crystal

原本由三个"星"字，而非三个"日"字合而会意，表"明亮"之意。依据是"星"的古体为三个圈中各有一点，属形声字。参见下文 212。

Originally this word was written not with three "suns" but with three "stars", to give the idea of "brightness". The proof for this is that in the Archaic Script the word for "stars" is written in three circles with dots inside, a harmonic word. See 212 below.

星

212

星 <ruby>星<rt>ㄒㄧㄥ</rt></ruby>

xīng/*Sing*₂

星星

Stars

此为古体。参见上文 211。

This is Archaic Script. See 211 above.

暴

213

pù, bào/*Pao*₄, ₅

在阳光下晾晒；炎热；暴力

To dry in the sun;

a scorching heat; violence

"日" "出" 之时，人们 "廾" （表拿） "米" 出来晾晒——故由此四字组成。
参见 II. 1，63，102 和上文 37。

When the "sun" has "come out" one "takes" the "rice" to be dried— a combination of four
words. See II. 1, 63, 102 and 37 above.

214

皕

bì/*Pi*₅

两 百

Two hundred

由两个"百"字组成。参见下文 215。

This is the word for "a hundred" written in a double form. See 215 below.

215

百

bǎi/*Bê*₅

一 百

One hundred

属形声字。上横表示"一"；下部表音，参见下文 216。

This is a harmonic word. The horizontal line on top indicates "one"; the word beneath, given in 216 below, gives the sound.

白

216

bái/*Bê*₅

白色
White

属指事字。字形表示指日出前天空的白光。

This is an indicative word. The drawing indicates the white light of the sky just before the sun rises.

皋

217

gāo/*Kao*₂

卓越的；沼泽，荒地
Eminent; marsh, wilderness

属形声字，表示"白光或阳光照耀"；由此引申出"卓越"之意。当其他地方尚于黑暗之中，日光最先照到旷野，故转而也指"旷野"。参见上文216及下文218，分别为该字的上部和下部。

This is a harmonic word meaning "white light or sunlight shining forth"; from this came the idea of "eminence". The open country gets the light first while other places are still dark, so by a turn of the idea it came also to mean "wilderness plains". See 216 above 218 below for the upper and lower portions of the word, respectively.

218

tāo/*T'ao*₂

前进，发展

Advance, progress

字形表示个人的能力增长为之前的 10 倍。参见 I. 18 和 II. 23。

The idea of the picture is that of one man's ability multiplied ten times. See I. 18 and II. 23.

戋（戋）

219

cán/*Tzien*₂

伤害
To hurt

原意指"用两支戈刺伤"，如字形所示。该字为"残"（下文 220）的字源，读音稍有变化。参见 II. 95。

Originally this word meant "to hurt with two spears", as the picture indicates. This is the original of the next word, 220 below, which is pronounced with a slight inflection. See II. 95.

残（残）

220

cán/*Ts'an*₁

损害，伤害；残余，野兽吃剩的残骸
**To injure, to hurt; remnant,
the remains of a carcass eaten by wild animals**

属形声字，由"戈"（上文 219）表音。左部为"歺"（上文 198），表残骸。

This is a harmonic word which has taken its sound from the word in 219 above. On the left is the word for "skeletal remains", 198 above.

穿

221

chuān/*Ch'uan*₂

刺穿，穿透

To pierce, to bore through

由"牙"中有"穴"（表示洞）而会意。参见 II. 30，158。

In this picture a "tooth" or "teeth" have made "holes". See II. 30, 158.

啟（启）   **222**

戶　啟　〈   qǐ/*Ch'i*₃

开启 ， 教导 ， 启发
To open, to teach, to enlighten

ₐ 戸 ᵦ 啓

字形表示敞开之"户"（表门），"敞开"之意由"口"字表示，指"入口"。
参见 II. 29，77。"a"和"b"字义相同。

The idea of the picture is that the "door" is "open", "open" being indicated by the word for
"mouth", meaning "entrance". See II. 29, 77. "a" and "b" have the same idea.

闖（闯）   **223**

闖　闖　⺅乂尢   chuǎng/*Ch'uang*₃

突然闯入或闯出
To rush suddenly in or out

字形象一匹马穿门而过，由此会意。参见 II. 78，131。

The idea of the word is represented here by the picture of a horse passing through a door. See II. 78, 131.

閑 （闲）

224

xián/*Hsien*₁

闩上；围栏

To bar; an enclosure

由"木"梁闩上"门"而会意。参见 II. 78 和 V. 6。

Here a "door" is shown barred with "wooden" beams. See II. 78 and V. 6.

閒（间）   **225**

jiān/*Hsien*₁

空隙，间隔，狭小的空间

A breach, an interval,
a narrow space

象月光从两扇门间照进来。参见 II. 2，78。

In this picture moonlight is shown passing between the leaves of a door. See II. 2, 78.

漏   **226**

lòu/*Lou*₄

渗漏

A leak

上部为简写的"屋"字；下部为"雨"字。由此表示雨水从屋顶漏进来。参见 II. 5 和下文 227。

The upper portion of this word is an abbreviated form of the word for "house"; below it is the word for "rain". This indicates that rainwater is leaking through the roof. See II. 5 and 227 below.

屋

227

wū/*Wu*₅

房 屋

A house

上部为"人"的侧面；下部为"至"（表到达）。人所到之处或居住的地方即房屋。参见 II. 24 和 III. 23。

On top here is a "man" in profile; the word for "to arrive at" is below. Where a man arrives at or resides is a house. See II. 24 and III. 23.

舍

228

舍　舍　尸
　　　　せ

shè/*Shê*~4~

客舍，临街的房屋

A hotel, a house on the street

下部（口）象地基；中部（十）表众多房屋之一，上部（亼）表集合。参见上文 82。

The lower portion of this word represents the foundation; the middle part indicates one house among many, and the upper portion signifies collectivity. See 82 above.

　　《段注》："市居曰舍也。此市字非买卖所之，谓宾客所之也。"

　　"舍"又假借为舍弃义，读 shě。

赤

229

chì/*Ch'ih*₅

红色；火的颜色

Red; the colour of fire

由上部的"大"和下部的"火"字组成。参见 II. 13，23。"a"和"b"字形相同。

This is a combination of the word for "large" written on top of the word for "fire". See II. 13, 23. "a" and "b" are the same picture.

炎

230

yán/*Yen*₂

火焰；燃烧起来

Flame; to flame up

炎 a

由两个"火"（II. 13）并列组成。"a"为古体，由两个火字重叠组成，更为
形象。

This is a double form of the word in II. 13. "a", which is Archaic Script, is another double

form; it shows the fire more clearly.

炙

炙 ㄓ

231

*zhì/Chih*4, 5

烧烤，在火上烤

To broil, to toast before a fire

由"火"字上面加"肉"字组成。参见 II. 13，106。

Here the word for "meat" is on top of the word for "fire". See II. 13, 106.

熒（荧）

232

熒 熒 ㄥ

yíng/Yung₂

闪闪发光；闪烁

Lights shining; to shimmer

象烛光或灯光从屋里或掩蔽物中透射出来。

This picture represents the light of candles or lamps issuing from a house or from under a cover.

黑

233

黑 黑 ㄏㄟ

hēi/Hêh₅

黑色，黑暗

Black, dark

上部表墙上的开口、窗户或烟囱；下部的"炎"（表火焰）将其熏黑。参见
II. 13，79。

The form on the top of this word represents an opening in the wall or a window or chimney;
the "flames" below it are making it black. See II. 13, 79.

234

熏

xūn/*Hsün*₁

熏 制 ， 熏 香 或 烟 熏
To fumigate, to scent or to smoke

由"黑"（上文 233）加"中"部而会意，表烟向上升起之意。

This is the word in 233 above with an addition on the top which gives the idea of the smoke
going upwards.

墨

235

mò/*Mê*₅

（黑）墨水
Ink (black)

由"黑"下面加"土"字组成，表煤烟，今之黑墨水仍是煤烟制成。参见
I. 9。

Underneath the word for "black" is the word for "soil", indicating "soot", out of which
black ink is manufactured even today. See I. 9.

赫

236

hè/*Hêh*₅

光辉的，显赫的
Brilliant, glorious

由两个"赤"（上文 229）组成。"a"取自古体。

Here two words for "red", given in 229 above, are combined. "a" is from the Archaic Script.

灰

237

huī/*Hui*₁

灰烬，灰尘；（故表颜色）灰色

Ashes, dust; (and hence in colour) grey

由"火"熄灭后可用"手"拿起的那一部分而会意。参见 Ⅱ. 13，39a。

The idea of the picture is to indicate that part of a "fire" which can be taken by the "hand".
See Ⅱ. 13, 39a.

烦（煩）

238

*fán/Fan*₁

烦 𠘰

使烦恼，使不安，使恼怒
To trouble, to disturb, to annoy

象"头"有"火"或发烧。参见 II. 13，24b，32a。
"Fire" or fever of the "head" is represented here. See II. 13, 24b, 33.

光

239

*guāng/Kuang*₂

光 𡆠

光明，明亮，喜爱
Light, brightness, favour

由"火"或光照在"人"身上而会意。参见 II. 13，24b。
This is the picture of a "fire" or light shining upon a "man". See II. 13, 24b.

真

240

zhēn/*Chën*₁

真　眞

正 确 的 ， 真 实 的 ， 真 正 的
True, real, genuine

"圣贤变形而升天"——此为古代对该字的释义。上部为"匕"（表变化），用法与上文 14 和 74 相同；中部为"目"字，而曲线（"乚"）表"隐藏"或"消失"；下部两撇表圣人所乘之物。该字原意指"人的真身"。

"A transfigured sage ascending to heaven" — so runs the ancient explanation for the formation of this word. On the top is the word for "transformation", as used in 14 and 74 above; in the middle is the "eye" and the curve meaning "hidden" or "disappearance"; the two strokes beneath this word indicate the thing on which the sage rides. Originally this word meant "the real or true being of a man".

得

241

dé/*Tê*₅

得到，取得，影响，有能力

To obtain, to acquire,
to effect, to be capable of

a

b

将上部所"见"置于"寸"（表测量，亦表示"用手拿"）上，合而表"取得"之意。参见Ⅲ.9和上文104。"a"为小篆，字形相同、唯左部增加部首"彳"。参见Ⅱ.51。

The idea of acquisition is indicated by drawing what is "seen" above what is "measured", which means also "taken by hand". See Ⅲ. 9 and 104 above. "a", which is in the Minor Script, is the same except that another sign has been added on the left. See Ⅱ. 51.

喜

242

xǐ/*Hsi*₃

喜　喜　Ｔ

愉 悦 ， 快 乐 ； 对 …… 满 意

Pleasure, joy; pleased with

喜

a

由上部的"壴"（表音乐）和下部的"口"合而会意，表示聆听音乐后开口表达喜悦之情。参见 II. 29 和 IX. 68。"a"为古体，"口"换作"欠"字，表示"气从口中散出"。参见上文 160。

The idea of the word is that the joy which is obtained by hearing "music", represented by the word on top, and which is expressed by the "mouth", written below it, is pleasure. See II. 29 and IX. 68. In "a", which is Archaic Script, the word for "mouth" is expressed by the word meaning "breath going out from the mouth". See 160 above.

某

243

某　某　又

mǒu/*Mou*₃

梅子，梅干
Plums, prunes

梅，槑

243a

梅
槑

méi/*Mei*₁

由"甘"和"木"字组成，表示结梅子的果树。现为假借字，表示"等等"，"某人或某物"；"243a"读作"méi"，仅表示"梅子，梅干"。参见 III. 27 和 V. 6。

The words for "sweet" and "wood" are combined here, meaning the tree that bears such fruits. Today as a borrowed word it means "so and so", "a certain person or thing"; the word pronounced "Mei", which is given in "a", means only "plums, prunes". See III. 27 and V. 6.

擊（击）

244

*jī/Chi*₅

击 打 ， 击 溃
To strike, to rout

左部为"軎"（V. 26），表示车轴；右部为"殳"（IX. 161），表示用棍子敲击，两字合而会意，指车轴相互撞击。

This word represents the axes of carts striking against each other by a combination of V. 26, which indicates the axis, and IX. 161, on the right, which means "to strike with a stick".

表

245

*biǎo/Piao*₃

表 达 ； 明 显 的 ， 表 面 的
To express; manifest, external

原意指"外衣",即罩在皮衣外的薄外套,与外面的皮毛一起穿。由"衣"中间加"毛"字组成。参见 II. 105,114。

Originally this word meant "overcoat", referring to a thin external coat used to cover the fur coat, which was worn with the fur outside. It is a combination of the word for "fur" inserted inside the word for "dress". See II. 105, 114.

索

246

suǒ/*So*₅

绳索

A rope

由两个字组成,表示某些草木的茎、叶或纤维,可拧成绳子。参见 II. 113 和下文 247。

This is a combination of two words, representing the stalks or leaves or fibers of certain plants which can be twisted into rope. See II. 113 and 247 below.

朿

247

pìn/*Pin*₄

剥离茎皮或分剥麻秆的皮

To strip a stalk or to peel hemp

该字今已少用。中部象麻秆；左右两撇或表示剥离的麻皮，或取自"八"，表"分开"。

This word is now rarely used. The plant is drawn in the middle portion of the word; the two outer curves either represent the outer layer of the plant or come from the word meaning "to divide".

孫 （孙）

248

sūn/*Sun*₁

孙子

△ grandson

由左部的"子"（表儿子）和右部的"系"（表家系）合而会意，表示某人归属于家系。参见 II. 49 和上文 176。

The idea of the word is that he belongs to the "genealogy", on the right, of the "son", on the left. See II. 49 and 176 above.

249

měi/Mei₃

美丽的，标致的，极好的，美味的，美好的

Beautiful, comely, admirable, delicious, good

上部为"羊"字，是"祥"的简写；下部为"大"字。参见 II. 23，122。

The word for "sheep", which is on the top, is an abbreviated form for "auspicious"; beneath it is the word for "great". See II. 23, 122.

羹

250

羹 《乙

gēng/*Kêng*₂

浓汤，肉汤
Soup, broth

a 羹 b 羹 c 羹

由一只羊"羔"——上部为"羊"字——放入下面的"鬲"（表大锅）中烹煮
而会意。左右两撇表示蒸汽。参见 II. 71，122。"b"取自小篆，下部为"美"
字，表美好，美味——参见上文 249。

The idea represented here is that of a "lamb" — the word for "sheep" in the upper half —
being boiled in a "cauldron", beneath it. The curved lines on either side indicate the steam.
See II. 71, 122. In "b", which is from the Minor Script, the lower half is the word for "good"
or "delicious" — see 249 above.

251

羌

羌 〈一尢

qiāng/*Ch'iang*₂

中国西部部族，藏人

Tribes in West China, Tibetans

a 羌

由"羊"和"人"合而表牧羊人，是对中国西部游牧部落的统称。参见 II. 24b，122。"a"左边加上"犬"部。参见 II. 123。

The words for "sheep" and "men" are here combined to signify shepherds, which was a general term for the nomads in the western part of China. See II. 24b, 122. In "a" the dog is pictured on the left. See II. 123.

*南方"蛮"族，其字从虫；北方"狄"族，其字从犬；

东方"貉"族，其字从"豸"；西方"羌"族，其字从羊；均含歧视意味。

羌指代藏人，不准确。

臭

252

臭 ㄒ一ㄡˋ

xiù/*Hsiu*₄

嗅到；强烈的臭味

To smell; strong-smelling

a

由"犬"上加"自"（表鼻子）而会意。狗的嗅觉灵敏。参见 II. 28，123。"a"
的造字方式相同。

The word for "nose" is written here on top of the word for "dog". Dogs have a sharp sense of
smell. See II. 28, 123. "a" is formed in the same way.

羴

253

羴 ㄕㄢ

shān/*Shan*₁

绵羊或山羊的膻味

The rank odour of sheep or goats

由三个"羊"组成。参见 II. 122。

This word is made up of three words for "sheep". See II. 122.

善

254

*shàn/Shan*₄

善　善　尸号

好，善于，善良

Good, apt, virtuous

"羊"字表示"吉兆或好兆头"，同上文 249。左右均为"言"字，表说话或言语。参见 II. 122 和 VII. 4。"a"取自竹简。

The word for "sheep" here means "auspice or good augury", as in 249 above. On either side is the word for "saying" or "speech". See II. 122 and VII. 4. "a" is from the bamboo slips.

轟（轰）

255

*hōng/Hung*₂

ㄏㄨㄥ

车 或 雷 的 隆 隆 声 ， 咆 哮 声 ； 爆 炸

**The rumbling of carts or thunder,
roaring; to explode**

由三个"车"组成。参见 II. 89。

Three words for "cart" are combined here to form this word. See II. 89.

麤（粗）

256

cū/Ts'u

ㄘㄨ

大 的 ， 粗 糙 的 ， 粗 略 的

Bulky, coarse, rough

由三个"鹿"组成。原意指"长途跋涉"，今已弃用。参见 II. 130。

This is three words for "deer" combined. The original sense of the word was "to cover a great distance", now obsolete. See II. 130.

塵（尘）

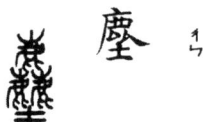

257

chén/*Ch'ên*₁

尘土
Dust

由三个"鹿"下面加"土"字而会意，表示群鹿疾驰使尘土飞扬。参见 I. 9 和 II. 130。

The idea of the dust raised by the running of a group of deer is represented by writing the word for "earth" beneath three words for "deer". See I. 9 and II. 130.

堯（垚）

258

yáo/*Yao*₂

高远，卓越
High, eminent

由三个"土"字叠写而表示一大堆土之意。参见 I. 9。

The word for "earth" is written three times to give the idea of a large mound of earth. See I. 9.

天

259

tiān/*T'ien*₂

天空；老天，神
The sky; Heaven, God

_a

由象形字"人"和顶部的横（表示天）组成。亦属象形并指事字。参见 I. 1 和 II. 23。"a"为该字的另一写法。

This word is made up of the pictograph for "man" with a horizontal line drawn on top to indicate the heavens. This word could also be classified as a pictograph-indicative. See I. 1 and II. 23. "a" is another form of the same word.

产

260

wěi/*Yen*₂

面朝上，仰望
To face upwards, to look up to

由"人"在"厂"（表悬崖）上而会意。参见 II. 15，24。

A "man" is drawn on top of a "cliff". See II. 15, 24.

危

261

危 ㄨㄟˊ

wēi/*Wei*₁

危险的，冒险的，高耸的

Dangerous, perilous, lofty

a 危

原意指"人在高处，心生恐惧"；由"巳"（表节制自己）和"厂"（上文 260）合而会意。"a"取自竹简。

The original idea of this word was "having fear on a precipice"; the sign meaning "to check oneself" has been added to the word in 260 above. "a" is from the bamboo slips.

雪

262

霅　雪　ㄥㄩㄝ

xuě/Hsüeh₅

雪　，　冰

Snow, ice

由"雨"和"彗"（表扫帚）组成。表示从天降而可彗扫者，雪或雹也，而非水。参见 II. 5 和 V. 15。

This word is a combination of the words for "rain" and "broom". The idea is that that which rains down and can be swept by a broom is not water but snow or hail. See II. 5 and V. 15.

帚

263

帚　ㄓㄡ

zhǒu/Chou₃

扫把，扫帚

A besom, a broom

朱

由"又"（表手）持握"巾"（表一块布）扫除净"囗"（表围墙）内之地而会意；故有"清扫"之意。参见 II. 39a 和 III. 18。

In this picture the "hand" is taking a "piece of cloth" to wipe clean a place within an "enclosure"; this gives the idea of "sweeping". See II. 39a and III. 18.

陟

264

zhì/*Chih*₅

登升， 前进

To ascend, to advance

由左部的"阜"（表山）和右部的"步"（表步伐或步行）合而会意。参见 II. 18 和上文 47。

The idea of the word is represented here by writing the word for "hill" on the left of the word for "steps" or "to walk". See II. 18 and 47 above.

劫

*jié/Chieh*₅

抢 劫 ， 掠 夺 ， 侵 犯

To plunder, to rob, to violate

由人欲"去"——左部，却以"力"胁止——右部，合而会意；故表示暴力。参见 II. 44 和下文 267。

The idea here is that someone wants to "go" — on the left — but is stopped by "force", on the right; this indicates violence. See II. 44 and 267 below.

凵

*kǎn/Chü*₁

盛 米 的 容 器

A receptacle for rice

象形字，今很少使用。

This is a pictograph now rarely used.

去

267

去 去 ㄑㄩ

qù/*Ch'ü*₄

离开；经过，逝去

To go away; past, gone

该字字源有两说。一说，上部表"人"，下部表音；另一说，象带盖的"凵"
（表容器）。作为转注字，表示"离开"等意——是"隐藏"或"贮存"在
"凵"中的引申义。

There are two explanations for the origin of this word. One is that the form on top
represents a man and the lower portion gives its sound; the other is that it is a pictograph of
a "receptacle" with a lid. Used in the sense of "to go away", etc., it is a transmissive, — an
extension of the idea "to hide" or "to store away" in a "receptacle".

审（审） **268**

宋 審 卩丂

shěn/*Shên*₃

审判，检查，审查，正式调查

To judge, to examine,
to investigate, to hold an official inquiry

在"宀"（表厅堂）中进行正式的调查；中间为"釆"（表辨别）。参见 II. 128，157。

Official inquiries were made in a "hall"; inside this word is the word for "discrimination". See II. 128, 157.

悉 **269**

悉 悉 厶丶

xī/*Si*₅

理解，悉知

To comprehend, to know

由"采"（表辨别）在"心"上而会意。参见 II. 38，128。"a"取自古体，上部可能为"囧"（表窗户或光亮）。

The idea is represented here by writing the word for "discrimination" above the word for "mind". See II. 38, 128. In "a", which is from the Archaic Script, the upper portion is probably the word for "window" or "light".

華（华）

270

huā/*Hua*₂

繁茂，开花；辉煌的，华丽的；（也指花朵）

To bloom, to flower;
glorious, resplendent; (also "a flower")

顶部的"艸"旁表示与植物相关；参见上文114。该字由"艸"和"a"（表花）组成，读音与后者相同。"a"上部象叶和花，下部为"于"字，表感叹。参见 V. 5。"b"为形声字。

The classifier on the top shows that this word belongs to the category dealing with plants; see 114 above. It is combined with the form given in "a", which means "flowers" and has the same pronunciation. "a" is a picture of leaves and flowers with the word for "outgoing breath" written beneath, indicating exclamation. See V. 5. "b" is a harmonic word.

*后读 huá，以区别于花。

甜   **271**

                                                                    tián/*T'ien*₂

甜的，宜人的，愉快的
Sweet, agreeable, pleasant

由"甘"（表甜味）和"舌"组成。参见 III. 27 和上文 88。

This is a combination of the words for "sweet taste" and "tongue". See III. 27 and 88 above.

香

香　丁
　　尢

272

xiāng/*Hsiang*₂

芳香
Fragrant

由"黍"和"甘"（表甜味）而会意。参见 III. 27 和下文 273。

The idea is represented here by a combination of the words for "millet" and "sweet taste". See III. 27 and 273 below.

黍

黍　ㄕ
　　ㄨ

273

shǔ/*Shu*₃

黍稻
Millet

黍可酿酒，由"禾""入""水"而会意。参见 I. 10 和 II. 9，64。

The idea here is that that "grain" which by "entering" into "water" changes it to wine is millet. See I. 10 and II. 9, 64.

*张舜徽《约注》引米育仁说：

"禾属之不黏者谓之稻，禾属之黏者谓之黍"。

慶（庆）

274

qìng/*Ch'ing*₂

庆祝；好运，祝福

To congratulate; good luck, blessings

上部为简写的"鹿"，因吉礼常以鹿皮作为礼物。中部为"心"字，下部为"夂"字，表示从后至。参见 II. 38，130 和上文 10。

The abbreviated word for "deer" is written in the upper portion of this word because, by the rules of hospitality, the skin of a deer was usually offered as a gift. In the middle is the word for "heart", and below it is the word for "coming from behind". See II. 38, 130 and 10 above.

V.

Ideatives cum Pictographs

会 意 并 象 形

日

1

曰　曰 _{ㄩㄝ}

yuē/*Yüeh*₅

发言，讲话

To speak, to say

a

象气从口中上升。参见 II. 29。"a" 字形相似。

This is a picture of a current of air going upwards out of the mouth. See II. 29. "a" is a similar picture.

兮

2

兮　兮 _ㄒ

xī/*Hsi*₁ (*Ah*₁)

（虚词）

(An interjection)

象一缕气上升并分散。参见 I. 16，23。

A current of air is represented here going upward and being divided. See I. 16, 23.

只

3

zhī/*Chih*₃

只　　屮

（表示语气停顿的虚词）；

只有，但是，然而，仅仅

(An interjection denoting a stop);

Only, but, yet, merely

a

象气从口中下引之形。参见 II. 29。"a"字义相同。

This word shows the breath from the mouth going downwards. See II. 29. "a" has the same idea.

乎

4

hū/*Hu*₁

乎 乎 ㄏㄨ

（表疑问的虚词）

(An interjection in questioning)

由"兮"（上文 2）加一撇，表示气越发上扬。

One more stroke has been added to the word in 2 above to indicate the air going further up.

于，吁

5

yú, xū/*Ü*₁, *Hsü*₁

于 于 ㄩ

吁 ㄒㄩ

（虚词，叹气）

(An interjection, a sigh)

上短横象口气之舒展平直。

In this word the breath is shown going straight out, which is indicated by the short horizontal line on top.

木

6

木　木　又

mù/*Mu*₅

树木，木材，树林；（故表）麻木，没有知觉
Trees, timber, wood;
(hence) numb, without feeling

上象树枝，下象其根。

The upper portion of the word represents the branches and the lower portion the roots of a tree.

果

7

果　果　己

guǒ/*Ko*₃

果实；（故表）结果，效果，后果；当然
Fruits; (hence) result, effect, consequence;
certainly

"木"（上文6）上有果实。"a"字形相似。

The form of a fruit is drawn on top of the word for "tree". See 6 above. "a" is similar.

朵（朵）

8

duǒ/*To*₃

一簇花

A cluster of flowers

与花或云搭配使用的量词。上部表簇，下部为"木"（上文6）。

This is a particle used with the words for flower or cloud. The cluster is indicated above the word for "tree", 6 above.

束

9

cì/*Ts'u*$_4$

束　ㄘ

刺，触须

A thorn, a tentacle

象"树"（木）两侧生刺。参见上文 6。

Thorns are shown growing on both sides of a tree. See 6 above.

巢

10

cháo/*Tzao*$_2$

巢　ㄔㄠ

树上的鸟巢

A nest in a tree

象树上的鸟巢，三只雏鸟在顶端。

The nest is shown in the tree, with three fledglings indicated on top.

*据《说文》，鸟在树上的窝叫巢，在洞中的窝叫窠。

漆

11

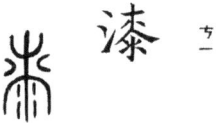 漆

qī/*Ch'i*₅

漆树，生漆

The varnish tree, lacquer

a

下部的"水"表示"木"（表树）的汁液流下。参见 II. 9。"a"的左边另加一"水"旁。

The word for "water" on the bottom denotes the sap of the "tree" flowing down. See II. 9. In "a" another classifier for water has been added on the left.

樂（乐）

12

 樂

yuè, lè/*Lo*₅, *Yo*₅

音乐；快乐的；享乐

Music; happy; to take pleasure in

象一大鼓和四小鼓置于木架上。

This is a representation of a large drum and four smaller drums placed on a wooden stand.

*据《段注》，鼓大鼗小。

廩

13

lǐn/*Lin*₃

官仓或筒仓

A government granary or a silo

ₐ ᵦ

下部（回）象贮藏粮食的屋子，其墙上开有小窗。上部表屋顶。"a"中可见"水稻"（禾）。

The lower portion of the word represents the building for storing rice with the small openings in the wall. The roof is indicated above it. In "a" the rice plant is shown.

箕［其］ 14

jī [qí]/*Chi*₁

簸箕，筛子

［他，她，它，这，那，他们，他们的，它的］

A winnowing basket, a basket for dust

(He, she, it, this, that,

they, their, theirs, its)

上部表篮子为竹制；中部象其形；底部为其垫座，亦表音。参见 II. 75，100。"b"为古体，象双手持握簸箕。"c"亦为古体；上部两撇"八"（表分开），亦表"分散"或"展开"。"d"和"e"均取自大篆；"e"加上另一形旁。参见 II. 61a。[] 中的第二种字体常用作关系代词、人称代词和物主代词。

The top portion of the word indicates that the basket is made of bamboo; the middle portion represents its form; the lower portion shows the support but also gives the sound. See II. 75, 100. In "b", which is Archaic Script, two hands are pictured holding the basket. "c" is also Archaic; the two strokes on top form the word for "division", which also means "dispersion" or "spread out". "d" and "e" are both from the Major Script; another pictograph has been added to "e". See II. 61a. The second form (in parentheses) is used always as a relative, personal and possessive pronoun.

彗

15

彗 彗 ᄃ

hui/*Fei*₄

扫帚
A broom

篲

15a

篲 篲

由"又"（表手）持握"丱"（表一束竹竿）会意。参见 II. 39a。"a"为古体，表示竹杆制成的扫帚。参见 II. 100。

This picture represents bundles of stalks held in the hand. See II. 39a. "a", which is Archaic Script, indicates a broom made of bamboo branches. See II. 100.

履

16

履 ㄌㄩˇ

$l\check{u}/Li_3$

鞋；步履；（故表）履行

A shoe; to walk; (hence) conduct

原意指"步行"。中部为"彳"（表步行），"夂"（表蹒跚）和"舟"（表船），而舟象鞋履之形；外部（尸）表音。参见 II. 37，51，87，159。

"To walk" is the original sense of this word. The words for "to walk" and "to stagger", as well as the word for "boat", which has the shape of a shoe, form the inner portion; the pronunciation is derived from the outer sign. See II. 37, 51, 87, 159.

17

裘

qiú/*Ch'iu*₂

袭 〈又

皮 衣

A fur garment

求

求

字形由"毛"在"衣"中构成。参见 II. 114。"a"取自古体，未有"衣"旁。参见 II. 39a。四撇为"尾"的简写（下文 18）。该字原意指"请求，恳求"；"b"下部的"从"字含义相同。

This word is made up of the word for "fur" placed in the middle of the word for "garment". See II. 114 and 18 below. In "a", which is from the Archaic Script, the word for "garment" has not been added. See II. 39a. The four strokes indicate an abbreviation of the word for "tail". The original idea of this word was "to ask for, to beg"; the word for "to follow" in the lower portion of "b" has the same connotation.

尾

18

wěi/*Wei*₃

尾巴；尾随

A tail; to follow

中部表示鸟或禽的尾巴，用来装饰衣服；上部为"人"字。

The inner sign represents the long tail of a bird or an animal used as an ornament of dress; a word for "man" is above it.

衰

19

shuāi/*Shuai*₁

干草编成的雨衣

A raincoat made of dried, woven fibres

[suō]/(*Ts'ui*₁)

衰 服

A mourning garment

象草（艸）在"衣"中间。参见 II. 114。"a"和"b"象衰服之形，其锥形帽子尤可见。

The fibres are pictured inside the word for "garment". See II. 114. "a" and "b" give a clear picture of the object, showing also the conical hat.

弁 ［卞］

20

biàn/*Pien*₄

锥形帽（弁帽）

A conical cap

由八（I. 16）和兒（II. 48）两个字组成。"a"为大篆，象弁帽之形，加上
"廾"（表双手）。"c"和"d"象头戴弁帽之形。

This is a combination of two words, I. 16 and II. 48. "a", which is Major Script, gives a picture
of the object, adding the form of "two hands". "c" and "d" clearly show the head wearing
the cap

市

21

fú/*Fu*₅

古 代 礼 服 前 皮 制 的 蔽 膝

A leather kneepad
used in ancient ceremonial dress

上横表丝带；下部为"巾"字。参见 III. 18。"b"为蔽膝上的图案，该字是
本书唯一取自明代杨慎收录的字。此字被公认为可靠的。

The horizontal line on top indicates a lace; the word for "kerchief" is below it. See III. 18.
"b", which gives the form of a design used on the kneepads, is the only word in this book
which has been taken from Yang Shěn's collection, Ming Dynasty. This form is universally
acknowledged as authentic.

带（帶）

22

dài/*Tai*₄

腰带，饰带

Girdle, sash

ᵃ   ᵇ   ᶜ

上部象腰间垂下的带子和丝带；下部为双写的"巾"。参见 III. 18。"a"、"b"和"c"中，腰带所挂之物尤可见。

The upper portion of this word represents ties and laces hanging from the waist; a doubled form of "kerchief" is below it. See III. 18. "a", "b", and "c" are all clearer pictures of things hanging from the waist sash.

*古时男子佩皮革的衣带，妇人以丝为衣带。

敝

23

bì/*Pi*₄

破 旧 的
Worn-out

"巾"为衣服的统称，周围四短撇表其破旧之处，故有衣衫褴褛之意。

The idea of raggedness is represented by four short curved lines indicating torn places in the "kerchief", which stands for clothes in general here.

兜

24

dōu/*Tou*₂

头 盔 ， 头 罩
A helmet, a head covering

中上的左右两撇象头盔盖住头的两边。参见 II. 48。

The curved lines on either side of the upper portion of the central word indicate the helmet projecting on both sides of the head. See II. 48.

匹

25

匹 匹 $\frac{\mho}{\frown}$

pǐ/$P'i_5$

一 匹 布 帛（合 40 尺 长）

A roll of cloth
(of the length of 40 Chinese feet)

由"八"（表分开）在"匸"（表卷）中会意。参见 I. 16。40 尺布帛常分为两卷，10 卷 200 尺的布帛即为一束。

The word is written in the form of the roll, with the word for "to divide" inside it. See I. 16. 40 feet of cloth were divided into two rolls, 200 feet in 10 rolls equalling a "bundle".

曹

曹 曹 〔ㄨˋ〕

26

wèi/*Hui*₄

车 轴 露 出 于 车 毂 外 的 末 端
The covering of the outer
projection of the axis of a wheel

由"车"字（II. 89）引申而来。

This is an extension of the word in II. 89.

鬥（斗）

鬥 鬥 〔ㄉ ㄡˋ〕

27

dòu/*Tou*₄

争 斗， 打 斗
To contest, to fight

象双手争斗，各持一物。

This is a picture of two hands fighting, each holding something.

＊区别于"斗"（dǒu），表 10 升。

巨

28

巨   巨   ㅂ

jù/*Chü*₄

木工用的方尺（矩），规矩

A carpenter's square, a rule

a 巨

象在"工"字内用手握住矩。该字由古体"a"演变而来。参见 I. 8。

This is the word for "work" with the form of a hand gripping the tool drawn inside it. It is derived from the word in Archaic Script given in "a". See I. 8.

筁

29

筁   筁   ㄏㄨ

hù/*Hu*₄

收绞丝绳的工具

An instrument for twisting ropes

互

互

互

中部象手推握"筕"的部分。上部为"竹"字。参见 II. 100。"a"为古体，无"竹"旁。作转注字，今表示"相互"或"互惠"，因捻绳时必须两端同时扭转。

The middle portion of this word represents the part of the "twister" which is turned by hand. Above it is the word for "bamboo". See II. 100. "a" is Archaic Script, without the classifier "bamboo". As a transmissive it now means "mutual" or "reciprocal", because the rope is made by twisting the strands equally from both ends.

巫

巫

巫 x

30

wū/U₁

巫师
A wizard

象人两袖起舞的样子，引神祇降临。

This picture represents a man with two long sleeves twirling in a dance in order to induce the descent of spirits.

兆

31

zhào/*Chao*₄

预 兆

An omen

中部两笔表灼烧龟甲的裂纹；左边曲线表灼龟甲之人。右部为后加的"卜"（表占卜）。参见 II. 59。

The two lines in the middle portion of this word represent the cracks on the tortoise shell when it was scorched; the curved lines on the left represent the burner. The word for "divination" on the right was added later. See II. 59.

昔

32

xī/*Hsi*₅

往昔， 旧的

Formerly, of old

象太阳晒干的肉条。参见 II. 1。

This was originally a picture of pieces of meat dried in the sun. See II. 1.

皀

33

jí, xiāng/*Hiang*₂

稻香

The fragrance of rice

象勺置于一袋米之下。

This is a picture of a packet of rice with a spoon drawn beneath it.

豐（丰）

34

fēng/*Fêng*₁

丰满，丰硕的，丰盛的

A bundant, fruitful, luxuriant

由"豆"（表礼器）盛物丰满会意。中部的"山"表高而大之意，其内的双"禾"（表谷物）指祭品。参见 II. 14，69。

The idea of the picture is that of a sacrificial vessel filled to the brim. The "grains", representing the offering, are shown inside and the word for "mountain" in the middle gives the idea of largeness and height. See II. 14, 69.

* "豐"和"丰"分为二字，"丰"释为"草木丰盛"。
后"豐"简化为"丰"。参见 X. 13。

畫（画）

35

 畫 ㄏㄨㄚˋ

huà/*Hua*4, (5)

绘画，图画

Painting, drawing

a 画

原意指"划分界限"，由上部的笔在下部的"田"上画出四周的界线而会意。参见 II. 20 和 IV. 137。"a"为简写。

Originally this word meant "to draw the boundary lines of a field", the picture showing the "field", on the bottom, with its four borders, being drawn by the pen above it. See II. 20 and IV. 137. "a" is a simplified form.

腦（脑）　　　　　　　　　**36**

nǎo/*Nao*₃

大 脑
The brain

象头顶长发，整个右部表示大脑。参见 II. 27。

The hair is depicted here on top of the head, the whole sign on the right representing the brain. See II. 27.

眉　　　　　　　　　　　　**37**

méi/*Mei*₁

眉 毛
The eyebrows

下部为"目"，曲线之上为额头的纹理，表眉毛。参见 II. 25。

The eye is drawn below and the wrinkles of the forehead above the curved line representing the eyebrow. See II. 25.

肱

38

肱

gōng/*Kung*₂

上臂，手臂

The upper arm, the arm

左下曲线表示肌肉。参见 II. 39a。

The curved form in the lower left portion of the word indicates the muscles. See II. 39a.

肩

39

jiān/*Chien*₂

肩 膀
The top of the shoulder

a

上部象肩形，下部为"肉"字。参见 II. 106。"a"字形相似。

This is a picture of the shoulder with the word for "flesh" drawn below it. See II. 106. "a" is a similar picture.

胃

40

wèi/*Wei*₄

胃
The stomach

上部象斜体的"米"在椭圆中；下部为"肉"字。参见 II. 63，106。

The word for "rice" is placed in a diagonal position inside the oval form in the upper portion of the word; the word for "flesh" is given below it. See II. 63, 106.

41

fǎn/*Fan*₃

翻覆，撤退，返回，反抗

To turn over, to retreat, to turn back, to rebel

外部表音，亦表翻覆手掌。参见 II. 15，39a。

The pronunciation of this word is derived from the outer sign, which also indicates that the palm of the hand is turned over. See II. 15, 39a.

足

42

zú/*Tsu*₅

脚；完全的，足够的，满足的

The foot; complete, enough, satisfied

上部圆形象膝盖骨；下部（止）表示脚趾。参见 II. 52。

The round form on top of the word represents the kneecap; the toes are pictured beneath it. See II. 52.

夬

43

guài/*Kuai*₄

分裂或决断

To part or parted

a

象手拉弓弦之形，中部竖笔表示弓弦，已经搭在箭尾的弧口上。参见 II. 39，83。"a"更为象形。

In this picture the hand is represented drawing a bowstring, indicated by the vertical line in the middle, which is shown attached to the nock at the end of the bow. See II. 39, 83. "a" is even more clear.

*据《字源》，又作"决"（jué），指古代射箭时用以钩弦的扳指。

牟

44

móu/*Mou*₂

牟叫声；哞哞叫

Lowing of bovine animals; to moo

顶部曲线表示公牛发出的声气。参见 II. 121。

The curled form on top represents the sound and the breath issuing from the ox. See II. 121.

牢

45

láo/*Lao*~2~

养牲畜的栏圈

A pen for cattle

象牛在栏里，大门已上闩。参见 II. 121。

The ox is shown inside an enclosure with the door barred. See II. 121.

芻（刍）

46

chú/*Ch'u*~2~

干草，饲料

Hay, fodder

象草割下后包捆好，以饲养牲畜。参见 II. 55 和 IV. 115。

The picture shows grass cut and packed in bundles for feeding cattle. See II. 55 and IV. 115.

兑

47

兑 ㄉㄨㄟ

duì/*Tui*₄

说话，祝福，感到喜悦

To speak, to bless, to rejoice

"口"在"人"上，顶部两撇象气从"人"的"口"中散出。参见 I. 16 和 II. 24b，29。

The two strokes on top of the word indicate that air is dispersing from the "mouth"— in the middle — of a "man" below it. See II. 16 and II. 24b, 29.

閉（闭）

48

閉 ㄅㄧ

bì/*Pi*₄

关闭，闭塞

To close, to stop up

中部象关门上闩。参见 II. 78。

The sign in the middle of the word indicates that the door is closed and barred from within. See II. 78.

開 （开）   **49**

kāi/*K'ai*₁

打 开

To open

象双手将门闩移开。"a"为古体，以形表意，上文小篆为其仿体，尽管原字形已无法辨识。"b"象两人推开门。

The picture shows that the bar of the door is being removed with both hands. The Archaic Script in "a" gives the exact idea while the Minor Script (above) is a copy of it, although the original form is no longer recognizable. "b" shows two people pushing open a door.

冤

50

yuān/*Yuan*₁

压抑，冤屈

Oppression, injustice

由兔在覆盖之下表曲折不伸。参见 II. 125 和 IX. 48。

The picture of a rabbit held under a cover gives the idea of oppression. See II. 125 and IX. 48.

彪

51

biāo/*Piao*₂

虎猫，花纹；高雅的

A tigercat, stripes; elegant

左部为"虎"字，右部（彡）象其身上的花纹。

The word for "tiger" is on the left and the stripes on its skin are indicated on the right.

52

后

后 后 ⌐ㄡ

hòu/*Hou*₄

君 主 ， 国 王 ， 皇 后 ， 女 皇

A ruler, a king, an empress, a queen

上部象一端坐的人，下部为"口"字，表示发布口令和命令。

The form on top represents a man sitting, and the word for "mouth" below it means here to give oral commands and orders.

53

磬

磬 磬 ⟨ㄥ

qìng/*Ch'ing*₄

一 种 叩 击 乐 器

A percussive musical instrument

a 𡔫

底部（石）表示该中式乐器由贵重的石头制成。左边的两偏旁表示其形如木工的矩尺，自顶端垂挂；右部两偏旁表示手持仗敲击。参见 II. 16 和 IX. 161。"a" 取自大篆，象磬之形。

This is a Chinese musical instrument made of precious stone, which is denoted by the word on the bottom. It is shaped like a carpenter's square and hung from its apex, which is represented by the two signs on the left half of the word; the two on the right indicate that it is struck with a stick held in the hand. See II. 16 and IX. 161. "a", which is from the Major Script, gives the form of the instrument.

淵（渊）　　　　　　　　　　**54**

𣶒 淵 ㄩㄢ

yuān/*Yüan*$_2$

深渊，涡流，深泉

An abyss, a gulf, a deep spring

a 𤀁

"a"取自大篆，省去左边的"水"旁；但水岸和水流在上文字形中尤可见。
参见 II. 9。

In "a", which is from the Archaic Script, the left indicator for "water" is omitted; but both banks and the waves of water are pictured, as in the form above. See II. 9.

谷

55

谷 谷 《x

*gǔ/Ku*₅

山 谷 ，　沟 壑 ，　峡 谷

A valley, a ravine, a gorge

字形中一部分水流自"口"（表峡谷）中流出。由此表山谷之意。参见 II. 29。

In this word waves of water are partially shown rushing forth from a gorge, which is indicated by the word for "mouth". From this comes the idea of a valley. See II. 29.

畴（畴）　　　　　　　　　　　56

chóu/*Ch'ou*₂

可耕地，田地

Arable land, field

左部为"田"字，右部表犁沟。参见 II. 20。

The word for "field" is written on the left, and the furrows are represented on the right. See II. 20.

卤（卤）　　　　　　　　　　　57

lǔ/*Lu*₃

盐 碱 地 ， 天 然 的 盐

Alkaline soil, natural salt

由大篆"西"字的简写，加上表盐粒的点组成。中国西部（现西北地区）有此类盐碱地。

This is an abbreviated form of the word for "west" in the Major Script, combined with dots which represent grains of salt. This type of soil is found in the west (now the northwest) of China.

*据《说文》，东部称盐碱地作斥，西部叫作卤。

[靈（灵）]

58

líng/*Lin*₂

连绵雨

Continuous rain

"雨"字下部尤见雨滴之形。参见 II. 5。

Here drops of rain are indicated below the word for "rain". See II. 5.

雷　　　　　　　　　　**59**

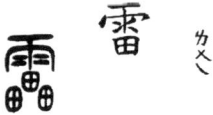

léi/*Lei*₁

打雷
Thunder

下部三个"田"表大地；上部为"雨"字。参见 II. 5，20。"a"和"b"均为大篆。"a"上部为"雨"字简体，中间两个圈表回旋之物；"b"中螺旋形部首表四"田"中回旋之物，如雷之回响。

The three words for "field" on the bottom represent the earth ; the word for "rain" is above. See II. 5, 20. "a" and "b" are both Archaic Script. In "a" the word for "rain" is still on top, in an abbreviated form, and the two circles represent something turning around ; in "b", the spiral forms indicate something whirling around within four "fields" ; i.e., the reverberations of thunder.

60

cuàn/*Ts'uan*₄

烹煮；炉灶

To cook; a cooking stove

上部象双手持炊具置于灶上；中部象在灶里放入燃料（木材），下部为点燃
的火。该字由五个字组成。参见 II. 13，71；IV. 37，171 和上文 6。

The upper portion of this word shows the cooking pot being placed on the stove by two
hands; fuel is being fed into the oven, in the middle, and a fire has been started underneath.

Five signs combine to form this word. See II. 13, 71; IV. 37, 171, and 6 above.

61

jīng/*Ching*₂

高大

Great

原意指"人筑起的高丘"。上部为"高"的简体。参见 II. 111。下部的竖线由底至顶，为指事字。国之首都（京都）表"高大"之意；日常使用时只取"京"字，如北京、南京等。

The original idea of this word was "a very high mound built by men". The upper portion is an abbreviated form of the word for "high". See II. 111. The vertical line below it is written from the bottom to the top, an indicative word. The term for the capital of a state (King Ssu,) means "a great multitude"; in ordinary usage only the first word is retained, e.g. Peking, Nanking, etc.

VI.

Harmonics

形 声

形声字为数最多，占词汇总量的 90%。其造字原则简单，此处不再赘述。许慎之定义如下："**以事为名，取譬相成**"。

"事"此处表示显而易见，亦表示所指事物或行为；"名"简单说即由其他部首或字配合组成的字。也可作如下解：首先，有一字表音作为基础；然后，添加其他的字或部首。

（a）在左边

（b）或右边

（c）在上边

（d）或下边

（e）在里边

（f）或外边（通常为一圈形结构）

新造的字其字义有所不同，但通常与表音的部首无关，而与所加部首或字相关，也有少数例外（如下文的"形声并指事"等）。据汉语规定，表音的旁称为"声"，所加部分称为"形"。新字的读音往往与声旁相同，即便不完全一致，也仅仅是音调变化，或是声母变化而保留韵母和复韵母，抑或是"声"旁变调而原音仍可识。严格来说，这是重要的一支知识，今称语音学，专治声音和韵律，无论在古代还是现代，这与历史上文字发音的几次——至少三次——巨变有很深的渊源，如方言的地域分布等。此处不宜展开论述。

此类汉字，许慎列举有二："江"（jiāng）和"河"（hé），均为拟声词，即字的构造源于对自然之物声音的模仿。此二字均表"河流"，前者指长江，位于中国中部，后者指黄河，位于北方。所谓"事"，即江河流淌之声。黄河在泥岸间疾速冲刷，发出"he-he-he"的声音，故由"可"（kě）作声旁，取其音"ke"。长江的两岸为岩石和山丘，波涛撞击中空的岩石，发出"kong...kong...kong"的声音并伴有回声，故由"工"（gōng）作声旁。因二字皆表河流，故在其左边加"水"字或"水"旁——亦称为部首。"江"今读作"jiang"，古时读作"gong"。[1] 显然，"工"表工作，"可"表可能或可以，这两个声旁的原意与"河流"毫无关联。

此二字作为范例，很好地说明了形声字以及拟声词的造字原则。但此类汉字很少，因自然之物并不都发声。即便其能发声，造新字时抑或采用，抑或不用。除开此类数量有限的拟声词和会意并指事字，还有一些问题有待回答，例如为何以特定的音表特定的字，换而言之，为什么一个字要如此发音，进而为什么以特定的偏旁构造这个或那个字，等等。所有这些都触发我们思考，这些问题本身是否值得一提，因为在分析字音时，总会遇到最基本的元素，即以最简单的符号表最基本的音，此后便无法继续分析。然而语言起源的秘密却值得进一步探究，但其研究应归入哲学范畴。去探寻答案，满意或不满意，都应当对文化史、音乐、心理学作深入研究，在人类最基本的声音及发声机能相关的比较文字学领域牢固确立一些普遍原则，无论比较文字学能否成为世界公认的一门科学。显然，如此广泛的领域非个人研究所能及，并已超出现有的认知范围。我们只好在已

.

1. 这一原则于梵文"Ganga"或"Ganges"的造字是否有所提示？

讨论的范围内，关注此一简单原则或造字方法。

为说明此类汉字，列举一些例字足以。此处专论字音，故省去字义。音调用数字 1—5 表示。在不同地区的方言中，音调不尽相同，有些地区有六、七、八甚至九种音调，然而这些方言并非我们关注的重点。本书只取五种标准音调。但并非每个音调都有对应的汉字，每个汉字也并非都有五个音调。无论口头语或书面语，每次使用时只有一个声调。毋庸置疑，许多字的音和调相同，只宜结合上下文理解，但在书面语里不会弄错。此处所列例字，不必一一记住。

Harmonic words are the most numerous, amounting to ninety per cent of the entire vocabulary. Not much need be said, since the principle is a simple one. The definition given by Hsu Shên is as follows:

> Words "formed with the fact taken as an appellation, and the sound harmonized in a similitude".

The meaning of the word "fact" here is somewhat obscure, yet we can take it as expressing the thing or action designated, and "appellation" simply as the word formed through the combination of another sign or word in harmonization. We may explain it in the following way: first, a certain word is taken as the basis for pronunciation; next, other words or signs may be added,

a) on the left,

b) or on the right;

c) on top,

d) or below;

e) inside,

f) or outside (often of a circle).

A new word is thus formed with a different meaning that may have something to do with the sign or word added, but, with the exception of a small group of words (given below as "cum ideatives" etc.) the meaning is generally not related to the basis of pronunciation. Technically in Chinese the basis of pronunciation is called the "sound", and the addition to it the "form". The pronunciation of this new word is then often the same as its basis, or if not exactly the same, there is only a variation of the tone, or the vowel or diphthong is retained but the consonant is changed, or there can be an inflection of the "sound", the derivation of which is still recognizable. Strictly speaking, this is part of a great branch of knowledge which we now call phonology, the study of sound and rhyme, both ancient and modern, which delves deeply into the history of the several — at least three — great changes in the pronunciation of words in the past, the topographical distribution of dialects, etc. That need not be treated here.

The two words given by Hsu Shên as examples of this category, Chiang 江 and Ho 河, were both onomatopoeics, that is to say, words formed by imitating the sound of natural objects. Both these words mean "river", but the former refers to the long Yangtze River in the middle part of China and the latter refers to the Yellow River in the north. The "fact" here used is the sound of the river flowing. The Yellow River, flowing swiftly within its mud banks, gives a sound like "ho-ho-ho", so the word K'o (kho) 可 was taken as its basis because of its "ho" sound. The Yangtze River with its rocky and hilly banks gives a sound like "kung... kung... kung" when the waves dash under hollowed cliffs, reverberating with echoes, so the word Kung 工 was used as its basis. Since they were used to designate rivers, the word or radical — called also "classifier" — for "water" was added to both words on the left. The word now read as Chiang was in ancient times pronounced Gung 江 [1]. Obviously the original meaning of these two bases, one meaning "work" and the other "may" or "can", has nothing to do with the idea of a river.

These two words taken as examples are clear enough for the explanation of the harmonic principle, inasmuch as they are at the same time onomatopoeics, but such words are few, because not every natural object has a sound, and even if it has a sound, it may or may not have been used in the formation of a new word. Now, apart from a limited number of such onomatopoeics and a limited number of ideatives cum harmonics, there are questions that remain to be answered, such as: why a certain sound was used to denote a certain word, or to put it in another way, why a word was so pronounced, and further, why a particular basis was used to form this or that new word, etc. All this may lead one to ask whether these questions can be posited at all, because in analyzing the pronunciation of a word we come to the final element, the fundamental sound represented by the simplest sign, after which we can proceed no further. Yet there must be secrets of the very origins of language which can be investigated even further, but that investigation must be relegated to the realms of philosophy. To obtain any answer at all, satisfactory or unsatisfactory, the fields of cultural history, music, and psychology must be deeply explored and certain generalizations in comparative philology concerning the fundamental human sounds and vocal faculties must be firmly established, whether

.

1. Could this principle give any suggestion to the formation of the Sanskrit word "Ganga" or Ganges?

comparative philology be a universally acknowledged branch of science or not. Evidently, this is too vast a field for individual research, being beyond our present scope. We can only limit ourselves to the field already explored, taking this simple principle or rather this method of word formation into consideration.

To illustrate this category, a few examples may be enough. Since sound alone is to be dealt with here, the meaning need not be given. The numbers mark the tones, from the first to the fifth. Tones vary in number with different dialects in different localities, and in some places there may be six, seven, eight or even nine tones, but we need not concern ourselves with these dialects. We shall take only the five standard tones into consideration. It is not that a particular tone must have its own word, nor that a word must be pronounced in all the five tones. Only one tone is used at a time, both in the written and in the spoken language. Needless to say, since so many words have the same sound and the same tone, they can only be understood in the context of the words heard, although in the written language they cannot be mistaken. It is not necessary to commit every word to memory in the examples given here.

東   dōng / *Tung*$_1$ 重   chóng, tóng, zhòng / *Chung*$_{2,3,4}$

凍   dòng / *Tung*$_4$ 動   dòng / *Tung*$_{3,4}$

涷   dōng / *Tung*$_4$ 徸   zhǒng, dòng / *Chung*$_3$

棟   dòng / *Tung*$_4$ 湩   dǒng, dòng, tóng / *Chung*$_{3,4}$

崬   dōng / *Tung*$_4$ 憧   zhòng / *Chung*$_3$

                                           埵   zhǒng / Chung$_3$

                                           緟   zhòng, chóng / Chung$_3$

                                           種   zhǒng, zhòng, chóng / *Chung*$_{3,4}$

                                           腫   zhǒng / Chung$_3$

                                           踵   zhǒng, zhòng / *Chung*$_3$

                                           鍾   zhōng / *Chung*$_1$

童　tóng, zhōng / $Tung_2$

僮　tóng, zhuàng / $Tung_2$

衝　chōng / $Chung_1$

幢　chuáng, zhuàng / $Chung_1, Chiang_1$

撞　zhuàng / $Chiang_1, Chung_1$

憧　chōng, zhuàng / $Chung_3$

潼　chōng, tóng, zhōng / $Chung_1, Tung_1$

橦　chōng, chuáng, tóng, zhōng / $Chung_1$

穜　zhòng, tóng, zhǒng / $Chung_3$

疃　tuǎn / $Tung_2$

罿　chōng / $Chung_2$

瘇　zhǒng, tóng / $Chung_{1,3}$

董　dǒng / $Tung_3$

幰　chōng, chuáng / $Chung_1$

鐘　zhōng / $Chung_1$

VII.

Harmonics cum Indicatives

形 声 并 指 事

氏

1

dǐ/*Ti*₃

氒 氒 ㄅ

基础
Foundation

上部由"氏"（下文 2）演化而来，读音亦为其变形。中部横线表大地；其下曲线表根，顶部表叶芽。底部短横强调主根。

The upper portion of this word is derived from the word in 2 below, and the pronunciation is an inflection of its sound. The horizontal line in the middle represents the earth; the curving line below it is the root, and the leaf-bud is shown on top. Here the short horizontal line on the bottom of the word gives emphasis to the taproot.

氏

2

shì/*Shih*₄

氒 氏 ㄕ

姓氏或族名
The family or clan name

为"氏"（上文 1）的字源；其释义见上文。原意指树木的根源，进而指人的
姓氏。"a"取自"古代碑刻经典"，其中破土而出的芽和底下的根尤可见。

This is the origin of the word in 1 above; its form is explained there. It is meant to represent
the origin of a tree, and thus, for a man, his family name. "a" is from the "Stone Inscriptions
of the Classics". It shows better the sprout coming out of the earth and the roots below.

3

yīn/*Yin*$_2$

声 音 ，音 调

A sound, a tone

由"言"（下文4）演化而来。"口"字中的短横表声音。"口"上为会意字——
辰，表示"冒犯上级"或"冒昧干预上级事务"。参见 I.4，11。

This word comes from 4 below. The short horizontal line in the word for "mouth" indicates
the sound. The form on top of the "mouth" is an ideative pronounced Chen, meaning "to
offend higher authorities" or "to intervene presumptuously in higher affairs". See I. 4, 11.

言

4

言　言

yán/*Yen*₁

言 说 ， 谈 话 ； 演 说

To speak, to talk; speech

"音"（上文3）的字源；其释义见上文。

This is the origin of the word in 3 above; its form is explained there.

＊直接讲话叫言，议论辩驳叫语。

宜   5

yí/I_1 (O)

正确的，相宜的，相配的，得体的；

应该，应当

Right, fitting, suitable, seemly;

ought, should

a

中部的夕（多之一半）位于屋檐（宀）之下地面（一）以上，故有"适宜"之意，进而指"相配"等。亦属会意字。参见 II. 157。"a"为古体，中部并非简写；其韵母在古代切"多"（IV. 75）。

The sign in the interior of this word represents that which is under the roof and above the earth, which gives the idea of "fit" and hence "suitable", etc. It is also an ideative. See II. 157. In Archaic Script, shown in "a", the central word was not abbreviated; it had the same vowel sound in ancient times as IV. 75.

VIII.

Harmonics cum Pictographs

形 声 并 象 形

齿（齿）

1

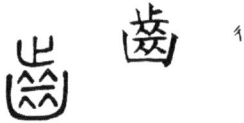

chǐ/*Ch'ih*₃

牙齿
The teeth

上部为"止"字（II. 52），表音。下部象牙齿的形状。

This word is pronounced in accordance with the word given in II. 52, which is the upper portion of the word. Below it is a picture of the teeth.

字

2

bèi/*Pu*₅

草木茂盛
Plants issuing forth exuberantly

中部象草木之形。字音切"八"（I. 16），表分开。

In the middle of this word is the picture of a plant. The pronunciation is derived from Pa, meaning "to divide", given in I. 16.

函

3

hán/*Han*[2]

厂
马

舌 头

The tongue

a

下部象舌头之形；字音切上部"马"（II. 97）。"a"仅象舌头之形。

The lower portion of the word is a picture of the tongue; it is pronounced in accordance with the word given in II. 97, which forms the upper portion of the word. "a" shows the tongue only.

4

彘

彘 ₁

zhì/*Chih*₄

猪
Swine

a

象猪的头和四肢；字音切上部"矢"（II. 84）。"a"字形相似。

This is a picture of the head and the legs of a swine; the pronunciation is derived from the word given in II. 84, seen in the lower middle portion of the word. "a" has a similar formation.

5

氏

氏 尸

shì/*Shih*₄

家族，氏族，姓氏
A family, a clan, a family surname

字的构造在 VII. 1 中已有释义。再次列出因其亦属此类造字原则。原字音切
"乀"(yí，I. 22)，表示流动。

The formation of this word is explained in VII. 1. It is given here again because it can also be classified under this category. The original pronunciation is derived from Yih, I. 22, meaning "to flow".

IX.

Harmonics cum Ideatives

形 声 并 会 意

芝

1

𡳐 芝 㞢

*zhī/Chih*₁

一种稀有菌类，柄为紫色，
人们相信其出现代表最幸福的时光，
会赐予人繁荣和长寿

A fungus with a purplish stalk,
very seldom found, the appearance of which
is believed to indicate the happiest of times,
with blessings of prosperity and longevity for everyone

字形原来的释义为"神草"；双"木"下面为"之"（表前进），表声。参见
III. 32 和 IV. 114。

"A divine plant" is the old explanation for the formation of this word; the word below the
two "plants" means "to progress" and gives the sound. See III. 32 and IV. 114.

莽

2

莽 尤

măng/*Mang*₃

困 惑 的 ， 无 序 的 ， 粗 鲁 的 ， 粗 野 的
Confused, disorderly, rude, rough

原释义为"中国南方称善于在丛中追逐兔兽的狗作'莽'"。由两个字组成；
参见 II. 123 和 IV. 117。会意字，亦属形声字。

"The hunting dog skilled in chasing rabbits through grassy fields is called 'Mang' in the
southern part of China" is the old explanation of this word. It is a combination of two words;
see II. 123 and IV. 117. It is an ideative as well as a harmonic.

曾

3

曾 勺

zēng/*Ts'eng*₂

已 经 ， 曾 经
Already, past

由三个字组成。中部表声；上部和下部表示说话声音的延续。等同于英文的虚词"then"。参见 I. 16，II. 79a 和 V. 1。

This is a combination of three words. The pronunciation is derived from the word in the middle; the words above and below it indicate the extension of the voice in speaking. It is an expletive something like "then" in English. See I. 16, II. 79a, and V. 1.

*《段注》："盖曾字古训乃子登切（zēng），后世用为曾经之义，读才登切（céng）。"

胖

4

胖

夂尢

pàn/P'ang₄

胖的，肥胖

Fat, corpulent

右边的"半"表声，稍有变音；左边为"肉"字。参见 II. 106 和 IV. 207。原意指（祭祀用的）半体牲。

The word for "a half" on the right gives the pronunciation with a slight inflection; the word for "flesh" is on the left. See II. 106 and IV. 207. The original idea of the word was half of an animal.

*据《说文》《字源》，"胖"后失其本义，乃假借表肥胖之意，读作 pàng。

胖又有宽舒之意，读作 pán，此义仅用于成语"心宽体胖"。

單（单）

5

單　單　召

dān/*Tan*₁

单一的，单独的，奇数的，简单的
Single, alone, odd, simple

Ｙ　Ｙ

以上字义为假借；许慎认为原意指"大的"或"伟大"。实际上应表示"夸口"或"自豪地说"，因上部为两个"口"字（吅），读作 xuān，表"喧闹"。下部为"華"的简体（II. 119），表"向前推"之意。形声字，上部表声。

The meanings given above are the borrowed senses of this word; the original idea was "large" or "great", according to Hsu Shên. Actually it should mean "to boast" or "to talk greatly", because of the two words on top for "mouth", pronounced Hsüan and meaning "clamourous". Below is an abbreviated form of the word "Po", II. 119, which gives the idea of "pushing forth". This is a harmonic word because of the word on top.

攴

6

pū/*P'u*₅

轻击，轻拍

To tap, to beat lightly

音同上部"卜"。下部表示用右手拍打。参见 II. 39a，59。

The pronunciation of this word is the same as the word in the upper half. The lower part indicates beating with the right hand. See II. 39a, 59.

吏

7

lì/*Li*₄

政府官员，官吏，差役

A clerk in government offices,

an officer, a deputy

顶部的"一"表示"高的"或"上级权威"。下部"史"字表声，指"史官"，亦指"政府官员"。官员总是执行上级的命令。参见 I. 1 和 IV. 138。

The word "I" on top means "high" or "high authorities". The pronunciation is derived from the word "shih" below, meaning a "historian" but also a "clerk in the government". The officials always followed the instructions from above. See I. 1 and IV. 138.

禮（礼）

8

lǐ/Li$_3$

礼节，典礼，仪式，礼拜，礼仪，习俗

Propriety, rites, ceremony, worship, good manners, mores

原意指"祭祀中用来求福的事"。左部为指事字"示"（参见 I. 7），右部象"礼器之形"，表音。不过古籍中尚未发现单独使用右部（豊）的记载。"a"为古体，字形更为简化；亦属形声字。

Originally this word meant "that which is done in worshipping the gods to invoke their blessings". On the left is an indicative, see I. 7, and on the right is the form of a "sacrificial vessel". No references can be found in the ancient classics for the separate use of the latter word, but it gives the sound. In the Archaic Script given in "a", the form is simpler; it is also a harmonic word.

9

碧

碧 碧 ㄅ
ㄧ

bì/*Pi*₅

碧色或青白的玉石
Greenish or bluish jade
with a white lustre

由三个字组成：左上为"玉"字，右上为"白"，指白色，表声，下部为"石"字。参见 II. 16，160 和 IV. 216。

Three words are combined here: the word for "jade" on the upper left, Bê, meaning "white", on the upper right, from which the sound is derived, and the word for "stone" below them. See II. 16, 160 and IV. 216.

社

10

社   社   尸
              せ

shè/*Shê*₄

土 地 的 神 主 ， 地 方 神 灵
The "master" or god of the soil,
the local deity

ₐ 祍

古音切右部"土"，表示土地。参见 I. 7，9。"a"为古体，加"木"字。周代，
每 25 户立一祭台供奉土地神，并在土地庙周围种植各种适宜在当地生长的
树木。所种之树称为社树。

The ancient sound of this word was derived from the word on the right, which means
"earth". See I. 7, 9. In "a", which is in the Archaic Script, the word for "tree" has been
added. In the Chow Dynasty, every 25 families worshipped together and built an altar to this
god, planting trees suitable to the soil beside the temple. That species of tree was then sacred
to that deity.

祟

11

suì/*Sui*₄

邪灵，鬼神给人的灾祸

An evil spirit,

evil influences of a demoniac nature

音切上部"出"字，表示出来。参见 I. 7 和 II. 102。

The sound of this word is derived from the word for "to come out" on top. See I. 7 and II. 102.

丧（喪）

12

sàng, sāng/*Sang*₂

丧失，丧亡，为死者奔丧

To lose, to die, to mourn for the dead

字义为"悲悼丧失的人或物";韵母切底部"亡"字。参见 IV. 36 和下文 13。

"To bewail someone or something lost" is the idea of the word; the word for "lost" on the bottom also gives its vowel sound. See IV. 36 and 13 below.

*《段注》:"亡部曰:'亡,逃也。'亡非死之谓。""凡丧失字本皆平声,俗读去声以别于死丧平声,非古也。"朱骏声《通训定声》:"《白虎通》:'人死谓之丧何,言其丧亡不可复得见也。不直言死,称丧者何,为孝子之心不忍言也。'"

13

哭

哭

kū/K'u₅

哀声,哭泣

To bewail, to cry

由"犬"悲痛地哀叫会意。

A "dog" barking in a mournful manner is the idea of this picture.

*哭,悲哀的声音。泣,无声出涕曰泣。

歸（归）

14

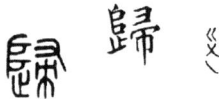

*guī/Kuei*₂

女子出嫁；回归，归去，返回

The marriage of women;
to return to, to send back, to go back

a

音切左上部"自"的韵母；左下部"止"表示停止之意。参见 II. 17，52。右部为"妇"（下文 15）的简体。"a"字形稍有不同。

The word on the upper left gives the vowel sound to this word; the word on the bottom left gives the idea "to stop". See II. 17, 52. The right side is an abbreviated form of the word in 15 below. The form of "a" is only slightly different.

婦（妇）

15

婦　婦　ㄷㄨ

fù/*Fu*~4, 3~

妻子，女性，妇女的统称
A wife, a lady, a woman in general

a

原意指"服从"或"服侍"。会意字，由"女""帚"两个字组成——参见 II.
45 和 IV. 263。"a"字形相似。

The original idea of this word was "to obey" or "to serve". It is an ideative made up of two
words — see II. 45 and IV. 263. "a" is very similar.

返

16

返　ㄈㄢ

fǎn/*Fan*~3~

返回，回去
To return, to go back

由左部"辵"（表走或步行）和右部"反"（表返回）组成，反表声。参见 IV.
47a 和 V. 41。

This is a combination of the word for "to go" or "to walk", on the left, and the word for "to
turn back" on the right, which also gives its sound. See IV. 47a and V. 41.

路 **17**

路 路 ㄌㄨ

lù/Lu₄

马 路 ， 道 路 ， 小 路
A road, a way, a path

由左部"足"（表脚）和右部"各"（表各自，每个）组成。音从"各"演化
而来。参见 IV. 9 和 V. 42。

This is a combination of the word for "foot" or "feet" on the left, and the word for "each"
or "every" on the right. The sound is derived from the latter word. See IV. 9 and V. 42.

嗣

18

sì/*Ssû*₄

嗣　　嗣　　厶

継承；子嗣

To inherit; heirs

由三个字组成。左上为"口"，其下为"册"。参见 II. 29，116。右部为"司"，表示主管。后辈继承爵位时，须在宗祠里朗读皇家的文书。音切"司"（下文 19）。

This is a combination of three words. The word for "mouth" is upper left, and the word for "documents" is below it. See II. 29, 116. On the right is the word for "to be in charge of". When the heirs inherited their dukedoms, the imperial documents had to be read in their ancestral temples. It is pronounced like 19 below.

司

19

sī/*Ssû*

司

主管
To be in charge of

为反写的"后"（V. 52）。表示与君主面朝相同的方向，故暗指其为君主的代表或大臣，主管皇家事务。

This word is the same as the word in V. 52 except that it is turned over. This indicates that the person is facing the same direction as the king, which implies that he is a delegate or minister of the king taking charge of imperial affairs.

拘

20

jū/*Chü*₁

拘

制止，拘捕，拘留，追随
To restrain, to seize, to arrest, to adhere

字义表示"用手制止"。参见 II. 39。音同右部"句"（下文 21）。

"To stop with the hand" is the idea of this word. See II. 39. The pronunciation is the same as the word in 21 below, which is the right hand portion.

句

21

句 句 ㄐ

jù/*Chü*₄

曲 线 ， 句 子 ； 钩 住
A curve, a sentence; to hook

音切"口"。两曲线为另一字"ㄐ"，表示弄弯或弯曲。古代以微曲的线表示完整表述之结束，如同今之句号或逗号。由此表示"句子"之意。参见下文 22。

This is pronounced like the word for "mouth". The other two curved lines form another word meaning "curved" or "curvature". In ancient times a slight hook was used to mark the end of a complete expression, as we put a dot or period today. From this the idea of "a sentence" arose. See 22 below.

钩（钩）

22

gōu/*Kou*₂

钩子

A hook

上文 21 和 22 原来都读作 gōu，但"句"后曲音作 jù。左部为"金"，表示钩子为金属制成。参见 X. 4。

"Kou" is the original sound of both 21 and 22, but by an inflection it came to be read as "Chǔ". Here a hook made of metal is designated by the radical for "metal" on the left. See X. 4.

* 据《说文》，"句"古音总如钩。

后人句曲音钩（gōu），章句音屦（jù）。又改句曲字为勾。

博

23

bó/*Po*₅

广博的，充足的

Extensive, ample

原意指"广阔地展开"。左部"十"表示繁多而量大。参见 I. 18。右部表声，参见下文 24 的释义。

"Broadly spread" was the original idea of this word. The word for "ten" on the left implies manifoldness and multiplicity. See I. 18. The pronunciation is derived from the word on the right which is explained in 24 below.

尃

24

𣄰　　ㄆ　　　fū/*Pu*₅

4 寸

A measurement of four inches

由两个字组成，"寸"（III. 9）和"甫"（下文 25）。

This is a combination of two words, the word for "inch" in III. 9 and the word in 25 below.

甫

25

甫 ㄈㄨ

$f\check{u}/Fu_3$

"风格"或姓名，

对 长 辈 ， 尤 其 是 老 年 男 性 的 尊 称

A "style" or name,

a title of respect for elders, especially old men

上部"父"表声，下部为"用"。参见 III. 7 和 IV. 16。作假借字，表"开始；刚才，最近；重要的，大的，有名的"。"博"（上文 23）的字义"广博"，其来源只合解释为长者或尊者的学识，即梵文的 pramana——常是明智而博大的。

The word for "father" on top gives the sound, and the word for "to employ" is below it. See III. 7 and IV. 16. As a borrowed word it means "to begin; just now, recently; great, large, eminent". We cannot but explain the origin of the sense "extensive" for the word Po in 23 above as coming from the idea that the measurement of the knowledge— in Sanskrit *pramana* — of old or respectable persons was wide and broad.

警

26

jǐng/*Ching*₃

警告，告诫，警醒

To warn, to caution, to arouse

原意指"用言语告诫"。下部为"言"（参见 VII. 4）。上部为"敬"（参见下文 27）。

"To caution someone with words" was the original idea of this word. See VII. 4 for the lower portion. The word on top is explained in 27 below.

敬

27

jìng/*Ching*₄

尊敬，崇敬，恭敬

To respect, to reverence, to honour

由"攴"（上文 6）和"苟"（下文 28）两个字组成，表示"约束或控制自己"，右部"攴"（表轻拍）表意。

This is a combination of two words, 6 above and 28 below, which gives the idea "to restrain or to control oneself", which is suggested by the word for "beating" on the right.

苟 **28**

苟 ₄¹ jì/Chi₅

小 心 的 ， 谨 慎 的 ， 恭 敬 的 ， 急 迫 的

Careful, watchful, respectful, urgent

为前面两个字的字源。上部为"祥"的简体，由"羊"字演化而来；下部为"口"被"包"住，紧闭而克制——即闭口不言。参见 II. 29，55，122。合而表示"慎言"。有别于下文 29，但现代书体中往往写法一样。

This is a word from which the two foregoing words were derived. On top is an abbreviated form of the word for "auspice", derived from the word for "sheep"; below it is the word for "mouth", but "enclosed and restrained" — i.e., to hold one's tongue. See II. 29, 55, 122. This combination means "to be good and careful in one's talk". This word must be distinguished from the word in 29 below, which is usually written in the same form in modern script.

苟

29

gǒu/*Kou*₃

不小心的，不正当的；如果，只，如若

Careless, illicit; if, only, if indeed

上部为"艸"，亦表示"粗笨"或"粗糙"之意；下部为"句"，表声。参见 IV. 114 和上文 21。"a"为古体，中有"艹"（莽）字。参见 IV. 117。

The word for "grass", on top here, has also the sense of "rustic" or "rough"; below it is the word for "hook", which has the same sound. See IV. 114 and 21 above. In the Archaic Script, given in "a", the word "mang" is used. See IV. 117.

誼（谊）

30

yì/I₄ → $yì/I_4$

合宜之物；仁义

That which is suitable; righteousness

原意指"言语适宜"。参见 VII. 4，5。右部"宜"表声，字义延伸指任何正当行为、善举，或正确的意思。

"The fit saying or words" was the original sense of this word. See VII. 4, 5. The sound is derived from the word on the right, and the meaning has been extended to include "any right action or virtuous conduct, or correct meaning".

晨

31

chén/Ch'ên₁ → $chén/Ch'ên_1$

破晓，早晨

Daybreak, morning

上部"臼"暗示"黑暗将散去",下部"辰"表示"夜里第五个时辰"(即早上 7 点至 9 点),亦表声。参见下文 47。

The use of the word Ch'u on top implies that the "darkness has lifted", and the word below it, meaning "the fifth period from midnight" (that is, 7 a.m. to 9 a.m.) gives the sound. See 47 below.

辰

32

chén/*Ch'en*₁

时 辰

A measure of time

象形字,原意指"妊娠"。上两横和左竖共同表示人形,下部"壬"表示怀孕。假借作为数量词,表示年、月或日之辰。由于此用法流传甚广,而失其原意,故在壬左边加"女"旁,组成一新字,表示"怀孕"。参见下文 33。

This is a pictograph originally meaning "pregnant". The two horizontal lines on the top combined with the vertical line on the left represent the form of a man, and the lower part is the word for "pregnancy". But as a borrowed word it is used as a numeral to denote a year or a month or a period of the day. Because this use prevailed, its original meaning was lost, and another word for "pregnant" was coded with a radical for "woman" added on the left of the original word. See 33 below.

娠

33

娠

shēn/*Ch'en*₁

妊娠，怀孕

Pregnant, having conceived

该字的历史演变，参见上文 32。

See 32 above for the history of this word.

晨

34

chén/*Ch'en*₁

晨

破晓，早晨
Daybreak, morning

应注意，字义与"晨"（上文 31）相同。中间带点的三个圈代表天蝎座，在中国，这几颗星星在晨光中格外明亮。此字也表示"明亮"或"光辉"，可能指其星群中最亮的天蝎座白星。"a"的上部替换为"日"字。

Note that this word has the same meaning as 31 above. The three circles with dots inside represent the stars of Scorpio, which are bright in the morning sky in China. This word means "bright" or "brilliancy", perhaps referring to Antares, the most brilliant star in the constellation. In "a", this word is written with the word for "sun" on top instead.

堅（坚）

35

jiān/*Chien*₂

坚实的，坚强的，坚固的，倔强的

Solid, strong, durable, obstinate

原意指"硬土"。音从上部"臤"（下文 36）。

The original sense of this word was "hard soil". The sound is derived from the word on top, 36 below.

臤

36

qiān/*K'êng*

紧紧抓住，紧握

A firm grasp, a tight grip

右部为"手"。音切左部"臣"（下文 37）。

On the right is the word for "hand". The sound is derived from the word on the left, 37 below.

臣

37

臣　臣　ㄔㄣ

臣服于；臣子，大臣

To be subject to; a subject, a minister

象形字，象人深鞠躬。

This is a pictograph showing a man bowing low.

賢（贤）

38

賢　賢　ㄒㄧㄢ

chén/*Chêng*₁

xián/*Hsien*₂

才能；贤德的，可敬的，贤良的

Talent; virtuous, worthy, good

该字表示"赠人以财富为贤德之举"。上部"臤"表声（上文36）；下部"贝"亦表示财富。参见 IV. 152。

"To impart wealth to others is a virtuous act" is the explanation for this word. The sound is derived from the word on top, 36 above; the word below it has also the meaning of "wealth". See IV. 152.

豎 （竖）　　　　　　　　　39

豎 豎 ㄕ
ㄨ

shù/*Shu*₄

竖立，建立；竖直的，直立的
To set up, to establish;
upright, perpendicular

原意指"稳稳立着"。下部"豆"表声，象直立的祭祀用具。参见 II. 69。

The original sense of this word was "to stand firmly". The sound is derived from the word on the bottom, which represents a sacrificial vessel that is always set upright. See II. 69.

整

40

zhěng/*Chêng*₃

整 㞢

整齐，整理

To put right, to set in order

下部为"正"（III. 2）；上部"敕"的释义参见下文 41。

On the bottom is the word for "upright", III. 2; the word on top is explained in 41 below.

敕

41

chì/*Ch'ih*₅

敕

皇帝的敕令

Imperial orders

原意指"发出命令或告诫"。会意字，由"束"（IV. 123）和"攴"（上文 6）
两个字组成。

"To give instructions or warnings" was the original sense of this word. It is an ideative formed by the combination of two words, IV. 123 and 6 above.

政

42

政　　政　　止乙

zhèng/*Chêng*₄

管 辖 ， 统 治 ； 政 治
To rule, to govern; politics

音同左部"正"。参见 III. 2 和上文 6。

The pronunciation of this word is the same as the word on the left. See III. 2 and 6 above.

改

43

gǎi/*Kai*₃

变更，改变，改正，改革

**To alter, to change,
to correct, to reform**

左部为象形字"已"（II. 154 a），表示"以……方式"或"使用"。右部"攴"亦表示"用手采取行动"，暗示更正之意。

On the left is the harmonic word meaning "by means of" or "to use", II. 154 a. The word on the right means also "the hand performing an action", by which correction is implied.

鼓

44

gǔ/*Ku*₃

鼓；击鼓

A drum; to beat drums

原意指"击鼓"，由右部"攴"（表击打）表意。左部"壴"表声（下文 68）。

The original sense of this word was "to beat a drum", clearly shown by the word on the right, "to beat". The sound is derived from the word on the left, 68 below.

教

45

鼓　教　ㄐ一ㄠ

jiào/*Chiao*₄

讲授，指导；教育，宗教

To teach, to instruct;
education, religion

原意指"上所施，下所效"。音从左部"孝"。参见下文 50。

"What is given by those above and followed as an example by those below" is the original explanation of this word. The sound is derived from the word on the left. See 50 below.

學（学）

46

xué/*Hsioh*₅

觉悟，学习；学识

To learn, to study; scholarship

原释义为"唤醒或启蒙"。由"教"（上文 45）加两个部首"臼"（表提起，下文 47）和"冖"（表覆盖，下文 48）组成。声从"臼"字演化而出。

"To awaken and to enlighten" is the original explanation of this word. Two more signs have been added to the word in 45 above, meaning "to uplift" "the covering", 47 and 48 below. The sound is derived from the former.

臼（臼）

47

jiù/*Chu*₃

提起

To uplift

象形字，象双手提物。字形为反"廾"（IV. 37）。

This is a pictograph showing both hands lifting something. It is an inverted form of IV. 37.

48

mì/*Mi*$_5$

覆盖；遮盖物

To cover; the covering

象形字。

This is a pictograph.

49

yáo/*Hsao*$_1$

交错，交织

To cross, to intermingle

象《易经》中八卦或六十四卦的横线，或断或续。

This word represents the horizontal lines, whether whole or broken, in the trigrams or hexagrams of the *Book of Changes*.

学

50

xué/*Hsiao*~5~

模 拟 ， 效 仿

To imitate, to emulate

形声字，可能为"學"（上文 46）的古体。上部"爻"（上文 49）表声。

This is a harmonic word, probably the word in 46 above in Archaic Script. The sound is derived from the upper portion, 49 above.

效

51

lǐ/*Li*₅

美丽

Beautiful

字形为交叉线图案，象窗户交纹之形。字形为"尔"的古体。参见下文 52。字义表"美丽"，现已很少使用。

This shows a design of cross lines, as used in a window. It is a form of the word Erh in the Archaic Script. See 52 below. As a word it means "beautiful", but it is now rarely used.

［你］

52

你

ěr/*Êrh*₃

于是，如此，所以

Thus, it is so, so

爾（尔）

句末助词，有时用作疑问词。由三部分组成：上部为"入"字；从下至上的竖画，表示向上之运动；左右各一撇的"八"，表示分开。参见 I. 10，16。气息及声音散去，即表示一句话结束。假借字，常用作代词，指"你"或"你的"。现在的"你"字是上文"尔"左边加"人"旁，但未收入许慎的字典。古文中常写为"a"，由上文的"尔"加交纹之形。"a"原意指"窗户上美丽的纹饰"。

This is a final particle, sometimes used as an interrogative. It is a combination of three signs: the word for "to enter" on top; the vertical line written from bottom to top, showing an upward movement; and the word for "division" on both sides. See I. 10, 16. The breath and hence the sound having been dispersed indicates the end of a sentence. As a borrowed word it is used as a pronoun meaning "you" or "your". The word used now meaning "you" has a classifier for "man" added on the left of the above form, but it is not found in Hsu Shên's Dictionary. In ancient texts this word is always given in the form shown in "a", designs of cross lines added to the above form. The original sense of "a" was "the beauty of window decoration".

雁

53

yàn/*Yen*₄

野 鹅

The wild goose

[鴈]

a

b

大雁常排成"人"字形，在寒冷的季节南飞，转暖后又北归，故而有人旁。中部为一只"隹"(表飞禽)。左上曲线"厂"表声。参见 II. 15，24，135。"a"中有"鸟"字。此字与 [ ] 中的字体，今已不加区分。参见 II. 137。"b"为更简化的字体。

The wild geese are arrayed like the word for "man", flying south in cold weather and north in hot weather, so this word is used. A "bird" is also drawn inside. The sound is derived from the curved line on the top left. See II. 15, 24, 135. In "a" the word for "fowl" is used. This word and the word in parenthesis are used today without distinction. See II. 137. "b" is a more abbreviated form.

*徐灏《段注笺》："凡远举高飞者，为鸿雁，为鳱鹅；养驯者，为鹅，为舒雁。古多通用。《礼经》单言雁者，即人所畜之鹅。"

瞿

54

*jù/Ch'ü*₁

鹰隼之视；惊视

The gaze of a bird; to gaze at

a   b

由二"目"在"隹"（表鸟）上会意。表示鹰和其他食肉飞禽。参见 II. 135。
"a"中双目正左右张望。

Two "eyes" are pictured above the word for "bird". This word refers to eagles and other
birds of prey. See II. 135. In "a" the eyes are looking towards the left and the right.

舒 55

舒 ㄕㄨ

shū/*Shu*₁

放松，伸展，展开

To relax, to stretch, to unroll

左部"舍"表声，右部"予"表给或拿之意。参见 II. 110 和 IV. 228。

The pronunciation is derived from the word on the left, while the word on the right represents the idea of giving and taking. See II. 110 and IV. 228.

剥（剝） 56

剥 ㄅㄛ

bō/*Po*₅

剥落，割羊毛，刻

To peel, to fleece, to cut

ₐ

左部为"录"（下文 57）。右部为"刀"字。参见 II. 85。有时亦写作"a"，左部"卜"表意，亦表声。参见 II. 59。

The sound is derived from the word on the left, 57 below. The "knife" is on the right. See II. 85. This word is sometimes written as given in "a", since the word on the left gives its meaning and pronunciation. See II. 59.

彔 （录）   **57**

lù/Lu_5

刻 木

To carve wood

象形字，亦为"剥"（上文 56）的古体。

This is a pictograph, and also an antique form of the word Po in 56 above.

"《投注》："象丁云，'刻木录录也'，破裂之音。"

劃（划）

58

ㄏㄨㄚ

huá, huà/*Hua*₄

划开，分割，刻画，标记

To rive, to divide, to cut, to mark

用刀或锥划破或分割。参见 II. 85。左部"画"表声。参见 V. 35。"a"取自古体。

A knife or an awl is used to rive or divide. See II. 85. The word on the left gives the sound. See V. 35. "a" is from the Archaic Script.

劑（剂）

59

ㄐㄧ

jì/*Tsi*₄

剪齐，调整，制药剂；一剂

To trim, to adjust,
to compound medicines; a dose

原意指"用刀剪齐"。字音与左部"齐"（III. 36）基本相同，但有变调。

"To cut evenly with a knife" was the original meaning of this word. The pronunciation is almost the same as the word on the left, III. 36, but with an inflection of the tone.

刺

60

cì/*Tz'u*$_4$

刺伤，杀死

To stab, to kill

左部"朿"表意，亦表声。参见 V. 9。

The word on the left gives the idea and the sound. See V. 9.

＊据《说文》，君主杀死大夫叫刺。

可

61

kě/*K'o*₃

可能，可以；能够

May, can; able

助动词或动词，源于自然的叹气声；象气息自"口"中散出。参见 I. 23 和 II. 29。

This is an auxiliary verb or verb originally derived from a sound exclamatory in nature; the picture shows the breath coming out from the "mouth". See I. 23 and II. 29.

吁

62

xū/*Hsü*₁

类似"哎"的感叹词

An interjection something like "alas"

右部"于"表示气息上升，故暗示从"口"中发出叹气声。参见 V. 5。

The sound of a sigh escaping from the "mouth" is indicated by the word on the right, which represents the breath going upwards. See V. 5.

恺（恺）

63

kǎi/*K'ai*₃

和善的，康乐的，高兴的，安乐的

Kindly, joyful, delighted, contented

左部"心"旁为后加；最初写作下文 64。参见 II. 38b。

The classifier for "heart" on the left is a later addition; originally this word was written like the word in 64 below. See II. 38b.

豈（岂）

64

qǐ/Ch'i₃ (K'ai₃)

军队得胜或凯旋时演奏的乐曲

Music played at a victory
or triumphant return of an army

假借字，现在指"如何"。由下文 65 和 68 的简体组成。

Used as a borrowed word this word now means "how". It is a combination of the abbreviated
forms of the words in 65 and 68 below.

微

65

wēi/Wei₁

细微的

Subtle

上文 64 的上部取自该字，该字又由下文 66 和 67 组成。

The upper portion of the word in 64 above is taken from this word, which is again a combination of 66 and 67 below.

66

duān/*Chuan*$_2$

顶 端；独 自，唯 一

The heading; alone; solely

象植物刚破土出芽之形，故表示微小，横线表示土地；其下表示根系。原为名词，现常用作副词。

The picture of the sprouts of a plant just appearing above the earth, which is indicated by the horizontal line in the middle, gives the idea of "minuteness"; the roots are shown below the line. Originally a noun, it is now used often as an adverb.

攸 67

yōu/*Yu*₂

悠远的，遥远的；很长时间

Fai-reaching, distant; for a long time

原意指"使水平稳地流行"，但"水"字只保留了中间竖笔。"a"省去"人"旁，"水"字则完整保留。虚词，指"那样""由此"。

The original sense of this word was "conducting water in a peaceful flow", but only the middle line is left of the word for "water". In "a" the word for "man" has been omitted but the entire word for "water" remains. As an expletive it meant "that which", "whereby".

壴 68

zhù/*Shu*₄

演奏乐器

A display of musical instruments

象陈设鼓乐，既立则远而可见。为庆祝胜利而奏乐，总是让人"满足"，故"微微"感到快乐。该字可参阅上文 63，64，65。

The picture represents musical instruments displayed, set upright and visible at a distance. Joy is always something "subtle" and that felt at a musical performance celebrating a victory makes one "contented". This word refers back to 63, 64, and 65 above.

69

jǐng/*Tsing*₃

陷阱，深井

A pitfall, a pit

左部为"阜",表山丘或土堆；右部为"井",表声。捕兽的陷阱往往设在丘
陵地带。参见 II. 18, 81。"a"上部为"穴"。参见 II. 158。"b"为古体,加
"水"旁,表示井中有水。参见 II. 9。

The word for "hill" or "mound" is on the left; the "well" on the right has the same
pronunciation as this word. A pit for wild animals is usually dug in hilly terrain. See II. 18, 81.
In "a" the word for "hole" is on top. See II. 158. In "b", which is in the Archaic Script, the
word for "water" has been added, showing that water is within the well. See II. 9.

饗（饟） 70

xiǎng/*Hsiang*₃

饟食，享用

To offer food in a ceremony,
or to enjoy it

上半部为"乡"字，表乡下，而乡下的某些场合，长者会一起聚餐；故底部加"食"字。参见 V. 33 和 IV. 84。该字与"a"可通用。其上部为"高"的简体，下部表示"供奉的食物"。"b"中对称的两部分为"高"的简体，表示祭祀时供奉的神和王。参见 II. 111。

The top half of this word is the word for "country districts", where on certain occasions the elders gathered for feasts; hence the word representing "food" has been added below it. See V. 33 and IV. 84. The above word and "a" are mutually interchangeable. On top is an abbreviated form of the word for "high" and the form on the bottom indicates "the food offered". In "b" the two opposing halves are abbreviated forms of the word for "high", by which God and King were designated in the sacrificial offerings. See II. 111.

馈（馈）

71

kuì/*K'uei*₄

祭 献 食 物

To make a present of food

左部为"食"旁，右部为"鬼"（表祖先的魂魄），表声。但凡节日须向祖先献祭。"鬼"表示"魂魄"，现在仅用来指"鬼魂"或"鬼怪"，而其原意"祭献食物"则引申为赠礼给他人。

On the left is the classifier for "food" and on the right is the word for "the departed sould of ancestors", from which the sound is derived. An offering is made to the ancestors on any festive occasion. But the word for "departed souls" has now degenerated to mean only "ghosts" or "demons", and the original sense of offering food has been enlarged to mean the offering of any gift to anyone.

勺（勺）   72

sháo/Sho₅

长柄勺，（杯）把

A ladle, a handle (as of a cup)

象"长柄木勺"，据考古研究，其形如杯，口径长6寸深3寸（中国古代的度量），中部直径3寸，柄长24寸，漆为红色。参见 II. 91 和 V. 6。

The picture represents "a wooden ladle", which, according to archaeological researches, was a cup-shaped ladle six inches — by ancient Chinese measurement — in diameter at the mouth, three inches deep and three inches in diameter in the middle, with a handle twenty-four inches long, lacquered red. See II. 91 and V. 6.

梁

73

梁

梁

ㄌㄧㄤ

liáng/Liang₂

跨溪的桥，横梁，桥梁

A bridge over a brook,
a beam, a ridge

ₐ 梁

字中有"水"和"木"；右上部"刅"（"创"的简写）表声。"a"为古体，有
二"木"，其间横线表示桥。

The words for "water" and "wood" are here; the sound is derived from the word in the upper
right portion, which is an abbreviated form of the word meaning "to create". In "a", which is
in the Archaic Script, two words for "wood" are used, and the line between them indicates
the bridge.

剙（创）　　　　　　　　　74

chuàng/*Ch'uang*₃

创造，创建，发明

To create, to make, to invent

原意指"挖井"；右部"㓞"表声。参见 III. 14。

"To dig a well" was the original sense of this word; the word on the right gives the pronunciation. See III. 14.

貧（贫）　　　　　　　　　75

pín/*P'in*₁

贫穷，贫困

Poor, impoverished

上部为"分"（表分开的），表声，也指减少；下部为"贝"，表示钱，也指
财富。参见 IV. 70，152。

The word for "divided" on top from which the sound is derived means also "lessened";
below it is the word for "money" or "coins" which means also "wealth". See IV. 70, 152.

贵（贵）

76

guì/*Kuei*₄

高贵的，贵族的，珍贵的，贵重的

Honourable, noble,
precious, expensive

原意指"物不贱"，即"贵重"等意。上部"臾"表声，其释义参见下文 77。
"a"为占体，应另有起源。"a"取自竹简，"b"则为同一字的另一书体，下
部多加一短横，上部竖画和两撇可能表示头巾上的贵重饰品。该字形的另一
用法参见下文 78a。

The original sense of this word was "things that are not cheap"; that means "expensive", etc. The word on top gives the sound, which is explained in 77 below. "a" is Archaic Script, and must be of another origin. It is copied from the bamboo slips, differing from "b", which is another form of the same word, in having one more short stroke underneath. The vertical line and the two curved lines on top probably indicate precious ornaments on a turban. See 78a below for another use of this form.

史（蕢）

77

kuì/*Kuei*₄

草编的篮或筐

A basket or casket made of grass

古体的象形字。此草筐用来提物，较大者可装运土。草筐本身很简朴，但与"贝"（表钱财）组合后，表示须花重金购买，故而指贵重之物，如上文76。

This is a pictograph in the Archaic Script. This type of basket is used for carrying things, and if large, for carrying earth. It is a simple thing, but when this form is combined with the idea of "money", meaning that much money is required to purchase it, an expensive object is meant, as in 76 above.

妻

78

妻　妻　ㄑ一

qī/*Ts'i*₁

法定的妻子

A legal wife

a

小篆体由两个字组成：上部为"捷"（下文 79）的简体，其下为"女"，表示一妇人正在"留心"服侍。"a"为古体；"女"在"贵"（上文 76b）之下。

This is in the Minor Script, a combination of two words: an abbreviated form of the word in 79 below on top, and the word for "woman" below it, signifying a woman "alert" in her services. "a" is Archaic Script; the word for "woman" is below the form given in 76b.

捷

79

*jié/Ts'ieh*₅

ㄗㄧㄝ

警觉的，敏捷的，迅速的，聪明的，机灵的

Alert, nimble, prompt, clever, smart

a

"妻"（上文 78）音切捷，稍有变调。原意指"草迅速生长"。"a"为另一字体，表示织布机的脚踏板。该字由三部分组成。

This word gives the pronunciation to the word in 78 above with a slight inflection. "The prompt growth of grass" was its original sense. "a" is another form of this word which represents the foot pedals on a weaving machine. It is a combination of three forms.

冒

80

mào/*Mao*₄

蒙眼前行，冒险，冒昧行事

To go forward with the eyes covered,
to risk, to rush upon

参见 II. 25 和 III. 29。

See II. 25 and III. 29.

最

81

zuì/*Ts'ou*₄

武力取得

To take by violence

参见 III, 29 和下文 125。

See III. 29 and 125 below.

寶（宝）

bǎo/*Pao*₃

珍宝，财宝；宝贵的

A jewel, a treasure; precious

由四个字组成。参见 II. 70，157，160 和 IV. 152。音切"缶"字（II. 70）。"a"
为古体，省去"贝"旁。"b"至"f"均取自古青铜器。

This word is a combination of four forms. See II. 70, 157, 160, and IV. 152. The
pronunciation is in accordance with the word Hou in II. 70. In "a", which is in the Archaic
Script, the word for "shells" has been omitted. "b–f" are all taken from the ancient bronzes.

窃（窃）

83

窃　ㄊㄧㄝ

qiè/*Ts'ieh*₅

偷；盗窃，偷窃

To steal; theft, larceny

原意可由字形看出，"一动物在米窖中挖洞偷吃"。蠕虫也包括在"动物"的总称之下。参见 II. 63，158 和 IV. 1。各部分合而表声。

This form represents the original sense of the word, "an animal stealthily digging a hole into a cache of rice and eating it". Worms are also included in the general term "animals". See II. 63, 158 and IV. 1. The pronunciation is a composite of the sounds of the component parts.

室

84

室　ㄕ

shì/*Shih*₅

房间，宁

A room, a home

由人"至"（表进入和居住）"宀"中（表房间）会意，由"至"表音。参见 II. 157 和 III. 23。

The "house" where one "enters and dwells" is the idea of this word, while the word for "to enter" gives its pronunciation. See II. 157 and III. 23.

害

85

hài/*Hai*₄, ₅

弄伤，损害；伤害

To injure, to do harm to; injury

底部为"口"（表言语），顶部为"宀"（表房屋），故传统释义为：惹事生非之言常起于家里。中部的"丰"表声。参见 II. 58。

The traditional explanation for this word is that the word for "mouth" on the bottom represents "words", which cause many troubles, and that these usually begin in the "family", represented by the word for "house" on top. The pronunciation is derived from the word in the middle. See II. 58.

定

86

dìng/*Ting*₄

固 定 ， 安 定 ， 决 定
To fix, to settle, to decide

由两个字组成，"宀"（II. 157）和"正"（III. 2）。字义明晰；中间"正"字表声。

This is a combination of two words, II. 157 and III. 2. The idea is clear; the pronunciation is

derived from the word in the center.

两

87

liǎng/*Liang*₃

中 国 古 代 重 量 单 位 一 两 ， 等 于 2 4 铢 ；

亦 表 示 一 双 ， 一 对 ； 两 个 都

One ounce

in ancient Chinese measurement,

equal to 24 grains;

also, a pair, a couple; both

両

由 "一" 和 "a" 组成，后者同声。"a" 现已弃用，由上文 "两" 代替。象形字，表示 "双方保持平衡"，由此指 "平分" 和 "一双" 等意。"b" 与 "a" 相似。

This is a combination of the word for "one" and the word in "a", which has the same pronunciation. "a" is now obsolete and the word above is used in its stead. It is a pictograph showing "a balance hanging on both sides", hence the idea of "equal division" and "a pair", etc. "b" is similar to "a".

敝

88

bì/*Pi*$_4$

破败的，贫穷的，无价值的

Worn-out, poor, unworthy

左部 "㡀" 表声，原意指 "破败的衣服"。参见 V. 23 和上文 6。

This word has the same pronunciation as the word on the left, which originally meant "worn-out clothing". See V. 23 and 6 above.

保

89

bǎo/*Pao*₃

保护，保证，养育，看护
**To protect, to guarantee,
to nourish, to nurse**

左部为"人"旁，右部表声，为下文 90a 的简体。参见 II. 24。

Here the classifier for "man" is on the left and the pronunciation is derived from the word on the right, which is an abbreviated form of the word in 90a below. See II. 24.

孚

90

fú/*Fu*₁

孵蛋；诚信
To brood over eggs; confidence

原读作 bǎo。会意字，表示鸟孵蛋时用"爪"在蛋上翻动；下部"子"表示后代。参见 II. 49，107。"诚信"之意源于"孵蛋"，因为如期发生的事会激发信任。"a"为古体，下部左右两撇表示"蛋"。

This word was originally pronounced Pao. It is an ideative showing that the "claws" on top are turning the eggs while the bird is brooding; "offspring" is meant by the word in the lower half. See II. 49, 107. The meaning of "confidence" comes from the sense "to brood over eggs" because any event which takes place at the appointed time inspires confidence. In "a", which is Archaic Script, "eggs" are represented by the two strokes on each side of the lower word.

91

仲

zhòng/*Chung*₄

三个或四个兄弟中的老二，
或一季度中的第二个月

The second of either three or four brothers
or the second month of any season

中

该字两种用法都表示位于"中"（表中间）；中表意，亦表声。参见 II. 24 和
III. 1。

Both the usages of this word have the idea of being in the "middle"; the word with this
meaning has the same sound. See II. 24 and III. 1.

伍

92

wǔ/*Wu*₃

伍 X

五人为伍，五家为比，伙伴
A file of five men,
a group of five families, a comrade

参见 I. 13 和 II. 24。

See I. 13 and II. 24.

什

93

什 什 尸

shí/*Shih*₅

十人为联，十家为联

A file of ten soldiers,
a group of ten families

据许慎，该字亦表示以十人或十户为单位相保相安。参见 I. 18 和 II. 24。

According to Hsu shên this word means also "to give guarantee to each other among the ten" members or families for mutual protection and security. See I. 18 and II. 24.

＊《段注》："《族师职》曰：五家为比，十家为联，
五人为伍，十人为联，使之相保相安。"

佰

94

băi/*Pê*₅

一百；百夫长

A hundred; a centurion

亦表示"百人之队长"。参见 II. 24 和 IV. 215。

This word means also "a leader of one hundred men". See II. 24 and IV. 215.

化

95

huà/*Hua*₄, ₂

熔化，转化，变化，教化

To smelt, to transform,
to change, to influence

a

右部"匕"为倒"人"，表示"改变"或"去世"，亦表声。"a"字形更为简化。

The word on the right is the sign for "man" inverted, meaning "changed" or "dead". It gives its pronunciation to the word. "a" is an even simpler form.

係（系） 96

xì/Hi₄

属于，捆绑，相联系，是

To belong to, to bind, to be attached to, to be, is, are

传统字义为"是"，因人说"就是这个"，暗示"属于""捆绑"等意。参见 IV. 176。

The conventional sense of "to be" comes from the idea that when we say "it is this", it implies "to belong to", "to bind", etc. See IV. 176.

倾（倾）

97

qīng/*Ch'ing*₂, ₃

倾倒，倾覆，危及

To upset, to be overthrown, to endanger

右部为"顷"字（IV. 35），表示"偏斜，偏向"。转注表示"倾倒"等意。

The word on the right is the word for "to lean, to incline", IV. 35. As a transmissive this word means "to upset", etc.

像

98

xiàng/*Siang*₄

外形，类似，形象；好像

Appearance, resemblance, image; like

上文所列均为引申意，原意指"形态或式样"，读作 yǎng。大象大而可识，故表示"外形"等意。然大象在中国很少见，故只能通过图画认识其样子，由此表"形象"等意。参见 II. 133。

The meanings given above are derivatives; the original sense of this word was "a form or pattern", and it was pronounced Yang. The elephant is a huge animal easily seen, so there came the idea of "appearance", etc. But since a living elephant is rarely seen in China, its appearance could only be known through pictures, so there came the idea of "image", etc. See II. 133.

僊 ［仙］ **99**

xiān/*Hsien*₂

长 生 不 老 、 升 天 离 去 的 人
"An immortal man transformed
who has left the mundane existence"

音同"a"，表示上升。a 的中上部"凶"（II. 27）表声。其余四部分合为一个字，表示"上升"。有时在下面加"巳"（表记号），如"b"。参见 IV. 37—39a。
This word has the same sound as "a", which means "to ascend". The sound is derived from the word in the upper middle portion of "a", II. 27. The other four parts form one word, meaning to "uplift". Sometimes another word for "token" is added beneath this word, as in "b". See IV. 37–39a.

製（制）

100

製 ㅗ

zhì/*Chih*₄

裁剪或制作（衣服）

To cut out or to make (as garments)

由"制"（IV. 66）和"衣"（II. 114）组成。

This is a combination of IV. 66 and II. 114.

覽（览）

101

覽 ㄌㄢ

lǎn/*Lan*₃

视察，近看，目击，细阅

To inspect, to look at,

to witness, to examine

由下部的"见"（IV. 104），和"监"（下文 102）的缩写组成，后者表声。

This is a combination of the word for "to see" on the bottom, IV. 104, and a condensed form of the word in 102 below, from which the pronunciation is derived.

监（監）

102

*jiān/Chien*₂

视察，监督

To inspect, to oversee

形声字，表示派人居上监督典礼，如祭祀时宰羊。参见 III. 25 和上文 37。

This is a harmonic word representing a delegated person supervising a ceremony from above, such as the slaughtering of sheep in a sacrifice. See III. 25 and 37 above.

息

103

xī/*Hsi*₅

息　厶

休息，停息，叹息，喘息
To rest, to desist, to sigh, to breathe

象气自"心"经过鼻（"自"）呼出。参见 II. 28，38。假借为"休息"之意，因人长时间劳累后会长长地舒一口气，为完成一项工作而感到轻松。上部"自"表声。

This picture represents the "breath" coming out of the "heart" through the "nostrils". See II. 28, 38. The borrowed sense is "to rest", as sometimes one heaves a long sigh after an exertion, feeling relieved that a certain work has been done. The sound is derived from the upper part of the word.

愚

104

愚

yú/*Yü*₁

愚笨的，愚蠢的，粗鲁的，迟钝的，呆滞的

Stupid, doltish, rude, obtuse, dull

上部表示"一种红眼的长尾猴"。亦属会意字，由头形在"脚印"之上会意。可与 II. 134 比较。"心"字也表示"智识"。参见 II. 38。

On top is the word for "a kind of monkey with red eyes and a long tail". This is also an ideative made up of the head shape written above the "footprint". Compare with II. 134. The word for "heart" meant also the "mind". See II. 38.

忘

105

忘

wàng/*Wang*₂

忘记，不记得，疏忽

To forget, to be unmindful of, to neglect

原意指"不记得"或"不放在心上"。上部"亡"表声。参见 II. 38 和 IV. 36。

"The loss of mind" or "escaped from the heart" is the original idea of this word. The pronunciation is the same as the word on top. See II. 38 and IV. 36.

决 （決）

106

jué/*Chueh*₅

决 定， 决 口， 疏 通 （水 流）

To decide, to burst open, to clear (as waterways)

"分开"或"使分离"暗示"做出决定"。左边加"水"旁，表示治理水流和河道。参见 V. 43。

"To part" or "to be parted from" implies "to make a decision". To indicate the regulating of watercourses and rivers, the classifier for "water" has been added on the left. See V. 43.

洄

107

huí/*Hui*₁

涡流，旋涡

An eddy, a whirlpool

参见 II. 22a。

See II. 22a.

汲

108

jí/*Chi*₅

从井中汲水

To draw water from a well

由"及"（表触到）"水"会意。参见 IV. 30。

"To reach to" "water" is the idea of this word. See IV. 30.

濕（湿） 109

shī/*Shih*₅

潮湿的，湿气重的，湿润的
Wet, damp, moist

右上横线表示"用来覆盖的物体"。右上其余部分为"显"（下文 110）的简体，表声。右下部为"土"，左部为"水"。

The horizontal line on top of the right side indicates "that by which it is covered". The rest of the upper right portion is an abbreviated form of the word in 110 below, from which the sound is derived. The word for "earth" is below it and "water" is on the left side.

㬎（显） 110

xiǎn/*Hsien*₃

阳光中的微粒；微小的，明亮的
Motes in a sunbeam; minute, bright

原意指"在日光下检查丝线";如此其细微处也清晰可见。引申指"观察事物的细微处或细节"。转而亦表示"在阳光下晾晒"。参见 II. 1 和 IV. 177。

The original idea of this word was "to examine silk in sunlight"; when this is done the silk can be seen in great detail and clarity. By extension this has come to mean "seeing anything in minuteness and detail". By a turn of the idea it means also "to dry in the sunshine". See II. 1 and IV. 177.

泰

111

tài/*Tai*₄

高尚的，可敬的，广阔的，极度的
Exalted, honourable,
extensive, extreme

上文为假借意，均源自上部"大"字，表示"巨大"，亦表声。该字原意指"滑溜"，现在已不使用。由三个字组成。参见 II. 9，23 和 IV. 37。

The borrowed senses given above all derive from the word on top meaning "great", which has the same pronunciation. The original meaning of this word was "slippery", now fallen out of use. This is a combination of three words. See II. 9, 23 and IV. 37.

漁（渔）

112

yú/*Yü*₁

捕鱼

To fish

有时右部为双"鱼"，一上一下。鱼表声。参见 II. 145。

Sometimes the word for "fish" on the right is written in a double form, one on top and another beneath it. It gives the pronunciation. See II. 145.

冬

113

dōng/*Tung*₁

冬天
Winter

上部为"夂"（表终），读作 zhōng，表示一束下端或中间用绳束结的丝。下部为"仌"（表冰）。参见 II. 10。一年之终会结冰，即冬天。

On top is the form of a bundle of silk tied at the "end" by a line or band in the middle, pronounced Chung. Below it is the word for "ice". See II. 10. At the "end" of a year when there is ice, that is winter.

否

114

fǒu/*Fou*₃

不，没有，相反
No, not, on the contrary

许慎的字典中出现过两次，一次归入上部的"不"旁，一次归入下部的"口"旁。参见 II. 29 和 III. 24。

This word appeared twice in Hsu Shěn's Dictionary, once under the heading of the word on top and again under the heading of the word on the bottom. See II. 29 and III. 24.

聽（听）　　　　　　115

tīng/*T'ing*₄

听从，听见，听任

To listen to, to hear, to allow

右部为"悳"（下文 116），左上为"耳"（II. 26），耳德即"听见"。左下部"壬"表声。

The "virtue", the word on the right, 116 below, of the "ear", upper left, II. 26, is "to hear". The pronunciation is derived from the word on the lower left.

德

惪　德　㣻

116

dé/*Tê*₅

道德，优点

Virtue, goodness

许慎之释义为"外得于人，内得于己也"。上部"直"（IV. 105）表声；下部
"心"参见 II. 38。

"Externally at one with other men and internally at one with oneself"; this is Hsu Shên's
explanation. The sound is derived from the word on top, IV. 105; for the word on the
bottom see II. 38.

　　　　　　*依《说文》，"德、惪"分为二字，"德"释为"升"。

　　　　　　桂馥《义证》："古升，登，陟，得，德五字义皆同"。

　　　　　　古道德字，只作惪，俗字假借德为之。现"德"为正体，"惪"为异体。

閨（闺）

117

guī/*Kuei*₁

閨 閨 《乂乀

闺房，家中独立的阁楼

Women's apartments,

private quarters in family residences

由"门"（II. 78）和"圭"（下文 118）组成，后者表声。门或闺房象下文 118 所述的玉圭之形。

This is a combination of the word for "door", II. 78, and the word in 118 below, which gives the sound. The door or such a compartment is like the piece of jade described in 118 below.

圭

118

guī/*Kuei*₁

圭 圭

玉 圭

A jade baton

珪

a 珪　珪　　　　　　　　　　　　b 圭

玉圭上端为拱形，下端为方形。天子将玉圭封给诸侯，以此为贵族和权力的
凭据，管理分封的土地。天子所持之大玉圭则两端均为方形。因圭与土地有
关，故两个"土"重叠；有时在左边加"玉"旁，如"a"。参见 II. 160。

The top of the baton was arch-shaped and the lower portion was square. It was conferred
upon feudal princes by the emperor as a symbol of nobility and authority over the land
alloted for government. The emperor himself held a large baton square at both ends. Since
it was connected with the land, the word for "earth" is given doubled; sometimes another
word for "jade" was added on the left, as in "a". See II. 160.

插

119

插　插　　ㄔㄚ

chā/Ch'a₅

插进，刺入

To insert into, to stick into

左部"手"字表示动作;"舂"(下文 120)表意,音同舂。

The word for "hand" is on the left showing the action; the idea is derived from the word in 120 below, and the pronunciation is the same as that word.

120

chā/*Ch'a*₅

舂去麦皮

To separate the grain from the husk

象臼和杵棒之形;舂舂的动作表示相同的意思。参见 II. 67。

This is the picture of a mortar and pestle; the action indicated has the same idea. Cf. II. 67.

受

121

*shòu/Shou*₄

受

ㄕㄡ
ㄡ

接受，忍受，遭受

To receive, to endure, to suffer

由"爰"（IV. 56）和"舟"（II. 87）的简写组成，后者表声。象交付物体给下面的"手"，故表示"接受"之意。

This is a combination of the word P'iao, IV. 56, and an abbreviated form of Chou, II. 87, from which the sound is derived. The picture represents something being given to the "hand" below, hence the idea of "to receive".

授

122

shòu/*Shou*₄

给予，授予，传授

**To give to,
to confer upon, to transmit**

由"受"（上文 121）左边加"手"旁，表示授予的动作；音同受。

The classifier for "hand" has been added on the left of the word in 121 above, showing action; the pronunciation is also the same as that word.

姓

123

xìng/*Sing*₄

姓氏，民族

A surname, a clan

右部的"生"表声，有变调，亦表意。在远古时代，姓氏源自母亲居住地的名称，故左边加"女"。参见 II.45 和 IV. 119。

The word for "birth" on the right gives the sound with an inflection as well as the idea. In very ancient times the surname came from the name of the land where the mother resided, so the word for "woman" was added on the left. See II. 45 and IV. 119.

娶

124

qǔ/*Ch'ü*₄

娶妻

To marry

音同上部的"取"（表选取，下文 125）；下部为"女"。参见 II. 45。

On top is the word for "to take", 125 below, which has the same pronunciation; below it is the word for "girl". See II. 45.

取

qǔ/*Ch'ü*₃

取 得 ， 获 取 ， 捕 获
To take, to obtain, to take hold of

左部为"耳"，右部为"又"（表手）。原字义取自古代部落的习俗，战斗结束后会割下所杀敌人的左耳，供奉于祠堂内作为战利品和胜利的象征。参见 II. 26，39a。

The word for "ear" is on the left and the word for "hand" is on the right. The original idea came from the practice of the ancient tribes of cutting off the left ear of a slain enemy after a fight and offering it to the ancestral temples as a trophy and proof of triumph. See II. 26, 39a.

婚

126

hūn/*Hun*₁

婚 婚 ㄏㄨㄣ

结婚
To marry

婚礼常在黄昏举行，故右边为"昏"（下文 127）。音同昏。参见 II. 45。

A marriage ceremony usually takes place at dusk, so the word on the right, 127 below, is used. It is of the same pronunciation. See II. 45.

昏

127

hūn/*Hun*₁

昏 昏 ㄏㄨㄣ

黄昏，昏暗
Dusk, dark

由"氐"（VII.1）的简体和"日"（II. 1）组成，表示"日落"。

This is a combination of an abbreviated form of VII.1 and II. 1, meaning "the sun is setting".

姻

128

yīn/*Yin*₁

姻 亲

Marriage connections

原意指"女婿的家"。右部为"因"（下文 129），表示"原因，手段"等；即女人所依就的对象。音同因。参见 II. 45。

"The family of the son-in-law" was the original sense of this word, The word on the right, 129 below, means "a cause, a means"; i.e., the means which the daughter depends on. The sound is the same as this word. See II. 45.

因

129

yīn/*Yin*₁

> 原因，理由；因此，因为，由于
>
> A cause, a reason;
>
> for this reason, because, in consequence of

许慎之释义不甚恰当。江永之释义更为可信，谓"因"是"茵"（下文 130）的古体。

Hsu Shěn's explanation of this word is not satisfactory. The one given by Kiang Yun is nearer to the truth, that this word is the Archaic Script of the word in 130 below.

* "因"甲骨文为象形字，朱骏声《通训定声》引江永说"象茵蓐之形，中象缝线文理"。此义后又作"茵"。

茵

130

yīn/*Yin*₁

垫 子

A cushion

指车中以干草填塞的垫子，故上部为"艹"旁。椭圆形的笔画象布或皮革做垫子时缝合的接缝。因垫子可以支撑人，故表示可以依靠或作为基础之物，进而表示"原因"之意。

This is a kind of cushion filled with dried grass and used in a carriage, hence the radical on top. The lines within the oblong form represent the seams between the pieces of cloth or leather which were sewn together to make the cushion. As a cushion is something which gives one support, this word came to mean something that could be relied upon or used as a base, hence it gives the idea of a "cause".

婢

131

bì/*Pei*₄

年 轻 的 侍 女
A young maid-servant

由两个字组成，右部为"卑"（下文 132），指地位低下或下等，亦表声，左部为"女"旁（II. 45）。

This is a combination of two words, "low or inferior" on the right, 132 below, which gives the sound, and the radical for "girl" on the left, II. 45.

卑

132

bēi/*Pei*₁

卑 贱 的 ， 低 下 的 ， 谦 卑 的
Low, inferior, humble

许慎的释义似乎有误。根据该字与其他部首组合之用法，卑应表示"一种椭圆形酒器，有柄，单手可携"。较典礼中使用的其他金属制酒具，卑是日常用的普通器具，常为木质。象形字，现仅用作转注字，表示"低下，谦卑"等意。可参看另一表示酒器的字"尊"，现用作转注字，表示"尊敬的，可敬的"，等等。

Hsu Shên's explanation seems to be wrong. This form, through its use in other combinations, has been found to represent "an oval-shaped wine container with a handle, which can be taken by one hand". In contrast to other wine vessels made of metal used on ceremonial occasions, this is a commonplace one in daily use, usually made of wood. This is a pictograph, but it is now used only as a transmissive, giving the idea of inferiority, humbleness, etc. Cf. the other word for "wine vessel" used now as a transmissive meaning "respectable, reverenced, etc.".

娣

133

dì/*Ti*₄

妹妹，弟媳

A younger sister,
the wife of a younger brother

左部为"女"，右部为"弟"（下文 134），指年幼的兄弟，音同弟。姐妹视如兄弟一般。

The word for "girl" is on the left and the word for "younger brother", 134 below, is on the right, for which the sound is the same. A sister is considered the same as a brother.

*据《尔雅·释亲》，古代姐妹共嫁一夫，长者为姒，幼者为娣；
兄弟之妻互称，年幼的为娣。

弟

134

dì/*Ti*₄

弟弟，少年

A younger brother, a junior

原意指"用革缕束物的次序"。现在仅能从古体"a"中看出。由"韦"（表皮革）的简体加一撇（读作 yì）。参见 I. 21。上文的小篆体加一撇，表示捆。当次第之意用于指人，则表示次第而生，指兄弟中后生或年幼者。

The original sense of this word was "the serial order of bundles bound by leather strips".
This can only be seen now in "a", which is the Archaic Script of this word. It is the word for
"leather" in an abbreviated form with a dash added, pronounced Yih. See I. 21. In the Minor
Script above there is one more curve, symbolizing the bundle. When the idea of "serial
order" is applied to men, it has the sense of succession, and, referring to brothers, it indicates
the next or a younger brother.

韋（韦）　［圍（围）］　　　**135**

wéi/*Wei*₁

加工好的兽皮，皮革，皮带
Dressed hides, leather, a thong

音同中间的"口"（表围绕）。参见 II. 21。上部和下部合而为另一字"舛"，
表意。原意指"相违背或矛盾"，因为兽皮可"扭曲"或随意折叠。参见下文
136。"a"取自古体。

In the middle is the word for "enclosure", which has the same pronunciation. See II. 21. The combination of the forms above and below it forms another word from which the sense is derived. "To oppose or to contradict" was the original idea of this word, because hide can be "twisted" or folded one way or another. See 136 below. "a" is from the Archaic Script.

136

舛

chuǎn/*Ch'uan*₃

相对；相反，矛盾

To oppose; opposite to, contradictory

象二人背对背相互依靠。亦属会意字。

Two persons are pictured reclining with their backs toward each other. This is also an ideative word.

坪

137

坪 坪 ㄆㄥ

píng/*P'ing*₂

平原，平坦之地

A plain, a level place

左部为"土"，右部为"平"，表声。参见下文 138 和 I. 9。

The word for "earth" is on the left, and the word for "flat" which gives its pronunciation is on the right. See 138 below and I. 9.

平

138

吞 平 ㄆㄥ

píng/*P'ing*₂

平直的，平和的，平坦的，

平等的，公平的，平均的，平常的

Level, even, flat,

equal, just, average, common

由感叹词"兮"（V. 2）和上部指事字"一"组成，表示语气平直舒展。

This is a combination of an interjection, V. 2, with the indicative for "one" on top showing that the air going upwards levels out.

均

139

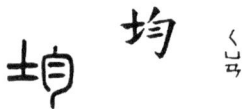

jūn/*Ch'ün*₁

平均 的 ；均 衡 ， 调 整

Equal; to balance, to adjust

左部为"土"字；右部为"匀"（下文 140），表声，字义相同。

The word for "earth" is on the left; the sound is derived from the word on the right, 140 below, which has the same idea.

匀

140

yún/*Yün*₁

平 均 的 , 均 匀 的 , 相 等

Equal, even, in equal parts

原意指"少";"二"在"勹"中,表示分开。物因二分而少。用作"均"(上文 139)的假借字,表示土地或土壤"平均"或"均匀"地展开。

The original idea of this word was "less"; the word for "two" inside the "fold" indicates division. When anything is divided, it becomes less than it was. It is used as a borrowed word for 139 above, meaning that the earth or soil is "equally" or "evenly" spread out.

城

141

chéng/*Ch'eng*₂

城 市

A city

a 　　　　　　　　　　　　　　b

音同右部的"成"（表完成）。由"茂"（下文 142）的简体加表声的象形字"丁"组成。参见 II. 60。"a"为大篆体，"土"字换作"郭"，表示"都城的外墙，其上筑有炮塔"。

The word for "accomplishment" is on the right with the same pronunciation. It is an abbreviated form of 142 below with the pictograph Ting added to give its sound. See II. 60. In "a", which is Major Script, the word for "earth" is substituted by the word Ku'o, meaning "the outer walls of a city on which turrets are built".

茂　　　　　　　　　　　　　142

茂　又

mào/*Mou*₄

繁 茂 的 ， 茂 盛 的 ， 丰 盛 的
Prosperous, flourishing, exuberant

形声字，下部"戊"表声。字义为"植物生长丰盛"。原意指"繁茂的"，转注表示"完成"。亦表示"容纳"，这就不难理解许慎对"城"（上文 141）的释义为"用来盛受容纳臣民"。

This is a harmonic word, its sound derived from the word on the bottom. It means "the exuberant growth of plants". The meaning of "accomplishment" is transmissive, while "prosperous" is the original idea. But this word means also "to contain", so Hsu Shên's explanation of a "city" (see 141 above) as "that by which the people are contained" is understandable.

酒 **143**

jiǔ/*Tsiu*₃

酿 造 的 酒 ， 酒 ， 烈 酒
Fermented liquor, wine, spirit

右部"酉"象酿酒的器具，转而指"酒"本身。左边加"水"旁，表示酒液。象形字"酉"表声。

The word on the right side is a pictograph of the container in which wine is brewed, which by a turn of the idea came to mean "wine" itself. The classifier added on the left shows that it is a liquid. The pronunciation is derived from the pictograph.

酣

144

hān/*Han*₂

微醉，陶醉
Merry with drink,
pleasantly inebriated

左部为"酉"（表酒），右部为"甘"，表声。参见 III. 27。
The word for "wine" is on the left and the word for "sweetness", from which the sound is derived, is on the right. See III. 27.

醉

145

zuì/*Tsui*₄

喝醉的
Drunk

右部为"卒"，表声，假借指"到达尽头"。人喝醉，即是到达限量。参见 III. 19。

The word on the right, from which the sound is derived, means "to come to an end" as a borrowed word. When one is drunk one has come to one's limit. See III. 19.

酱（酱）

146

jiàng/*Tsiang*₄

豆酱，肉酱，酱油

Bean sauce, gravy, soy

音切左部（爿）的韵母。参见下文 147。右上为"肉"，其下为"酉"（表酒）。肉汁拌酒以便保存。"a"为古体，未加"肉"旁。"b"为大篆体；亦无"肉"旁，但左下加"皿"字。参见 II. 68。

The radical on the left gives its vowel sound in the pronunciation. See 147 below. Upper right is the word for "meat", and below it "wine". Gravy is mixed with liquor for preservation. In "a", which is Archaic Script, the word for "meat" has not yet been added. b is Major Script; the word for "meat" was not used, but another word for "vessel" was added on the lower right. See II. 68.

147

爿

jiàng/*Ts'iang*₂

将树干或木片一分为二

To halve a tree trunk

or a piece of wood

指事字，未收入许慎的字典。而是从注释中收入。

This is an indicative not found in Hsu Shĕn's Dictionary. It has been collected from annotations.

*另一说读 pán。

148

缀（綴）

zhuì/*Chiu*₅

连在一起，串起（如项链）

To paste together,

to connect (as pendants)

叕

左部为半个"丝"字（II. 113），右部象串起的项链。"a"据信为其古体。

Half of the word for "silk", II. 113, is on the left, and a pictograph of pendants connected together is on the right. "a" is supposedly this word in the Archaic Script.

塞

149

sài, sè/*Sê*~5, 4~

堵 塞 ， 阻 隔 ； （ 山 与 山 之 间 的 ） 通 道

To stop up, to block;

a pass (as between mountains)

许慎的释义为"分开";原意指"阻隔"。"a"表示用双手将空隙填满。中部为"展"(下文 150)。

"To separate" is the meaning given by Hsu Shên to this word; "to block" is the original sense. The picture in "a" shows that both hands are working to fill up an empty space. The word in the middle is 150 below.

*现也读 sāi。

展

150

工工
工工 展 ⬚

zhǎn/Chên₃

展 开 , 打 开 , 展 示
To unroll, to open, to exhibit

许慎的释义为"看见"或"极巧地视察"。会意字,四个"工"(gōng)重叠,表示工艺。参见 I. 8。

Hsu Shên's interpretation of this word is "to see" or "to examine very minutely". It is an ideative representing craftsmanship, the word "kung" being repeated four times. See I. 8.

功

151

gōng/*Kung*₁

工丿功 《ㄨㄥ

功劳，成就，工作

Merit, achievement, task

会意字；由"工"和"力"组成。参见 I. 8 和 II. 44。音同工。

This is an ideative; the words for "work" and "strength" are combined. See I. 8 and II. 44. It has the same pronunciation as the word for "work".

铃（铃）

152

líng/*Ling*₂

铃 铃 ㄌㄧㄥ

铃铛，小而圆的铃

Bell, small round bells

左部为"金"，表示用金属制成。参见 X. 4。音同右部"令"，暗示"发出命令"。铃常系于马或旗帜上。参见 IV. 85。

The word on the left denotes that something is made of "metal". See X. 4. This word has the same pronunciation as the word on the right in which the idea of "to give orders" is implied. These bells are used on horses or on flags. See IV. 85.

*据《说文》，铃又称为令丁。

陳（陈） 153

chén/Ch'en₁

铺陈，安排，陈列，陈述（通常是对上级）

To spread out,
to arrange, to expose,
to state (usually to someone superior in rank)

上文所列字义均为假借意；原指今河南省的丘陵地区的地名。左部为"阜"（表山丘），右部为"木"，右边中间为"申"，表声。"a"为大篆体，省去"木"。参见 II. 18，V. 6 和 X. 9。

All these are borrowed senses of this word; the original is the name of a hilly district in what is now the province Honan. The word for "hills" is on the left, "trees" is on the right, and the word for "extension", from which the sound is derived, is in the middle of the word on the right. In "a", which is Major Script, the word for "trees" is deleted. See II. 18, V. 6, and X. 9.

隙

154

xì/*Hsi*₅

裂缝，缝隙，由此引申出：
（1）间隔，空闲，（2）朋友生间隙，不和，怨隙

A crack, a fissure,
from which come the meanings:
1) an interval, leisure
2) a fissure in friendship,
a quarrel, a grudge

原意指峭壁间的孔隙。参见 II. 18 和下文 155。

"A crack between the cliffs" is the original sense of this word. See II. 18 and 155 below.

155

xì/*Hsi*₅

陈 缝 里 露 现 的 光 线

The light that issues through a rift

由中部的"白"和上下两个"小"组成，表示只有一缕光线从缝隙里透出来。参见 IV. 68，216。

This word is made up of the word for "white" in the middle between two words for "small", one on the top and one at the bottom, indicating that only a ray of light is issuing from a crack. Light is considered to be white. See IV. 68, 216.

疑

156

疑

yí/I_1

怀 疑 ，不 信 任

To doubt, to distrust

左部为"矢"（表箭）的古体。右下为"止"字。右上"子"表声。参见 II.
49，52，84。由箭射中预定目标会意，故而无可"怀疑"；字义表示"确定
的"或"固定的"。现在的字义恰好相反，而"㠯"（下文 157）的原意才指
怀疑。

The left portion of this word is the word for "arrow" in antique script. The word for "to
stop" is on the lower right. The sound follows the word in the upper right. See II. 49, 52,
84. The idea is that the arrow has reached the designated target, therefore there is no sense
of "doubt"; its meaning is "settled" or "fixed". Today the meaning of this word is just the
opposite, and the word in 157 below originally had this definition.

疑

157

yí/*Shi*₁

疑惑，不信任；不确定的
To doubt, to distrust; unsettled

左部的"矢"（表箭）为古体，表声，右部的"匕"表示改变或变换。如若目标不断变换，人就会疑惑，不确定箭该射向何处。该字现已弃用，常用"疑"（上文 156）。

The word for "arrow" in the Archaic Script on the left gives its pronunciation, and the word on the right means "to change or transform". If the target is changing, one is in doubt as to where the arrow should be shot or aimed at. This word is now obsolete, since the word in 156 above is in frequent usage.

陆 （陆）

158

lù/*Lu*₅

干 的 土 地
Dry land

许慎的释义为"高平地"。音同右部"坴"，兼表意。参见 II. 18 和下文 159。

"An elevated plateau" is Hsu's explanation for this word. The pronunciation is the same as the word on the right from which the idea is derived. See II. 18 and 159 below.

坴

159

lù/*Lu*₅

一 块 或 许 多 土 块
A clod or clods of earth

大块的"土"——字的底部——像"尗"（表菌）一样多。参见 I. 9 和下文 160。

Clods of "earth" — the word on the bottom — are like "mushrooms" in being so numerous. See I. 9 and 160 below.

尗

160

lù/Lu₅

菌，霉或霉菌

Mushroom, mould or mildew

象"大"在芽上，会意字。菌类的芽大而多。

The word for "big or large" is written above the form of a sprout. This is an ideative. Mushrooms as sprouts are large, and they are numerous.

殳

161

殳

shū/*Shu*₁

用 棍 子 打 ， 用 手 势 指 挥 ； 以 殳 为 武 器

To beat with a stick,

to direct with a movement of the hand;

a club used as a weapon

音同 "攵"（下文 162）。可与 "支"（上文 6）相比较。

The pronunciation of this word is the same as the word in 162 below. Compare with 6 above.

*《周礼》说：殳用积竹制成，八条棱，长一丈二尺，

竖立在兵车上，车上的先锋队拿着它在前面驰驱。

162

shū/*Shu*₁

ㄕ
ㄨ

短 羽 鸟

The short feathers of birds

象飞翔时鸟羽的样子。

The word represents the shape of the feathers as seen in flying.

X.

Ideatives cum Harmonics cum Pictogaphs

会 意 并 形 声 并 象 形

俎，且

1

zǔ/*Tsu*₃

宴请或祭祀时盛肉的几具，盘子

A stand for meat
as feasts or sacrifices, a tray

左部为"肉"的简体；右部象"且"之形。参见 II. 106 和 III. 26。

The word for "meat" is abbreviated on the left here; on the right is the pictograph for "stand". See II. 106 and III. 26.

禽

2

qín/*Ch'in*₂

走兽（和鸟）的统称

Animals (and birds) in general

底部为"内"（下文 3）；可参考更确切的字形。其上的中间部分抽象地勾勒
出兽首。上部"今"（下文 5）表音。

The word on the bottom is the word in 3 below; its more exact form is given there. The
middle portion, written just above it, is an abstract representation of the head of an animal.
On top is the word that gives its pronunciation, 5 below.

*《段注》："《释鸟》曰：'二足而羽谓之禽，四足而毛谓之兽'。"

3

róu/*Jou*₁

兽足蹂地

The treading of the feet
of animals on the ground

"a"为另一个字，字音和字义均与该字相同，为后造。

"a" is another word with the same sound and meaning, a later invention.

金

4

金　金　ㄐ丨ㄣ

jīn/Chin₁

黄 金 ， 金 属 的 统 称

Gold, metal in general

金　金
a　b

下部为"土"字；左右的竖笔表金属在矿土中之形。上部为"今"（下文5），
表声。"a"取自古体。

The word for "earth" is on the bottom; the vertical strokes on the left and right of it
symbolize the metal in mines. The word on top, 5 below, gives its pronunciation to this word.
"a" is from the Archaic Script.

5

今

今 今 ㄐㄧㄣ

jīn/*Chin*₁

现在，目前
Now, present

由上部的"亼"（表集合）和下部的古体字"上"组成。上文 2 和 4 的音皆从今，故列于此。

This is a combination of the word for "to gather" on the top and the word for "up to" in the Archaic Script below it. This word is given here because of the pronunciation it gives to the words in 2 and 4 above.

嶲

6

guī/*Hsi*₁ (*Fui*₃)

嶲　工ㄧ

一种燕子或周燕

A kind of swallow or martin

上部象其头冠；中部为"隹"（表鸟）；下部"冏"表声。有两个读音，均正确。参见 II. 135 和 IV. 89。

On top is the crest of the bird; in the middle is the word for "bird"; the sound is derived from the lower part. This word has two pronunciations, both correct. See II. 135 and IV. 89.

冠

7

guān/*Kuan*₁

冠　《ㄨㄢ

帽子，冠冕，鸟的头冠或羽冠

A hat, a cap,

the comb or crest of a bird

由三个字组成，"冖"（表覆盖），"元"（表来）和 "寸"（表措施和法规）。元表声。参见 III. 9，IV. 79 和 IX. 48。

This is a combination of three words, the words for "covering", and "the head", and the word for "inch", meaning measures and statutes. It is pronounced like the word for "head". See III. 9, IV. 79, and IX. 48.

8

身

shēn/*Shên*₁

身体，人

The body, the person

上部为"人"字；中部象人的身躯，底部的撇画为"申"（下文 9）的简体，亦表声。

On top is the word for "man"; the middle part represents the trunk of the body in a pictograph, and the slanting stroke on the bottom is an abbreviated form of the word in 9 below, which gives its pronunciation.

9

申

shēn/*Shên*₁

伸展
Extension

a

b c d

原为指事，表示两"手"支撑身体。"a"为大篆体，中部笔画弯曲。"挺直身体"转注表"伸展"或"扩展"之意。

Originally this was an indicative showing two "hands" holding up the body. In the Major Script shown in "a", the middle line is curved. "To straighten the body" in a transmissive sense means "to extend" or "extension".

10

牽（牵）

qiān/*Ch'ien*₁

拉，拖，牽引，拖拽
To pull, to haul, to draw, to drag

象底部的"牛"由中间马蹄形的绳索牵引着。上部为"玄"字，表声。参见 II. 121 和 IV. 188。

An "ox", on the bottom, is being led by a rope, represented by the horseshoe-shaped line in the middle. This word is pronounced in accordance with the word on top, Hsüan. See II. 121 and IV. 188.

11

gōng/*Kung*₁

身体，自己；亲自

The body, oneself; personally

上文的小篆体由两个字组成，左部的"身"（表身体）和右部的"吕"（表脊椎）。参见上文 8 和 II. 42。"a"右部为"弓"字。象人屈体时，脊椎显露出来。也可能表示身体像弓一样弯曲；弓表声。参见 II. 83。

Two words are combined in the Minor Script given above, the word for "body" on the left and the word for "vertebrae" on the right. See 8 above and II. 42. In "a" the word on the right is the "bow". When the body is bent, the vertebrae appear, as shown above. Or perhaps it is meant that the body can be bent like a bow; it also follows the pronunciation of the word for "bow". See II. 83.

奉

12

fèng/*Fêng*₄

双 手 奉 上 ， 侍 奉

To offer with both hands, to serve

顶部 "丰"（下文 13）表声。参见 II. 39 和 IV. 37—39a。

The pronunciation is in accordance with the word on the top, given in 13 below. See II. 39 and IV. 37−39a.

丰

13

fēng/*Fêng*₁

草木丰盛

The exuberance

of the growth of vegetation

由"生"（表生长或生命）向上和向下延伸，表示繁茂之态。参见 IV. 119。

This is the word for "growth" or "life" extended both upwards and downwards, signifying a

flourishing state. See IV. 119.

能

14

néng/*Neng*₁

才能，能力；能够

Talent, ability; able to

左上部"以"表声，偏斜后形如字母"e"。参见 II. 154。原意指一种凶猛的熊类野兽，其足像鹿，"肉"丰美。能兽强壮，似有才能的人，故而表贤能之意。参见 II. 106。

The word in the upper left gives the sound, which is here deflected into "e". See II. 154. This word originally repressented a stout wild animal like a bear, with legs like those of a deer, and it is "fleshy". A great animal is compared to a talented man, hence the sense. See II. 106.

旁

15

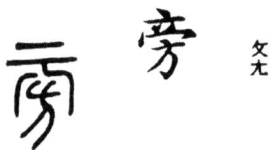

páng/*P'ang*₂

广 大 的 ， 包 罗 万 象 的 ， 伟 大 的
Extensive, all-embracing, great

象"上"面的东西从两边向下延伸；中间的"方"表音。参见 I. 4 和 II. 88。"a"为古体，表示"下"面的东西从两边或四周延伸；其余部分相同。参见 I. 5。"b"亦为古体，表示"一"包含万物。参见 I. 1。

The picture indicates that what is "above" has been extended, coming down on both sides; the pronunciation is derived from the word inside. See I. 4 and II. 88. In "a", which is Archaic Script, what is "below" is extended on both sides or on all sides; the rest is the same. See I. 5. "b", Archaic Script also, shows that what is "one" is embracing all. See I. 1.

16

pāng/*P'ang*$_2$

广大的，包罗万象的，伟大的；大雨

Extensive, all-embracing, great;
heavy rain

上部为"雨"，字义与"旁"（上文 15）相同。

Here the "rain" is on top the idea of the word is the same as in 15 above.

附 录

Appendix

规范的书写示例
INDICATIONS FOR CORRECT WRITING

1. 下列数页汉字均用线描出字形，数字代表笔画的书写顺序，箭头则表示书写方向。最后几页为复合字，由几个简单的部分组成。各部分的顺序用a，b，c 等标出。建议用钢笔或毛笔反复临摹。字的大小可根据需要调节。

   In the following pages the words are written in outline form, the sequence of the strokes being indicated by the numerals and the direction of the strokes by an arrow. In the last few pages complex words, composed of several simpler forms, are given. The sequence of writing each part is simply indicated by a, b, c, etc. Repeated copying, either with a pen or a brush, is advisable. The words may be written in any convenient size.

2. 字的中心仿佛有一隐形的重心，如此字的重量稳稳地落在竖轴线上，而不致向两边偏斜。

   An invisible centre of gravity must be found so that the weight of the word, so to say, rests stably in a vertical line not inclined towards either side.

3. 每个字书写时均自上而下，从左列右，先一笔横画再竖画小点。这是最为便的书写顺序。如若字为全包围结构，则应先写外面的三画，然后是中间部分，最后是底下的横线。

Every word is written from top to bottom and from left to right, as is every horizontal line and every vertical line. This is the most convenient way. If the word has four enclosing lines, three outer lines are written first, then the middle portion, and finally the bottom line.

4. 每个汉字的笔顺都是固定的。笔画的动向大体为环形，故前一笔的终点与后一笔的起点往往相邻。这样既省时，又省力。

The sequence of writing the strokes is fixed with each word. The movement is a circular one in general, so that the end point of one stroke is near the starting-point of the next. This saves much time and energy.

5. 每一笔画的长度和方向相对其他笔画也是固定的，一点细微的差别就会使此字变为彼字，尽管其笔画的数量是一样的。所选的例字正是为了说明这一点。

The length and direction of each stroke in proportion to other strokes are fixed, a slight variation of which would change one word into another though the number of strokes be the same. The examples have been chosen to illustrate this.

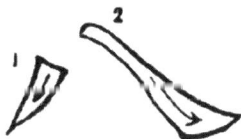
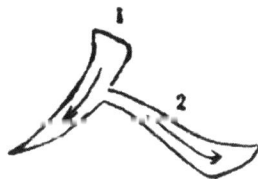

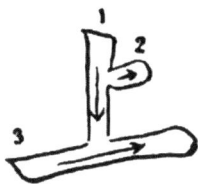

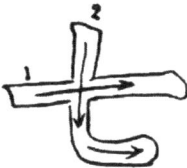

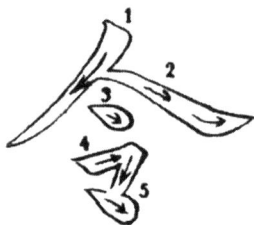

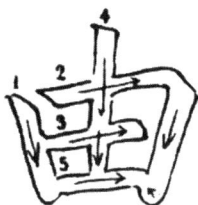

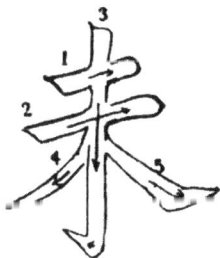
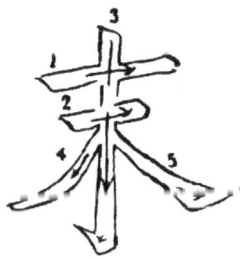

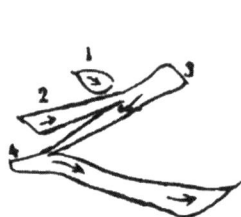

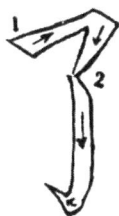

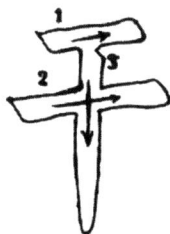

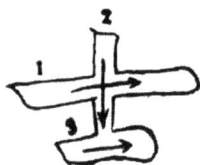
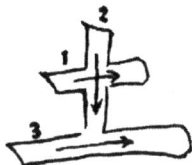

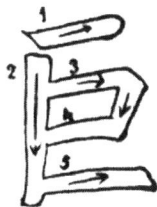

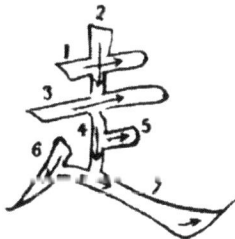

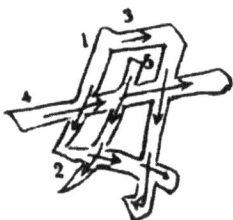

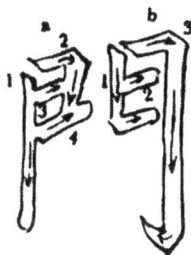

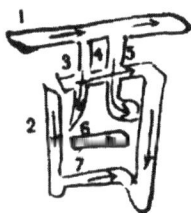

我 或

祭 登

夸 祭

卷 春

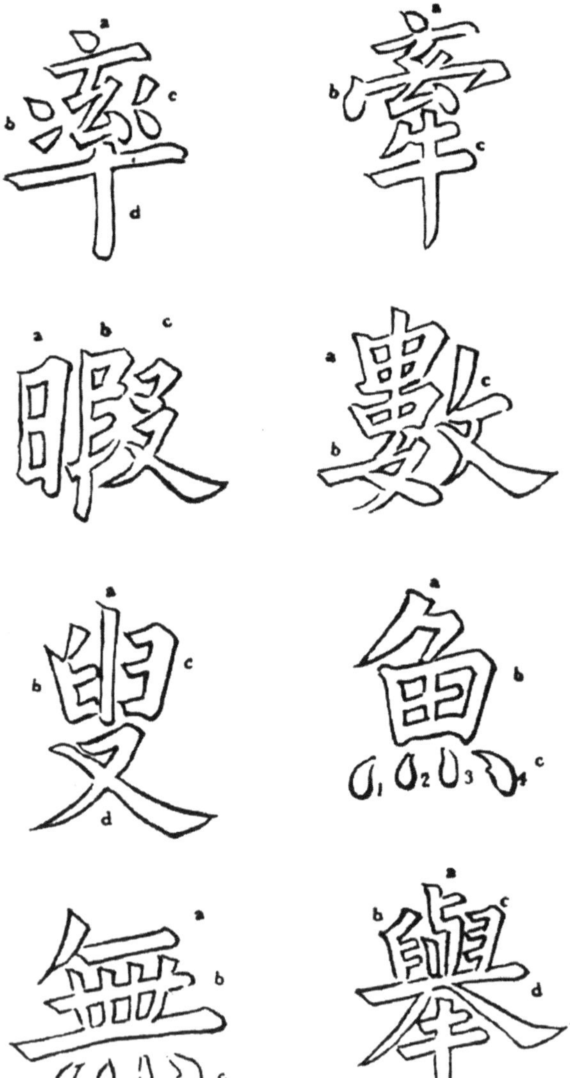

音标

THE PHONETIC SIGNS

为中国古籍作注释，是必须给出汉字读音的。在现代的欧洲语言中，如遇到不认识的字词，至少可以根据拼写将其读出，尽管这在很大程度上也取决于读者的水平。但汉语却无此便捷，不能据形发音；即使是形声字，至多也只能根据声部猜测其读音。在汉朝，公元前2世纪至公元2世纪，彼时还未尝有国家或国际性的语音符号。故一些不常用的字常注释为"音同"或"音切"另一个字。然无此相似性时，批注者就不知所措了。即使存在读音相同的情况，然批注的字若是晦涩或不常使用，那么问题仍未解决。直至2世纪末，人们才逐渐找到另一种注音的方法。据说发明者为三国时期魏朝（公元220—265年）一位名叫孙炎的学者，但最新研究表明，早在他之前这种方法已经开始使用了。方法很简单，取第一个字开头的声母，加上第二个字的韵母或复韵母，组成第三个音。如此，古籍和字典中的注音就不甚困难了。

公元9世纪末，一位名叫守温的佛家弟子发明了"三十六字母"系统，将汉字用作字母。但在他之前据说另有人已经编订了30个"字母"，守温仅增补了6个。这一系统复杂而完备，其优点在于使古代语音系统化了，这对于语音研究极有帮助，但于实际使用意义并不太大。

古代的语音系统可以给文本注音，通过标注正确的读音，为传统的语言确立了标准，然而对于消除口语的方言差异却并无帮助。南方人和北方人的交流只能通过书面语，因之书面语标准化已有两千多年。如若各自使用家乡的方言，则无法沟通。字形虽同，字音却各异。1913年春，中华民国教育部召集几乎所有知名的语音学专家，在北京召开了"国语标准化会议"。会议很成功，并确立了39个语音字母，以最简单的书写符号表示出来，此系统正式确立为"国家语音符号"。此处未沿用"字母"或字面的"字母表"这样的错误称谓。

但学者普遍不喜欢这一系统，因其并非不可或缺。学习汉语的词汇已经很困难了，此外再掌握一套语音符号，对普通人而言确实徒增麻烦。文法学校有教授此一系统的课程，但学习语言时却显得可有可无。此外，对于高年级学生而言，可查阅古代字书，而无须借助这一套系统。于此提出一重要现况，不仅存在于汉语中，也存在于其他外国语言中，即所谓的习惯性暴君。然而，对于学习中文的外国人而言，拼音也许有所帮助。现在采用此符号标注读音的字典随处可见。列表如下。

In annotating ancient Chinese texts, the sound of certain words must be given. If we meet a word which we do not know in any of the modern European languages, we can at least read it out according to its spelling, though that depends much upon the intelligence of the reader. But in chinese this privilege is not given. We cannot read it out phonetically; at most we can only guess from half of the word, taking it to be one of the harmonics. In the Han Dynasty, two centuries before and after the Christian era, there were as yet no national or international phonetic symbols. So to a certain word not commonly known, there was always annotated "to be read as" or "with the sound like" another word. But where no such likeness could be found, the annotator would be at his wit's end. Even if there was a phonetic equivalent, but it was a word obscure or rarely used, the difficulty was still not solved. Gradually towards the end of the second century A.D. people found another method of denoting the sound, putting two words together and pronouncing them as one. The inventor was supposed to be a scholar of the Wei Dynasty (220-264 A.D.) named Sun Yen 孙炎 , but recent researches reveal that this method was employed long before his time. It is a very simple method in which the initial consonant of the first word was taken and combined with the vowel or diphthong of the second word, so as to form a third sound. Henceforth, there was no more difficulty in noting the sounds of words either in ancient texts or in dictionaries.

At the end of the ninth century, a Buddhist monk with the name Shou Wen 守温 formulated a system of "thirty-six phonetic letters", using words as letters. But it was also said that another author before him had already compiled thirty such "letters", to which Shou Wen added only six. That system, a comprehensive and well-formulated one, had the merit of systematizing all ancient sounds and was helpful in phonetic studies, but it did not serve much practical purpose.

The ancient system can be used in denoting the sounds in texts, in giving the correct pronunciation and thereby bringing about a certain standardization of the traditional tongue, but it does not help in the abolition of different dialects of the spoken language. Hence, a man from the southern part of China can understand a man from the northern part only through the written language, since that has been standardized for more than two thousand years, but if each speaks the dialect of his native part they cannot understand each other. Though the words are the same, they are pronounced differently. So in the spring of 1913, the Ministry of Education in China summoned nearly all the eminent philologists of the nation to Peking and convened a "Conference on the Standardization of the National Tongue". The outcome was successful and thirty-nine phonetic letters were formed out of the most simple signs found in the written language, and this system was officially proclaimed as the "National Phonetic Symbols", no longer called "letters" or literally "alphabets", which was of course a wrong appellation.

But scholars generally do not like this system, since they can do without it, and the common people find extra trouble in mastering another system of phonetic sings superimposed upon a vocabulary which is already difficult enough. It is indeed taught in grammar schools, but the language has still to be learned separately with or without it. Moreover, for higher studies ancient lexicons can be resorted to without such a system. Here we come across one of the fundamental actualities not only of Chinese but of all languages, viz., *usus tyrannus*. Yet to foreigners learning Chinese this system may be useful, and dictionaries with notations of pronunciations using these signs are easily available nowadays. The tables are given below.

中国国家语音符号 I

CHINESE NATIONAL PHONETIC SYMBOLS I

1. 属声母的语音符号 Phonetic signs of the consonantal class
2. 对应的罗马字母 Corresponding Roman letters
3. 普通话的读音 Read as the Peking Mandarin or official tongue
4. 古代三十六字母系统的对照表 Correspondences with the ancient system of thirty-six phonetic letters

ㄅ	ㄆ	ㄇ	ㄈ	万	ㄉ	ㄊ	ㄋ
b	*p*	*m*	*f*	*v*	*d*	*t*	*n*
伯	迫	墨	佛	復	德	特	訥
幫	滂	明	非	微	端	透	泥
並	並		敷		定	定	娘
			奉				

ㄌ	ㄍ	ㄎ	ㄫ	ㄏ	ㄐ	ㄑ	ㄣ
l	*g*	*k*	*ng*	*h*	*j(i)*	*ch(i)*	*gn*
肋	格	客	頡	赫	基	欺	尼
來	見 羣	溪 羣	疑	曉 匣	見 羣	溪 羣	疑 泥 娘

ㄒ	ㄓ	ㄔ	ㄕ	ㄖ	ㄗ	ㄘ	ㄙ
sh(i)	*j*	*ch*	*sh*	*r*	*tz*	*ts*	*s*
希	知	痴	詩	日	資	雌	思
曉 匣	知 照 澄 牀	徹 穿 澄 牀	審 禪	日 娘	精 從	清 從	心 邪

中国国家语音符号 II

CHINESE NATIONAL PHONETIC SYMBOLS II

1. 属韵母的语音符号 Phonetic signs of the vowel class

2. 对应的罗马字母 Corresponding Roman letters

3. 普通话的读音 Read as the Peking Mandarin or official tongue

4. 与公元 1152 年刘元编订的《韵文字典》的韵母对照表 Correspondences with rhymes in the "Lexicon of Rhyme" composed by Liu Yuan in 1152 A.D.

一	ㄨ	ㄩ	ㄚ	ㄛ	ㄜ	ㄝ	ㄞ
i	*u*	*iu*	*a*	*o*	*e*	*e*	*ai*
衣	烏	迂	(啊)	痾	鵝	哀	哀
支微齊	魚虞	魚虞	麻	歌	質陌職	麻	佳灰

* 蘇音

** 寧音

ㄦ el	ㄥ eng	ㄤ ang	ㄣ en	ㄢ an	ㄡ ou	幺 au	ㄟ ei
兒	哼	昂	恩	安	歐	熬	呃衣
支 庚青蒸東	冬庚青蒸東	江陽	真文侵元	覃鹽咸 元寒刪先	尤	蕭肴豪	支微齊灰

进一步分类
FURTHER ANALYSIS

唇音	Labials	ㄅ ㄆ ㄇ
唇齿音	Labial-dentals	ㄈ 万
舌尖音	Tip consonants	ㄉ ㄌ ㄋ ㄊ
软腭音	Soft palate-back consonants	ㄍ ㄎ 兀 ㄏ
平舌音	Front consonants	ㄐ ㄑ 广 ㄒ
卷舌音	Raised-blade consonants	ㄓ ㄔ ㄕ ㄖ
前舌音	Fore-blade consonants	ㄗ ㄘ ㄙ

单韵母	Single vowels	ㄧ ㄨ ㄩ ㄚ ㄛ 古 ㄝ
复韵母	Diphthongs	ㄞ ㄟ ㄠ ㄡ
声母前的韵母	Vowels followed by consonants	ㄢ ㄣ ㄤ ㄥ
卷舌音	Curved tip vowel	ㄦ

读 音 示 例

INDICATIONS FOR PRONUNCIATION

本文采用的是威氏（威妥玛式）普通话拼音法，亦是最常用的拼音法。该系统中韵母和声母的发音规则如下：

In this book the Wade system of transliteration of Mandarin , the one most commonly used, has been adopted. In this system the vowels and consonants are pronounced as follows：

韵 母

Vowels

a：如 father　as in "father"

ê：如 under 中的 u　like the *u* in "under"

e：如 Edward　as in "Edward"

ih：如 her 中的 e（在英文中没有完全对等的发音）　like the *e* in "her" (no real equivalent in English)

i：如 machine　as in "machine"

o：如 saw 中的 aw（但常如 cut 中的 u）　like *aw* in "saw" (but often like the *u* in "cut")

ü：如法语中的 u 或德语中的 ü　like the French *u* or German *ü*

声母

Consonant

（不送气　Unaspirated）

ch：发音如 jam 中的 j　is sounded like the *j* in "jam"

k：如 gun 中的 g　like the *g* in "gun"

p：如 bat 中的 b　like the *b* in "bat"

t：如 doll 中的 d　like the *d* in "doll"

ts 和 *tz*：发音如 dz　are sounded like *dz*

j：介于法语 j 和英语 r 之间　between French *j* and English *r*

（送气　Aspirated）

ch'：如 chin　as in "chin"

k'：如 kin　as in "kin"

p'：如 pun　as in "pun"

t'：如 tap　as in "tap"

ts' 和 *tz'*：如 Patsy 中的 ts　like the *ts* of "Patsy"

其他声母大多数与英语的辅音类似。

Most of the other consonants are similar to those in English.

索 引

INDEX

běi	北	IV. 28	$P\hat{e}_5$
bèi	貝（贝）	IV. 152	Pei_4
bèi	孛	VIII. 2	Pu_5
běn	本	III. 3	$P\hat{e}n_3$
bǐ	比	IV. 11	Pi_3
bì	畢（毕）	II. 120	Pi_5
bì	皕	IV. 214	Pi_5
bì	㳊	V. 23	Pi_4
bì	閉（闭）	V. 48	Pi_4
bì	碧	IX. 9	Pi_5
bì	敝	IX. 88	Pi_4
bì	婢	IX. 131	Pei_4
biǎn	扁	IV. 173	$Pien_3$
biàn	釆	II. 128	$Pang_4$
biàn	弁［下］	V. 20	$Pien_4$
biāo	猋	IV. 98	$Piao_2$
biāo	彪	V. 51	$Piao_2$
biǎo	表	IV. 245	$Piao_3$
biào	受	IV. 56	$P'iao_3$
bīng	氷（冰）	II. 10	$Ping_2$
bīng	兵	IV. 145	$Ping_2$
bǐng	秉	IV. 135	$Ping_3$
bìng	竝（并）	IV. 10	$Ping_4$
bō	剝（剥）	IX. 56	Po_5

bó	博	IX. 23	Po_5
bǔ	卜	II. 59	Pu_5
bù	不	III. 24	Pu_5
bù	步	IV. 47	Pu_4
cái	才	III. 35	$Ts'ai_1$
cǎi	采	IV. 126	$Ts'ai_3$
cán	戋（戋）	IV. 219	$Tzien_2$
cán	殘（残）	IV. 220	$Ts'an_1$
cǎo	艸，草	IV. 114	$Ts'ao_3$
cè	册	II. 116	$Ts'ê_5$
chā	叉	II. 40	$Ch'a_2$
chā	插	IX. 119	$Ch'a_5$
chā	臿	IX. 120	$Ch'a_5$
chán	毚	IV. 100	$Tsan_2$
chǎn	弗	II. 57	$Ch'an_3$
chāng	昌	IV. 34	$Ch'ang_2$
cháng	長（长）	IV. 74	$Ch'ang_2$
chàng	鬯	II. 72	$Ch'ang_4$
cháo	巢	V. 10	$Tzao_2$
chē	車（车）	II. 89	$Ch'ê_2$
chè	屮	IV. 115	$Choe_5$
chén	塵（尘）	IV. 257	$Ch'ên_1$
chén	晨	IX. 31	$Ch'ên_1$
chén	辰	IX. 32	$Ch'en_1$

chén	晨	IX. 34	*Ch'en*₁
chén	臣	IX. 37	*Chêng*₁
chén	陳（陈）	IX. 153	*Ch'en*₁
chéng	城	IX. 141	*Ch'eng*₂
chǐ	齒（齿）	VIII. 1	*Ch'ih*₃
chì	彳	II. 51	*Ch'ih*₅
chì	赤	IV. 229	*Ch'ih*₅
chì	敕	IX. 41	*Ch'ih*₅
chōng	春	IV. 42	*Ch'ung*₁
chóng	虫［蟲］	II. 144	*Ch'ung*₁
chóu	畴（畴）	V. 56	*Ch'ou*₂
chū	出	II. 102	*Ch'u*₅
chú	刍（刍）	V. 46	*Ch'u*₂
chuān	川	II. 8	*Ch'uan*₂
chuān	穿	IV. 221	*Ch'uan*₂
chuǎn	舛	IX. 136	*Ch'uan*₃
chuāng	窗（窗）	II. 79	*Ch'uang*₁
chuāng	刅	III. 14	*Ch'uang*₂
chuǎng	闖（闯）	IV. 223	*Ch'uang*₃
chuàng	㓚（创）	IX. 74	*Ch'uang*₃
chuī	吹	IV. 93	*Ch'ui*₁
chuí	垂	II. 98	*Ch'ui*
chuò	辵	IV. 47a	*Ch'o*
cǐ	此	IV. 12	*Tz'u*₃

cì	束	V. 9	*Ts'u*$_4$
cì	刺	IX. 60	*Tz'u*$_4$
cóng	從（从）	IV. 27	*Ts'ong*$_1$
cū	麤（粗）	IV. 256	*Ts'u*
cuàn	竄（窜）	IV. 102	*Ts'uan*$_4$
cuàn	爨	V. 60	*Ts'uan*$_4$
cùn	寸	III. 9	*Ts'un*$_4$
dà	大	II. 23	*Ta*$_4$
dài	帶（带）	V. 22	*Tai*$_4$
dān	丹	II. 82	*Tan*$_1$
dān	單（单）	IX. 5	*Tan*$_1$
dàn	旦	III. 5	*Tan*$_4$
dāo	刀	II. 85	*Tao*$_2$
dé	得	IV. 241	*Tê*$_5$
dé	德	IX. 116	*Tê*$_5$
dǐ	氏	VII. 1	*Ti*$_3$
dì	娣	IX. 133	*Ti*$_4$
dì	弟	IX. 134	*Ti*$_4$
diǎn	典	IV. 172	*Dien*$_3$
diàn	奠	IV. 43	*Tien*$_4$
dīng	丁	II. 60	*Ting*$_2$
dǐng	鼎	II. 74	*Ting*$_3$
dìng	定	IX. 86	*Ting*$_4$
dōng	東（东）	IV. 130	*Tung*$_1$

dōng	冬	IX. 113	*Tung*₁
dōu	兜	V. 24	*Tou*₂
dǒu	斗	II. 65	*Tou*₃
dòu	豆	II. 69	*Tou*₄
dòu	鬥（斗）	V. 27	*Tou*₄
duān	耑	IX. 66	*Chuan*₂
duī	㠯［堆］	II. 17	*Tui*₁
duì	兑	V. 47	*Tui*₄
dùn	盾	II. 90	*Tun*₃
duō	多	IV. 75	*To*₂
duǒ	朶（朵）	V. 8	*To*₃
è	歺（歺）	IV. 198	*Wo*₅
ér	而	II. 34	*Êrh*₁
ér	兒（儿）	II. 47	*Êrh*₁
ěr	耳	II. 26	*Êrh*₃
ěr	［你］，爾（尔）	IX. 52	*Êrh*₃
èr	二	I. 2	*Êrh*₃
fá	乏	III. 17	*Fah*₅
fá	伐	IV. 23	*Fah*₅
fán	煩（烦）	IV. 238	*Fan*₁
fǎn	反	V. 41	*Fan*₃
fǎn	返	IX. 16	*Fan*₃
fāng	匚	II. 61	*Fang*₂
fāng	方	II. 88	*Fang*₂

fēi	飛（飞）	II. 142	*Fei*₁
fèi	吠	IV. 96	*Fei*₄
fēn	分	IV. 70	*Fên*₁,₄
fēng	豐（丰）	V. 34	*Fêng*₁
fēng	丰	X. 13	*Fêng*₁
fèng	奉	X. 12	*Fêng*₄
fǒu	缶	II. 70	*Hou*₃
fǒu	否	IX. 114	*Fou*₃
fū	夫	III. 15	*Fu*₁
fū	尃	IX. 24	*Pu*₅
fú	㇟	I. 20	*Fu*₅
fú	市	V. 21	*Fu*₅
fú	孚	IX. 90	*Fu*₁
fù	阜	II. 18	*Fiu*₄
fù, fǔ	父	III. 7	*Fu*₃,₄
fù	婦（妇）	IX. 15	*Fu*₄,₃
fǔ	甫	IX. 25	*Fu*₃
gǎi	改	IX. 43	*Kai*₃
gān	干	I. 11	*Kan*₁
gān	甘	III. 27	*Kan*₂
gāo	高	II. 111	*Kao*₂
gāo	皋	IV. 217	*Kao*₂
gǎo	杲	IV. 131	*Kao*₃
gào	告	IV. 7	*Kao*₄,₅

gē	戈	II. 95	Ko_2
gé	革	II. 108	$Kê_5$
gè	各	IV. 9	Ko_5
gēng	羹	IV. 250	$Kêng_2$
gōng	工	I. 8	$Kung_1$
gōng	弓	II. 83	$Kung_1$
gōng	公	IV. 17	$Kung_1$
gōng	肱	V. 38	$Kung_2$
gōng	功	IX. 151	$Kung_1$
gōng	躬	X. 11	$Kung_1$
gǒng	廾	IV. 37	$Gung_3$
gòng	共	IV. 39	$Gung_{3,4}$
gōu	冓	II. 109	Keo_2
gōu	鉤（钩）	IX. 22	Kou_2
gǒu	苟	IX. 29	Kou_3
gǔ	古	IV. 77	Ku_3
gǔ	骨	IV. 195	Ku_5
gǔ	谷	V. 55	Ku_5
gǔ	鼓	IX. 44	Ku_3
guā	瓜	II. 99	Kua_2
guǎ	咼［剐］	IV. 199	Kua_3
guài	夬	V. 43	$Kuai_4$
guān	冠	X. 7	$Kuan_1$
guàn, chuàn	貫（贯），串	II. 56, IV. 154	$Kuan_4$, Ch'uan
guàn	盥	IV. 167	$Kuan_3$

guāng	光	IV. 239	$Kuang_2$
guī	龜（龟）	II. 148	$Kuei_1$
guī	規（规）	IV. 106	$Kuei_1$
guī	歸（归）	IX. 14	$Kuei_2$
guī	閨（闺）	IX. 117	$Kuei_1$
guī	圭，珪	IX. 118	$Kuei_1$
guī	巂	X. 6	$Hsi_1(Fui_3)$
guì	貴（贵）	IX. 76	$Kuei_4$
guǒ	果	V. 7	Ko_3
hài	害	IX. 85	$Hai_{4,5}$
hān	酣	IX. 144	Han_2
hán	寒	IV. 129	Han_1
hán	函	VIII. 3	Han_2
hǎn	厂	II. 15	Han_2
hàn	马	II. 97	Han_2
háo, hào	號（号）	IV. 90	$Hao_{2,4}$
hǎo, hào	好	IV. 8	$Hao_{3,4}$
hē	乀	I. 24	$Ho_{1,2}$
hé	禾	II. 64	Q_2
hé	合	IV. 82	Ho_5
hè	赫	IV. 236	$Hêh_5$
hēi	黑	IV. 233	$Hêh_5$
hōng	轟（轰）	IV. 255	$Hung_2$
hòu	後（后）	IV. 53	Hou_4

hòu	后	V. 52	Hou_4
hū	乎	V. 4	Hu_1
hú	壺（壺）	II. 73	Hu_1
hù	户	II. 77	Hu_4
hù	笟，互	V. 29	Hu_4
huā	華（华）	IV. 270	Hua_2
huá, huà	劃（划）	IX. 58	Hua_4
huà	畫（画）	V. 35	$Hua_{4,(5)}$
huà	化	IX. 95	$Hua_{4,2}$
huī	灰	IV. 237	Hui_1
huí	回	II. 22	Hui_1
huí	洄	IX. 107	Hui_1
huì	卉	IV. 116	Hui_4
huì	彗／篲	V. 15/15a	Fei_4
hūn	婚	IX. 126	Hun_1
hūn	昏	IX. 127	Hun_1
huǒ	火	II. 13	Huo_3
huò [yù]	或［域］	IV. 150	$Ho_5[Yü]$
jī	丌	II. 75	$Ch'i_1$
jǐ	幾（几）	IV. 189	Chi_1
jī	撃（击）	IV. 244	Chi_5
jī [qí]	箕［其］	V. 14	Chi_1
jí	吕	IV. 6	Chi_5
jí	及	IV. 30	Chi_5

jiào	教	IX. 45	*Chiao*₄
jié	劫	IV. 265	*Chieh*₅
jié	捷	IX. 79	*Ts'ieh*₅
jiě	解	IV. 65	*Chiai*₃
jiè	丯	II. 58	*Chiai*₃,₅
jiè	戒	IV. 139	*Chiai*₄
jīn	斤	II. 86	*Chin*₁
jīn	巾	III. 18	*Chin*₁
jīn	金	X. 4	*Chin*₁
jīn	今	X. 5	*Chin*₁
jìn	晋（晋）	IV. 210	*Tsin*₄
jīng	晶	IV. 211	*Tsing*₂
jīng	京	V. 61	*Ching*₂
jǐng	井	II. 81	*Tsing*₃
jǐng	警	IX. 26	*Ching*₃
jǐng	阱，穽，井	IX. 69	*Tsing*₃
jìng	敬	IX. 27	*Ching*₄
jiǒng	囧	II. 80	*Chiung*₂
jiǔ	九	I. 17	*Chiu*₃
jiǔ	酒	IX. 143	*Tsiu*₃
jiù	臼	II. 67	*Chiu*₄
jiù	臼（白）	IX. 47	*Chu*₃
ju	菊（鞠）	IV. 54	*Chu*₅
jū	拘	IX. 20	*Chü*₁

jù	具	IV. 151	*Chü*₄
jù	巨	V. 28	*Chü*₄
jù	句	IX. 21	*Chü*₄
jù	瞿	IX. 54	*Ch'ü*₁
juàn	雋（隽）	IV. 143	*Ts'üan*₄
jué	爵	II. 92	*Tsio*₅
jué	決（决）	IX. 106	*Chueh*₅
jūn	君	IV. 78	*Chün*₁
jūn	軍（军）	IV. 149	*Chün*₁
jūn	均	IX. 139	*Ch'ün*₁
kāi	開（开）	V. 49	*K'ai*₁
kǎi	愷（恺）	IX. 63	*K'ai*₃
kān, kàn	看	IV. 103	*K'an*₁,₄
kǎn	凵	IV. 266	*Chü*₁
kǎo	丂	I. 23	*Kao*₁
kě	可	IX. 61	*K'o*₃
kè	克	II. 112	*K'eh*₅
kǒu	口	II. 29	*K'ou*₃
kū	哭	IX. 13	*K'u*₅
kuài	巜	II. 7	*Kuai*₄
kuì	餽（馈）	IX. 71	*K'uei*₄
kuì	臾（簣）	IX. 77	*Kuei*₄
kùn	困	IV. 31	*K'un*₄
lái	來（来）	II. 101	*Lai*₁

lǎn	覽（览）	IX. 101	*Lan₃*
láo	牢	V. 45	*Lao₂*
lǎo	老	IV. 14	*Lao₃*
léi	雷	V. 59	*Lei₁*
lěi	厽	II. 19	*Lei₂*
lǐ	里	IV. 109	*Li₃*
lǐ	禮（礼）	IX. 8	*Li₃*
lǐ	效	IX. 51	*Li₅*
lì	力	II. 44	*Li₅*
lì	鬲	II. 71	*Li₅*
lì	立	III. 16	*Lih₅*
lì	戾	IV. 99	*Li₄*
lì	吏	IX. 7	*Li₄*
lián	聯（联）	IV. 181	*Lien₁*
liáng	梁	IX. 73	*Liang₂*
liǎng	两，両	IX. 87	*Liang₃*
liè	鼣	II. 153	*Le₅*
liè	劣	IV. 71	*Lüeh₅*
lín	林	IV. 122	*Lin₂*
lǐn	㐭	V. 13	*Lin₃*
líng	［靈（灵）］	V. 58	*Lin₂*
líng	鈴（铃）	IX. 152	*Ling₂*
lìng	令	IV. 85	*Ling₂,₄*
liú	留	IV. 111	*Liu₂*

mào	冒	IX. 80	*Mao*$_4$
mào	茂	IX. 142	*Mou*$_4$
méi	梅，槑	IV. 243a	*Mei*$_1$
méi	眉	V. 37	*Mei*$_1$
měi	美	IV. 249	*Mei*$_3$
mén	門（门）	II. 78	*Mên*$_1$
měng	黽（黾）	II. 150	*Ming*$_3$
mǐ	米	II. 63	*Mi*$_3$
mì	冖	IX. 48	*Mi*$_5$
mián	宀	II. 157	*Mien*$_2$
mián	绵（绵）	IV. 180	*Mien*$_1$
miàn	面	II. 33	*Mien*$_4$
miáo	苗	IV. 120	*Miao*$_2$
mǐn	皿	II. 68	*Ming*$_3$
míng	名	IV. 81	*Ming*$_2$
míng	明	IV. 209	*Ming*$_2$
mìng	命	IV. 86	*Ming*$_4$
mò	末	III. 4	*Mo*$_5$
mò, mù	莫，幕	IV. 127	*Mo*$_5$
mò	墨	IV. 235	*Mê*$_5$
móu	牟	V. 44	*Mou*$_2$
mǒu	某	IV. 243	*Mou*$_3$
mǔ	母	II. 46	*Mu*$_3$
mù	目	II. 25	*Mu*$_5$

mù	牧	IV. 61	Mu_5
mù	木	V. 6	Mu_5
nǎi	乃	II. 50	Nai_3
nán	男	IV. 112	Nan_2
nǎo	腦（脑）	V. 36	Nao_3
nè	訥（讷）	IV. 89	$Na_5 (Nui_5)$
nèi	内	III. 30	$Nui_{4,5}$
néng	能	X. 14	$Neng_1$
niàn	廿	IV. 1	$Yü_5 (Nien_4)$
niǎo	鳥（鸟）	II. 137	$Niao_3$
niú	牛	II. 121	Niu_2
nòng	弄	IV. 38	$Lung_4$
nǚ	女	II. 45	$Nü_3$
pán	般	IV. 64	Pan_1
pàn	胖	IX. 4	$P'ang_4$
pāng	雱	X. 16	$P'ang_2$
páng	旁	X. 15	$P'ang_2$
pǐ	匹	V. 25	$P'i_5$
piàn	片	III. 12	$P'ien_4$
piě	丿	I. 19	Pi_3
pín	貧（贫）	IX. 75	$P'in_1$
pǐn	品	IV. 91	$P'in_3$
pìn	牝	IV. 247	Pin_4
píng	坪	IX. 137	$P'ing_2$

píng	平	IX. 138	*P'ing*₂

píng	平	IX. 138	*P'ing*$_2$
pū	攴	IX. 6	*P'u*$_5$
pù, bào	暴	IV. 213	*Pao*$_{4,5}$
qī	七	I. 15	*Ch'i*$_5$
qī	漆	V. 11	*Ch'i*$_5$
qī	妻	IX. 78	*Ts'i*$_1$
qí	齊（齐）	III. 36	*Ts'i*$_2$
qǐ	啟（启）	IV. 222	*Ch'i*$_3$
qǐ	豈（岂）	IX. 64	*Ch'i*$_3$ (*K'ai*$_3$)
qì	气	II. 4	*Ch'i*$_4$
qì	旱	IV. 92	*Ch'i*$_5$
qiān	僉（佥）	IV. 83	*Ch'ien*$_2$
qiān	臤	IX. 36	*K'êng*
qiān	牽（牵）	X. 10	*Ch'ien*$_1$
qián	前	IV. 52	*Ts'ien*$_2$
qiàn	欠	IV. 160	*Ch'ien*$_4$
qiāng	羌	IV. 251	*Ch'iang*$_2$
qiě	且	III. 26	*Tsu*$_3$
qiè	竊（窃）	IX. 83	*Ts'ieh*$_5$
qín	琴	II. 115	*Ch'in*$_2$
qín	禽	X. 2	*Ch'in*$_2$
qīng, qǐng	頃（顷）	IV. 35	*Ch'ing*$_{2,3}$
qīng	頃（顷）	IX. 97	*Ch'ing*$_{2,3}$
qìng	慶（庆）	IV. 274	*Ch'ing*$_2$

qìng	磬	V. 53	*Ch'ing*₄
qiú	囚	IV. 29	*Ts'iu*₂
qiú	裘，求	V. 17	*Ch'iu*₂
qū	曲	II. 62	*Ch'ü*₅
qǔ	娶	IX. 124	*Ch'ü*₄
qǔ	取	IX. 125	*Ch'ü*₃
qù	去	IV. 267	*Ch'ü*₄
quán	泉	II. 12	*Ts'uan*₂
quǎn	〈	II. 6	*Ch'üen*₃
quǎn	犬	II. 123	*Ch'üen*₃
què	舃	II. 138	*Hsi*₃
què	雀	IV. 140	*Ts'io*₅
qūn	囷	IV. 32	*T'un*₁
rǎn	冄（冉）	II. 35	*Nien*₂
rén	人	II. 24	*Jên*₁
rén	仁	IV. 19	*Jên*₁
rén	壬	IV. 206	*Jên*₂
rèn	刃	III. 13	*Jên*₄
rì	日	II. 1	*Jih*₅
róng	戎	IV. 146	*Jung*₁
róu	内，蹂	X. 3	*Jou*₁
ròu	肉	II. 106	*Ju*₅
rù	入	I. 10	*Ju*₅ (*ruh*)
sà	卅	IV. 2	*Sa*₅

sài, sè	塞	IX. 149	$S\hat{e}_{5,4}$
sān	三	I. 3	San_2
sàng, sāng	丧（喪）	IX. 12	$Sang_2$
sēn	森	IV. 121	$Shen_2$
shān	山	II. 14	$Shan_2$
shān	删	IV. 175	$Hsan_1$
shān	彝	IV. 253	$Shan_1$
shàn	善	IV. 254	$Shan_4$
shàng	上	I. 4	$Shang_4$
sháo	勺	II. 91	Sho_5
sháo	杓（勺）	IX. 72	Sho_5
shǎo	少	IV. 69	$Shao_{3,4}$
shé	舌	IV. 88	$Sh\hat{e}_5$
shé	折	IV. 118	$Ch\hat{e}_5$
shè	射	IV. 148	$Sh\hat{e}_{4,5}$
shè	涉	IV. 162	$Sh\hat{e}_5$
shè	設（设）	IV. 192	$Sh\hat{e}_5$
shè	舍	IV. 228	$Sh\hat{e}_4$
shè	社	IX. 10	$Sh\hat{e}_4$
shēn	娠	IX. 33	$Ch'en_1$
shēn	身	X. 8	$Sh\hat{e}n_1$
shēn	申	X. 9	$Sh\hat{e}n_1$
shěn	審（审）	IV. 268	$Sh\hat{e}n_3$
shēng	升	II. 66	$Sheng_2$

shēng	生	IV. 119	*Sheng*₂
shī	尸	II. 37	*Shih*₁
shī	濕（湿）	IX. 109	*Shih*₅
shí	十	I. 18	*Shih*₅
shí	石	II. 16	*Shih*₅
shí	什	IX. 93	*Shih*₅
shǐ	矢	II. 84	*Shih*₃
shǐ	豕	II. 124	*Shih*₃
shǐ	史	IV. 138	*Shih*₃
shì	示	I. 7	*Shih*₄
shì	世	IV. 3	*Shih*₄
shì	士	IV. 4	*Ssu*₄
shì	仕	IV. 5	*Ssu*₄
shì	是	IV. 108	*Shih*₄
shì	氏	VII. 2, VIII. 5	*Shih*₄
shì	室	IX. 84	*Shih*₅
shǒu	首	II. 32	*Shou*₃
shǒu	手	II. 39	*Shou*₃
shǒu	守	IV. 193	*Shou*₃
shòu	受	IX. 121	*Shou*₄
shòu	授	IX. 122	*Shou*₄
shū	舒	IX. 55	*Shu*₁
shū	殳	IX. 161	*Shu*₁

shū	𠂤	IX. 162	*Shu*₁
shú [shū]	尗 [菽]	III. 34	*Shu*₅
shǔ	鼠	II. 127	*Shu*₃
shǔ	蜀	II. 151	*Shu*₅
shǔ	黍	IV. 273	*Shu*₃
shù	戍	IV. 24	*Shu*₄
shù	束	IV. 123	*Shu*₅
shù	豎 (竖)	IX. 39	*Shu*₄
shuāi [suō]	衰	V. 19	*Shuai*₁ [*Ts'ui*₁]
shuài	率	II. 118	*Suai*₅
shuāng	雙 (双)	IV. 134	*Shuang*₁
shuǐ	水	II. 9	*Shui*₃
sī	厶	IV. 18	*Ssu*₁
sī	思	IV. 45	*Ssu*₁
sī	絲 (丝)	IV. 177	*Ssu*₁
sī	司	IX. 19	*Ssû*
sǐ	死	IV. 197	*Ssu*₃
sì	四	I. 12	*Ssu*₄
sì	兕	II. 126	*Ssi*₃
sì	巳	II. 155	*Ssu*₄
sì	嗣	IX. 18	*Ssû*₄
sòng	送	IV. 57	*Sung*₄
sù	粟	IV. 33	*Su*₅
suī	夊	II. 159	*Sui*₁
suì	祟	IX. 11	*Sui*₄

sūn	孫（孙）	IV. 248	Sun_1
suǒ	索	IV. 246	So_5
tā	它	II. 146	$T'o_2$
tà	少	III. 21	Ta_5
tà	沓	IV. 165	$T'a_5$
tài	泰	IX. 111	Tai_4
tāo	夲	IV. 218	$T'ao_2$
tǎo	討（讨）	IV. 191	$T'ao_3$
tiān	天	IV. 259	$T'ien_2$
tián	田	II. 20	$T'ien_2$
tián	甜	IV. 271	$T'ien_2$
tīng	聽（听）	IX. 115	$T'ing_4$
tíng	廷	IV. 205	$T'ing_2$
tóng	同	IV. 87	$T'ung_1$
tǔ	土	I. 9	$T'u_3$
tù	兎（兔）	II. 125	$T'u_4$
tún	屯	III. 31	$T'un_1$
wàn	萬（万）	II. 152	Wan_4
wáng	王	I. 6	$Wang_{2,4}$
wáng	亡	IV. 36	$Wang_2$
wǎng	网	II. 117	$Wang_3$
wàng	忘	IX. 105	$Wang_2$
wēi	危	IV. 261	Wei_1
wēi	微	IX. 65	Wei_1

wéi	口	II. 21	Wei_1
wéi	為（为）	II. 132	Wei_1
wéi	韋（韦）［圍（围）］	IX. 135	Wei_1
wěi	广	IV. 260	Yen_2
wěi	尾	V. 18	Wei_3
wèi	位	IV. 21	Wei_4
wèi	聚	V. 26	Hui_4
wèi	胃	V. 40	Wei_4
wén	文	II. 54	Wen_1
wū	烏（乌）	II. 136	Wu_1
wū	屋	IV. 227	Wu_5
wū	巫	V. 30	U_1
wǔ	五	I. 13	Wu_3
wǔ	武	IV. 147	Wu_3
wǔ	伍	IX. 92	Wu_3
wù	勿	II. 103	Fu_5
xī	夕	III. 6	Hsi_5
xī	析	IV. 125	Hsi_5
xī	悉	IV. 269	Si_5
xī	今	V. 2	$Hsi_1(Ah_1)$
xī	昔	V. 32	Hsi_5
xī	息	IX. 103	Hsi_5
xí	習（习）	IV. 196	Si_5
xǐ	喜	IV. 242	Hsi_3

xì	系	II. 113, IV. 176	Hsi_4
xì	係（系）	IX. 96	Hi_4
xì	隙	IX. 154	Hsi_5
xì	禊	IX. 155	Hsi_5
xià	下	I. 5	$Hsia_{3,4}$
xiān	先	IV. 80	$Sien_2$
xiān	僊〔仙〕	IX. 99	$Hsien_2$
xián [xiàn]	涎〔羨〕	IV. 161	$Hsien_{4,2}$
xián	閑（闲）	IV. 224	$Hsien_1$
xián	賢（贤）	IX. 38	$Hsien_2$
xiǎn	㬎（显）	IX. 110	$Hsien_3$
xiāng, xiàng	相	IV. 107	$Siang_{2,4}$
xiāng	香	IV. 272	$Hsiang_2$
xiǎng	饗（飨），享	IX. 70	$Hsiang_3$
xiàng	象	II. 133	$Siang_4$
xiàng	像	IX. 98	$Siang_4$
xiāo	梟（枭）	IV. 141	$Hsiao_2$
xiǎo	小	IV. 68	$Siao_3$
xié	叶，協（协）	IV. 76	$Hsieh_5$
xīn	心	II. 38	$Hsin_2$
xìn	囟	II. 27	$Hsin_4$
xìn	信	IV. 20	$Hsin_4$
xīng	興（兴）	IV. 171	$Hsing_2$
xīng	星	IV. 212	$Sing_2$

xíng	行	IV. 49	*Hsing*$_2$
xìng	姓	IX. 123	*Sing*$_4$
xiōng	凶	IV. 158	*Hsiung*$_1$
xiū	休	IV. 22	*Hsiu*$_2$
xiù	臭	IV. 252	*Hsiu*$_4$
xū	吁	IX. 62	*Hsü*$_1$
xuán	縣［懸（悬）］	IV. 179	*Hsüan*$_2$
xuán	玄	IV. 188	*Hsüan*$_1$
xué	穴	II. 158	*Hsüeh*$_5$
xué	學（学）	IX. 46	*Hsioh*$_5$
xué	学	IX. 50	*Hsiao*$_5$
xuě	雪	IV. 262	*Hsüeh*$_5$
xuè	血	III. 25	*Hsüeh*$_5$
xūn	熏	IV. 234	*Hsün*$_1$
xùn	迅	II. 143	*Hsin*$_4$
yá	牙	II. 30	*Ya*$_2$
yān	焉	II. 139	*Yen*$_2$
yán (chān)	延，延	IV. 50	*Yen*$_2$ *(Chen)*
yán	炎	IV. 230	*Yen*$_7$
yán	言	VII. 4	*Yen*$_1$
yǎn	㕥	II. 104	*Yen*$_3$
yǎn	广	III. 20	*Yen*$_7$
yǎn	衍	IV. 51	*Yen*$_3$
yàn	燕	II. 140	*Yen*$_4$

yú, xū	于，吁	V. 5	$Ü_1$, $Hsü_1$
yú	愚	IX. 104	$Yü_1$
yú	漁（渔）	IX. 112	$Yü_1$
yǔ	雨	II. 5	$Yü_3$
yǔ, yú	予	II. 110	$Yü_{1,3}$
yǔ	禹	II. 134	$Yü_3$
yǔ	羽	II. 141	$Yü_3$
yǔ	與（与）	IV. 72	$Yü_{3,1}$
yù	玉	II. 160	$Yü_4$
yù	聿	IV. 137	$Yü_5$
yuān	冤	V. 50	$Yuan_1$
yuān	淵（渊）	V. 54	$Yüan_2$
yuán	元	IV. 79	$Yüan_1$
yuán	原	IV. 163	$Yüan_1$
yuē	曰	V. 1	$Yüeh_5$
yuè	月	II. 2	$Yüeh_5$
yuè, lè	樂（乐）	V. 12	Lo_5, Yo_5
yún	云〔雲〕	II. 3	$Yün_2$
yún	匀	IX. 140	$Yün_1$
zàn	贊（赞）	IV. 156	$Tsan_4$
zàng	葬	IV. 128	$Tsang_4$
zào	噪	IV. 144	Sao_4
zé	則（则）	IV. 155	$Tsê_5$
zè	仄	IV. 44	$Ts'ê_5$

zēng	曾	IX. 3	*Ts'eng*₂
zhǎn	展	IX. 150	*Chên*₃
zhàn	占	IV. 94	*Chan*₂, ₄
zhāng	章	IV. 60	*Chang*₂
zhǎo, zhuǎ	爪	II. 41, 107	*Ts'ao*₃
zhào	兆	V. 31	*Chao*₄
zhé	乇	III. 33	*Choeh*₄
zhēn	真	IV. 240	*Chën*₁
zhěn	参	IV. 200	*Chên*₃
zhēng	争（争）	IV. 55	*Tzêng*₂
zhěng	整	IX. 40	*Chêng*₃
zhèng	正	III. 2	*Chëng*₄
zhèng	政	IX. 42	*Chêng*₄
zhī	之	III. 32	*Chih*₁
zhī	支	IV. 73	*Chih*₁
zhī	知	IV. 95	*Chih*₁
zhī	隻（只）	IV. 133	*Chih*₅
zhī	只	V. 3	*Chih*₃
zhī	芝	IX. 1	*Chih*₁
zhí	直	IV. 105	*Chih*₅
zhǐ	止	II. 52	*Chih*₃
zhǐ	夂	IV. 10	*Chih*₄
zhì	豸	II. 129	*Ch'ih*₄
zhì	至	III. 23	*Chih*₄

zhì	制	IV. 66	$Chih_4$
zhì	炙	IV. 231	$Chih_{4,\,5}$
zhì	陟	IV. 264	$Chih_5$
zhì	盭	VIII. 4	$Chih_4$
zhì	製（制）	IX. 100	$Chih_4$
zhōng	中	III. 1	$Chung_1$
zhōng	終（终）	IV. 178	$Chung_1$
zhòng	眔（众）	IV. 13	$Ch'ung_4$
zhòng	仲	IX. 91	$Chung_4$
zhōu	舟	II. 87	$Chou_2$
zhōu	周	IV. 15	$Chou_2$
zhōu	州	IV. 164	$Chou_2$
zhǒu	肘	IV. 194	$Chou_3$
zhǒu	帚	IV. 263	$Chou_3$
zhū	朱	III. 11	Chu_1
zhú	竹	II. 100	$Chuh_5$
zhǔ	主	III. 10	Chu_3
zhù	祝	IV. 169	Chu_5
zhù	壴	IX. 68	Shu_4
zhuàn	弅	IV. 59	$Tsin_4$
zhuī	隹	II. 135	Wei_1
zhuì	缀（缀），叕	IX. 148	$Chiu_5$
zǐ	子	II. 49	Tzu_3
zì	自	II. 28	$Ts\hat{u}_4$

zōng	宗	IV. 168	*Tsung*₁
zǒu	走	IV. 201	*Tsou*₃
zú	卒	III. 19	*Tsu*₅
zú	足	V. 42	*Tsu*₅
zǔ	俎，且	X. 1	*Tsu*₃
zuì	最	IX. 81	*Ts'ou*₄
zuì	醉	IX. 145	*Tsui*₄
zuǒ	左	IV. 40	*Tso*₃
zuò	坐	IV. 110	*Tso*₄

译后记

　　《小学菁华》是徐梵澄先生在 1963 年编撰的一部汉英字典，之后因种种原因，被搁置了 13 年之久，后来在法国友人的催促下，才于 1976 年出版。是书出版以后，他老人家有三句话，说这书"颇见赏于荷兰学界"，又"旋即销售一空"，还让"他们（学院）大赚了一笔"。可见这部书在海外受到了广泛的欢迎。

　　20 世纪 60 年代，是徐先生向印度乃至西方全面介绍与传播吾华古典学术思想之菁华的时代，而这部字典，乃是其中之"第一项任务"。因为"读书需先识字"，这就是我们的"小学"，也即汉字。对于我们的汉语而言，虽说文字是给语音加上了图形，但二者的来源究竟不同，晓后者（能说）未必识前者（能认），因为一属"空间"，一属"时间"，表空间者为"文"，表时间者为"声"，并由这两支脉络发展出两种不同的语文类型，一是"文教"，一是"声教"。文教重"眼识"，声教重"耳识"。"文教""眼识"，倚重者图画，故"文字起源于图画"（孙诒让）。如上，徐先生亦有论说。

　　打开书，不仅可知这是一浩大的工程，而且可想于此耗费了先生多大的心力。原本在南印度一隅的阿罗频多学院，中文铅字难说齐全，而这书又颇涉及甲骨文、石鼓文、金文等，需制作。于是先生一人"战斗"，重操技艺旧业，摹写、篆刻、形模，然后灌注铅字。此一过程极为烦琐、耗时，加之印度天气多酷暑难耐，那劳作之苦辛只合想象了。是书正文由三种字体组成，小篆、小楷和现代印刷体，前两者皆为先生手书作品，特别是篆体，还给出了异形者，如"子"字有

7种，"马"字有5种，一目了然，且赏心悦目。全书共收录744个汉字（除形声字只举出少数例字外），姑且每个字以3种字体计算，则需制出2000多个汉字的模型，果若将其排兵布阵，可真像兵马俑一样壮观了！这里不妨一问，先生为什么以小篆作词源的起始呢？因为小篆去古不远，是成熟的文字。许慎认为小篆是由古文省变而来的，并且小篆的形体已由笔意变成笔势，这笔势可以推迹古文，由此笔意才"可得而说"。"可得而说"什么？是说六国以前的"言语异声，文字异形"的语文。

依先生的心思，学习汉字，并非只是有用于一般性的各种交流，而是要在其中获得精神性，即由"字"而"文（化）"而"精神"。通过学习，进而能阅读和了解中文古籍，尤其是哲学古籍，这是"本书真正价值所在"。这就是说，汉字是通向中国智慧的第一台阶，对于我们的文化而言，它"有一种统摄作用，它统知，统情，统意，或一言以蔽之，统精神"（《徐梵澄传》第243页）。它有绝高的价值，因此先生对这自家的宝什是珍爱有加的，他决不允许汉字染污猥琐的言语，见其韦檀多学古典的翻译，多有删节者，如《行云使者》(南印度版) 第41页"此首甚有删改"，第55页"此首于原义甚有删改"，第93页、110页皆如是，第124页"此首大半删削"。他自己曾说："实在是太不堪了，没有必要译出来。"（《梵澄先生》第83页）而他自己的文字运用，却始终是那么纯洁，无论汉语还是英文，皆以雅言出之，真实、简明、生动、传神。如其英语释文解"巫"字，《说文解字》曰："祝也，女能事无形，以舞降神者也。象人两褎（袖）舞形。"先生译为："The picture represents a man with two long sleeve twirling in a dance in order to induce the descent of spirits"。"两褎"并未译作"two sleeves"，形容词"long"点明了中国古代服饰的特点，同时，英文注释使用了动名词"twirling"，描绘出长袖翩翩多姿的样子。由此，英语读者便犹如身临其境了。

这部《小学菁华》，采用的是"六书"之法，对汉字分类进行解释，体现出汉字的"文教"性格。六书，即象形、指事、会意、形声、转注和假借，就具体字而言，前四项或有"并"之交叉，如"会意并象声并象形"，例"俎"；后二项则是：异字同义为"转注"，异义同字为"假借"。这是古代讲授小学的传统，如果不通晓这六原则，那么"古文几不可读，更无从理解"。徐先生说："汉文的制作诚然早了几千年，原是以形为主。然六书中谐音之字，几占十分之九。二者并论，一在前，一在后，亦可谓一为主，一为客。文字居于上层。"（《异学杂著》第54、55页）而今之汉语字典，多以字母顺序安排检索，如《新华字典》和《现代汉语词典》，虽然亦有部首之检索，但主体还是字母之检索，这样在无形中就生出了"重音轻形"的倾向。当然，汉字拼音化的作用是巨大的，它不仅推动了汉语的标准化和普及化，而且直接促进了汉字的数字化和信息化。然而，汉字究竟是一"以形为主"的大道，如果字音"居于上层"了，那么它深邃的光辉是否就被遮掩了呢？再说，设若只从读音入手，而不结合字形、字义，汉语是很难掌握的，它要求的是形、音、义之三要素的完美结合。

与这部《小学菁华》结缘，是译者的幸运，而本人也从中所获良多。在以往的学习中，我们多借助拼音来查找生字或难字，而对字形的运用则是辅助性的。翻译这部书，可说是重习"小学"，因此对训诂有了一点入门知识。正是凭借这么"一点"知识，译者顺利地通过了国家汉办的考试，取得了孔子学院的任教资格，并赴德国图林根教学二年。教学期间，本人的重点向书写倾斜，因为先生说过：我们的"华文，终究以形为主体。从填写影本，蒙纸描书，以至临摹碑帖，是一长期训练。这训练有绝大的价值，因为人以此从幼年便养成了美的意识，如布置的适当，长短大小轻重浓淡的和谐，皆美术上的要素；这推及寻常生活行动，要和谐，皆不言而喻，有其良好效果。这便是生活的一重要部分，是教养之一端"（《异学杂著》第169—170页）。而西方的教学多以场景为平台，比较注重互动的效果，盖因其是"声教"的背景，只要能说出句子，那么大致便能拼写出字母。然要书写汉字，对于外国孩子就比较为难了，即便是外籍华人的子女，说的是一口流利的汉语，可是一落笔，仍是错字连连。汉字，对于他们而言，仿佛是一个陌生而又神秘的世界。

徐先生考虑到了这一困难，这部字典正文后，附有他亲自手书的"双钩"汉字书写样本，即"书法"入门。译者将其影印后作为习字的素材，让学生填摹，这一尝试果然奏效，平日里一写汉字就犯怵的孩子们，于"填摹"运笔却颇有兴致。每年6月的最后一个周末，是学校例行的"开放日"，这一天，学校的"书法角"总是挤满了充满好奇心的孩子，其中不少人甚至未曾学过汉语，但也特愿一试身手。在那当儿，他们每一个人都认真地一笔一画地填写着"神奇"的汉字，既不交头接耳，也无自言自语，教室里安静地仿佛只剩下"空间"了。而我们的汉字正是这占有空间的"渊默而雷声"的语言，其"动静"岂可谓小？然这"动静"是明，即"静固生明"之"明"。我想，如若在这一良好的氛围中久久熏习，会怎么样呢？似乎徐先生对孩子们的态度总是那么仁霭宛然，其要求也从不过苛，他只希望他们成为一个个的"佳弟子"而已。他说："若使一时代人士，即现代诸人的佳弟子，皆养成到那种地步，一个个'文质彬彬'，实是可憧憬的事。"（同上引第99页）"佳弟子"就是"君子"，"一个个'文质彬彬'"就是"君子群"乃至"君子国"，而这正是鲁迅的理想。

本书英文原版的装帧是由先生设计的，封面采用了金文作装饰图案，封背则嵌入了古体之"舟"字。这"舟"字，是我们汉字的寓意，它代表着中国人的人生观和世界观，是中华民族共同生命的承载体。阿罗频多说得好："若使作成一器皿的金子是真实的，我们当怎样假定此器皿本身是一幻相呢？"（《神圣人生论》第34页）也就是说，"数字"与"器皿"是一生命有体，而且是永恒性的生个有体。正如先生所指出的："以过去之发展看，一种基于构架和形式的语言会更有生命力。它犹如一永恒之舟承载着各种知识——物质的或精神的——不断前行，驶向远而愈远的前方，可以是人类最好的守护者。由此，人类可望赢得我们永不停步的朋友——时间。"（本书"序言"）我们的生命是在有限的岁月中的，而我们的文字却给了我们以无限的生命。这无限的"生命"是"道"，是"善生"，是"精神"。

贺 佳　记于 2017 年 10 月 26 日，徐梵澄先生 108 周年诞辰日

文景

社 科 新 知 　 文 艺 新 潮

Horizon

小学菁华

徐梵澄 著

贺 佳 译　孙 波 校

出品人	姚映然
策划编辑	李 頔
责任编辑	李 頔
营销编辑	胡珍珍
装帧设计	Timonium lake
设计协力	魏荣辰

出品　　　北京世纪文景文化传播有限责任公司

　　　　　（北京朝阳区东土城路 8 号林达大厦 A 座 4A 100013）

出版发行　上海人民出版社

印刷　　　山东临沂新华印刷物流集团有限责任公司

制版　　　北京楠竹文化发展有限公司

开本　　　890mm×1240mm　1/32

印张　　　23　字数：418,000

　　　　　2024 年 5 月第 1 版　　2024 年 5 月第 1 次印刷

定价　　　138.00 元

ISBN　　　978-7-208-17494-8/B · 1594

图书在版编目（CIP）数据

小学菁华 / 徐梵澄著；贺佳译；孙波校 ·-- 上海：
上海人民出版社，2022
　（徐梵澄全集）
　ISBN 978-7-208-17494-8

　Ⅰ. ①小… Ⅱ. ①徐… ②贺… ③孙… Ⅲ. ①汉语—
对外汉语教学　词典 Ⅳ. ① H195 61

中国版本图书馆 CIP 数据核字（2021）第 252113 号

本书如有印装错误，请致电本社更换 010·52187586